Women and Alcohol in Social Context

# Women and Alcohol in Social Context

## Mother's Ruin Revisited

Jan Waterson
*Lecturer*
*Department of Social Policy and Social Work*
*University of Birmingham*

Foreword by

Elizabeth Ettorre
*Professor of Sociology*
*University of Plymouth*

Consultant Editor: Jo Campling

First published 2000 by
PALGRAVE
Houndmills, Basingstoke, Hampshire RG21 6XS and
175 Fifth Avenue, New York, N. Y. 10010
Companies and representatives throughout the world

PALGRAVE is the new global academic imprint of
St. Martin's Press LLC Scholarly and Reference Division and
Palgrave Publishers Ltd (formerly Macmillan Press Ltd).

ISBN 0–333–66589–9 hardback
ISBN 0–333–66590–2 paperback

This book is printed on paper suitable for recycling and
made from fully managed and sustained forest sources.

A catalogue record for this book is available
from the British Library.

Library of Congress Cataloging-in-Publication Data
Waterson, Jan, 1949–
    Women and alcohol in social context : mother's ruin revisited / Jan
    Waterson ; foreword by Elizabeth Ettorre.
       p. cm.
    Includes bibliographical references and index.
    ISBN 0–333–66589–9 (cloth)
      1. Women—Alcohol use—Great Britain. I. Title.
    HV5137 .W38 2000
    362.292'082'094—dc21
                                                              00–034785

10    9    8    7    6    5    4    3    2    1
09   08   07   06   05   04   03   02   01   00

Printed and bound in Great Britain by
Antony Rowe Ltd, Chippenham, Wiltshire

*In memory of Winifred, who knew a different sort of 'mother's ruin', with a long after-taste*

# Contents

# List of Tables

# List of Figures

# Foreword

Most of us arc probably aware that women drink alcohol in a variety of ways, for a variety of reasons and in a variety of situations. In earlier work (*Women and Alcohol: A Private Pleasure or a Public Problem*, Women's Press, 1997), I put forward the view that among women who drink alcohol there is a difference between 'positive drinking' and 'negative drinking'. In using these terms, I was not imposing moral standards on women's drinking or saying that those involved in positive drinking were better than those involved in negative drinking, or that women who experience negative drinking should feel bad, guilty or negative about themselves as women. In that context, I focused primarily on women's use of alcohol as being experienced both negatively or positively. My main point was that when women experience problems with their use of alcohol, this inevitably leads to disapproval, negative feelings and discontent within themselves. The picture emerged that all women drinkers are constrained in many ways to conform to powerful social images, telling them what it means to be 'acceptable women' in society. Most, if not all, fail in their attempts to reflect satisfactory female images or to embody femininity.

In *Women and Alcohol in Social Context*, Jan Waterson 'revisits' my earlier ideas and develops them further with eloquence and strength. She sets the notions of positive drinking and negative drinking firmly within a social policy framework in which the voices of women are able to be heard clearly.

Emerging from original work carried out for a PhD, this book is based on an empirical study of 60 women. It offers an altogether refreshing approach, establishing a balance between the intricate micro and complex macro social processes involved in women's experiences of drinking. Jan Waterson's accounts of these women's narratives are critical, grounded in their daily ordeals and periodic episodes *vis-à-vis* alcohol. While the author acknowledges that gender is a complex matter, she provides for the reader a 'gender-sensitive story' that is engaging, as well as an overall picture of women and alcohol that is fluid. However, providing a gender-sensitive account in the alcohol field today is of the utmost importance. Why?

The reader should be aware that the field of alcohol studies has been consistently resistant to a gender-sensitive perspective. To the trained eye (that is, of a gender-sensitive researcher), this resistance is quite surprising, given that gender dynamics can be seen to permeate most if not all aspects of contemporary cultures of drinking. In the light of this widespread resistance, there has been and indeed is a need for good empirical work in which gender-sensitive perspectives are able to develop and, more importantly, aid practitioners in their everyday understanding of women who drink. As I hinted above, *Women and Alcohol in Social Context* is a book that fulfils this need. It offers a powerful intellectual intervention in the field of alcohol studies – an intervention which should have effects on everyday treatment and, in turn, healing processes for women who drink.

However, practitioners beware. You will not be offered the customary ideas on why and how women drink. You will not be led by traditional stereotypes of women alcoholics as 'diseased', 'polluted' or 'deviant' women. Rather, your everyday assumptions about gender and drinking will be challenged, as the pains as well as pleasures of drinking women become visible. You will be confronted to see as well as to understand not only how and why negative drinking leaves women feeling stigmatised, marginalised and demoralised, but also how it is fruitless for professionals to be guided by the stereotype of the 'fallen' woman. You will also learn how positive drinking is possible, as women, shaped by the constraints as well as freedoms of motherhood, are able to balance their joys and sufferings within the context of our risk culture.

Many of us are aware that the multitude of problems or poly-problems that women who drink encounter make them unable to fit comfortably within society. Nevertheless, this 'mismatch' between these women and society is contested throughout this book. *Women and Alcohol in Social Context* is a sincere attempt on the part of the author to create a much needed environment in which the production of gender-sensitive knowledge not only is a real possibility, but also is able to effect contemporary policies and practice towards women who drink too much. In today's academic world, this is no small feat, and thus the message of this book deserves thoughtful consideration by scholars and practitioners alike.

Elizabeth Ettorre
Professor of Sociology
University of Plymouth

# Acknowledgements

My primary debt is to all the women who shared their stories with me. The book could not have been written without them. The interest, stimulus and encouragement from colleagues who responded to drafts was invaluable, as was Jo Campling's belief that the book would eventually be completed. I am also grateful to colleagues who created the space for me to write. Finally, my thanks to all those who lived with its progress.

# 1
# Introduction: Have a Drink

Alcohol is a drug, legally sanctioned and widely used by most people in western countries, but nevertheless a drug. Unlike tobacco, its physical effects may have some benefits as well as dangers (Razay et al. 1992). The production of alcohol creates employment and revenue. Its use distinguishes and kills time, signals hospitality and reciprocity, and lubricates and structures social interaction. Drinking can be routine or ritualistic. Like food it functions as an indicator of gender, income, attitudes towards health, social preferences and social status (Merrell and Murcott 1992) and like food is a taken-for-granted part of daily life.

Consuming alcohol is part of life in western cultures and of interest to the majority of us, whether we have any professional interest or not, as occasional bursts of intense media interest indicate. For those of us who work in health and welfare, whether as policy-makers, academics or as practitioners, it is rarely far from the surface of current agendas. Alcohol issues reach where others do not necessarily go, that is right into all areas of public policy and services. They are important to criminal justice services, health services and welfare services caring for vulnerable adults and children.

Indeed, our patterns of consumption of all sorts of goods have become a way of measuring social inequalities. They indicate the differences in people's ability to participate as full citizens in society (Cahill 1994). As Townsend (1979) noted twenty years ago, relative poverty is all about not having easy access to the goods and way of life that are important to the majority. In this context, if being able to have a drink is part of generally accepted notions of the good life, being unable to do so becomes a deprivation.

Any policy or practice is partly created in the light of explanatory analysis. Thus differing analyses and perspectives on an issue will generate different policy recommendations and practices. Alcohol use can be harmful, but more frequently it enhances the quality of life. This dichotomy gives rise to difficulties in explaining alcohol-related harms (Kreitman 1977, Strong 1980), and creates policy and practice dilemmas. How can the needs of preventative and ameliorative health and welfare policies be reconciled with a need to provide sufficient information, for autonomous, informed decision-making for users, and the need to create equal opportunities of access to quality of life? In social terms, its use can be both beneficial, oiling the wheels of social exchange, but also potentially very harmful. But it is precisely this ambiguous nature which makes it so fascinating. Over twenty years ago it was said that alcohol is to social science what dye is to microscopy: it illuminates the structure of social life (Room 1975).

With this potential, it is remarkable that studies of women's everyday drinking apart from a few exceptions have until recently remained a largely unexplored area for social analysis (Ettorre 1992, 1997, Thom 1994). The increasing importance of lifestyle and consumption patterns as ways of expressing individual and group identity in terms of political style, sexuality, social status or class (Tomlinson 1990) make the absence of any detailed analysis even more noticeable. Perhaps it is because social scientists have seen their own drinking as a leisure pursuit, that is a non-work activity. However, leisure is now a legitimate topic of academic interest (Jarvie and Maguire 1994).

Most of the previous work on women and alcohol has been problem-oriented. This is the longstanding legacy of 'mother's ruin'. Any discussion of the positives that drinking behaviour can bring are rare (Waterson 1996). It is usually the dangers we hear about. Most commonly dangers are referred to as risks (Douglas 1992), but as Douglas (1985) reminds us, original concepts of risk were neutral, simply a matter of probability, so that the outcome of an action might be positive or negative. We live in what are now frequently characterised as risk societies (Beck 1992). Discussions of health and welfare services are often couched in notions of risk, risk assessment, risk management and protection from harm (Kemshall et al. 1997, Gabe 1995). Indeed Bunton and Burrows (1995) have argued that risk assessment is now the main focus of efforts to improve the health status of communities. It is no wonder that notions of alcohol-related risks and risk level of intake have dominated much of the writing about the topic.

Certainly there are many alcohol-related harms, but also time-honoured pleasures. Taking risks or weighing up the chances is part of everyday life (Giddens 1991).

*Normal people, as a matter of course, will happily sacrifice the possibility of an illness in the long term as against present enjoyment.* (Charlton 1993, p. 32)

It is the harmless pleasures that come from drinking that can easily disappear under the welter of problems it can bring. Much of the literature only looks at the problems arising from overuse. Manthorpe et al.'s (1997) review of the normality of drinking amongst people with learning difficulties, which outlines the risks of overuse, as well as the risks of not being able to partake in everyday activities like going for a drink, is a welcome exception. In that paper the authors pay a great deal of attention to what the people with learning difficulties wanted and thought. But we know from other contexts that policy-makers and other professional do not always 'hear' the voice of the user, as they define their own risks, but prefer to define the risks for them (Waterson 1999). Franklin (1998) has described risk as a dynamic force for change, arguing that the ways we manage it open up opportunities. For informed individuals it certainly offers the chance of greater empowerment as they make their own risk assessments, taking charge of their own lives and negotiating their own courses of action. 'Mother's ruin' needs revisiting so that the potentially negative connotations can be limited, but associated pleasures and benefits maximised as women enter into dialogue with policy-makers and professional health and welfare workers.

## Revisiting notions of mother's ruin

This book revisits our notions of 'mother's ruin'. What is the ruin – losing control of drinking or not being allowed to self-define risks? What are the dangers? What pleasures could be lost? Who is in danger? Who loses? Essentially this book tells a story – a story as told by 62 women, a story of their drinking experiences. An analysis of their differing situations will be used to compare their stories with those told by social scientists as they have tried to understand women's drinking to date.

When we speak of 'mother's ruin' we tend to think of gin. Most commonly we think back to the eighteenth and nineteenth centuries, recalling images of women consuming vast quantities of gin in an effort to terminate unwanted pregnancies:

*Hot gin and quinine, violent exercise or crawling upstairs backward were all said to work.* (MacMillan 1990, p. 126)

The other picture that springs to mind is that of drunken mothers neglecting their children as they pursue their own gratification (Gutzke 1984). Barr, (1995, p. 190), for example, cites a poignant case of Judith Dufour who, when visiting her two-year-old child in the workhouse, took him out for the afternoon in his new clothes provided by the workhouse, and killed the child in order to sell his clothes to buy gin.

Current medical evidence suggests links between drinking and spontaneous abortion are tenuous (Cavallo et al. 1995), and not many women would try to induce an abortion by drinking themselves stupid. However, women with small children or pregnant women who drink heavily are still stigmatised and suspected of child neglect, or worse. A recent survey of calls to a telephone help-line for children noted that a third of calls reporting child neglect referred to a parent abusing drugs or alcohol. Of those, 50 per cent referred to the mother only (Lewis 1997). But other surveys suggest this is an overestimation, and that mothers are more likely to be responsible in only about a third of instances (Houston et al. 1997). It seems that heavy paternal drinking is much more likely to go unreported than maternal drinking. Women who are pregnant or who have small children remain probably the most censored group amongst people with alcohol problems, who are themselves highly stigmatised.

Nevertheless, current estimates suggest that 800,000 children in England and Wales, a further 85,000 in Scotland and 35,000 in Northern Ireland are living in families where one adult has a drink problem (Brisby et al. 1997). Analysis of over 3,000 calls to a national telephone help-line for children between 1995 and 1996, where one or both parents were reportedly misusing alcohol, revealed a distressing picture of violence, abuse and neglect (Houston et al. 1992). Further evidence of these links comes from research on adult children of heavy drinkers who frequently recall significantly more traumatic and difficult childhoods than their contemporaries (Velleman 1993). But, as we have already noted, responsibility for this state of affairs is not simply a matter of maternal responsibility. In the telephone survey reported above, fathers were implicated in more cases than mothers. In fact, lone male parents were especially at risk (Houston et al. 1992). So, whilst 'mother's ruin' as traditionally conceived is no longer applicable, some vestiges of the traditional picture are accurate, albeit not widespread and not in a way that conforms to the two main stereotypes: drinking to abort an unwanted pregnancy or neglecting children through incapacity brought about by drinking.

More commonly, these days refusing a drink may be one of the first public signals of a pregnancy. Something like 42 per cent of women reported to a national survey that they had tried to cut down the amount they drank in the last five years; and of these, about a third did so because they were pregnant (GSO 1998). Not drinking, or at least cutting down, has become a pregnancy ritual, even assuming taboo status (Priest 1990). We know from surveys that the transition to motherhood for many women is a time of spontaneous decrease in their consumption (Breeze 1985; Waterson and Murray Lyon 1989a, 1989b; Burrows and Nettleton 1995). UK community surveys indicate that about a third of married women without dependent children exceed officially defined safe limits, but only about 18 per cent of those married with dependent children do so (GSO 1998). But, taboos, whilst offering protection from real dangers, can also exaggerate them. In other words, they can be mechanisms of social control for social elites. Medicalisation has been an issue for women as they have sought to regain control of their health matters (Roberts 1990) and resist the medical pathologisation of normal events, such as childbirth, which are not necessarily in need of medical treatment or supervision (Oakley 1993). For women involved in this struggle, the important thing has been to resist the dominant view of a male medical elite. Even now in the UK only 15 per cent of all medical consultants are women, and women account for only 25 per cent of all community and hospital doctors (Department of Health 1991). So, it is hardly surprising that a medical view should be male-dominated.

During the last three decades mainstream sociology, social policy and social work studies, especially those that relate to health and illness, have seen the development of a distinctive gendered perspective (Maynard 1990; Ungerson and Kember 1998). But although gender differentiation has begun to feature in the alcohol literature, many of the approaches have remained static over the last 20 years (Hands et al. 1995). Whilst it is accepted that women's reasons for drinking are different from men's, that they consume different beverages, drink in different ways and settings, have different difficulties with alcohol, access treatment differently and need different approaches (Hafner 1992), a fully gendered approach to women's uses of alcohol has not been fully developed. This would look for causes in an unequal and gender-differentiated society. We need to look at the realities of women's life experiences, in similar ways to work which has been done on the medicalisation of women's lives (Oakley 1980, 1993; Oakley and Graham 1981; Doyal and Elston 1986). Alcohol problems, far from being the price that women pay for emancipation, are frequently a rational response to their experience of a gender-differentiated society (Vogt 1984; Ettorre 1992, 1997). This book locates women's drinking within the context of their everyday lives.

More recently feminist literature has shifted to the epidemiology of women's health, drawing out the heterogeneity of women's experience and the impact of social advantage or exclusion (Blaxter 1990; Payne 1991; Doyal 1995). As Annandale (1998) has noted, much of the feminist debate about medical control of women's lives has centred on individual women's subjective experience, their work or their lifestyle, with relatively little emphasis on the impact of major social divisions, such as class or the distribution of power. We know from other research that women's experiences can be very varied according to their class position. Some of the studies that are relevant to women's drinking include Graham's (1994, 1995) discussion of smoking, Oakley and Rajan's (1991) survey of social support, and Wolfson and Murray's (1986) short collection of women's accounts of drug problems. This book follows in that tradition noting, as Ettorre (1992) says, that we need to understand both the structural (social) and processual (individual) influences which sustain or undermine women's drinking. But first, by way of introduction, an outline of the dominant perspectives on motherhood and drinking and women's drinking follows. In addition, I shall, by way of giving context, briefly review how drinking patterns have changed over the last few decades, shaping women's everyday drinking habits, and how concepts of drink-related harms have also evolved, influencing public and policy perceptions of appropriate or non-harmful drinking.

## Perspectives on motherhood and drinking

One indicator of the health of any research field might be a measure of the volume of publications about it (Carley 1981). Until 1980 little was written on the general topic of women and alcohol from either medical, epidemiological or social perspective. Between 1929 and 1970 only 28 English-language papers were written (Lisansky 1957), and even in 1972 Lindbeck was able to comment that although there was much mention of women's drinking problems, there was little work of depth.

Over the last two decades there has been a change. Interest has grown, starting in the US and later developing in the UK and the rest of the world. Several major literature reviews (Kalant 1980; Shaw 1980; Ettorre 1992, 1997; Plant 1997), and national reports on alcohol misuse in the UK (National Council of Women 1976, 1980) have been produced. In

1992 a government-sponsored conference was held in the UK (Department of Health and Royal College of General Practitioners 1992). But despite all this, even in 1995 most research on substance use still focused on men (Brett et al. 1995).

One topic has dominated above all others. Since 1970 over 3,000, mainly medical papers have been written on the effects of alcohol on pregnancy, far surpassing in quantity all other work on women and alcohol (Abel 1986). Concern has centred on potential congenital harm to the unborn child. Whatever control women have regained over childbirth, once the possibility of pregnant women drinking for pleasure was introduced a medicalised response was provoked and any drinking, however small, viewed as problematic.

When reviewing the current state of knowledge some years ago Edwards (1983, p. 248) commented:

> *Whatever the real biological problem, the story of Fetal Alcohol Syndrome (FAS) might be profitably be studied in terms of what the sociologists call the 'social construction' of a problem.*

Just why this issue has been dominant when the need for research into women's drinking problems unrelated to pregnancy is far greater (Waterson and Ettorre 1989) demonstrates public attachment to notions of women as child producers and protectors. This emphasis on the effects of drinking on pregnancy outcome took place after the rise of the women's movement in the late 1960s and 1970s on both sides of the Atlantic, so that by the late 1970s Gomberg was able to suggest that:

> *Fetal Alcohol Syndrome, by its rapid popularity, had become the locus of expression of a kind of projective rage and disapprobation towards women in North American Society, making FAS the ultimate feminine crime of foetal impairment.* (Gomberg 1979, p. 86)

Ideological portrayals of pregnancy and motherhood as self-denying, nurturing of men and offspring alike (Abbott and Sapsford 1987, Kaplan 1992; Smart 1992) inevitably conflict with notions of independent and stigmatised female drinking. After all: '*Nobody likes to think that the hand that rocks the cradle might be shaky*' (Curlee 1970, 247).

The desire to protect the 'unborn child' is deeply rooted in our society. A pregnant woman is prone to all sorts of potential environmental pollutants and even everyday activities may become problematic. There is a clear implication that the incapacity of a mother is threatening in a way that is not for fathers. Even in primitive societies there is an under-standing that the care of a field can be left, but the care of a child not. As there are very few occasions when men assume primary respon-sibility for childcare, we can assume that such concern is universal. Although women's position in general has shifted, society retains a deep-seated view of domesticity and subordination as fundamentally female (Doyal 1995).

A useful historical aside may be given here. Berridge and Edwards (1981) note that concern about opiate use first centred on middle-class female use for enjoyment, suggesting that social concern about the use of potentially addictive substances increases when they are used for female pleasure. Additional interpretations have included the sugges-tion that, at least in the USA, the topic, because of its emotive qualities, was used by alcohol agencies to attract public attention to alcohol prob-lems in general and to secure the continuation of their research (Fillmore 1985).

However, until 20 years ago, alcohol continued to be used for pain relief in labour and for preventing pre-term labour (Abel 1981). Popular obstetric texts encouraged its use during pregnancy (Bourne 1972) and when breast-feeding (Llewellyn-Jones 1978). Interestingly, until a decade ago, the content of alcohol in gripe water, a remedy for infantile colic, could be as high as 5 per cent, that is higher than many beers and lagers. As the *Guardian* (11 April 1989) pointed out, the permitted daily dosage for an infant was the equivalent of four gin and tonics.

But, by 1980, clear diagnostic criteria for Fetal Alcohol Syndrome (FAS) were established on the basis of 245 cases in the US (Rosett 1980). Follow-up studies of identified cases, confirming long-term effects, have since appeared and cases reported around the world (Waterson and Duffy 1992). There is now a consensus that increasing self-reported maternal alcohol use is positively associated with a continuum of birth damage from the relatively inconsequential to the very serious (Alcohol Health and Research World 1994).

At the most serious extreme is an irreversible combination of devel-opmental delay, growth retardation, neurological abnormalities and characteristic facial dysmorphology known as the Fetal Alcohol Syndrome which is associated with heavy alcohol consumption during pregnancy (over 35 units of alcohol a week). But, not all very heavy drinking mothers produce children with full-blown FAS (Abel 1984). In the UK cases have been reported (Beattie et al. 1983; Poskitt 1984), but to date none of the prospective studies of women's drinking during their preg-nancies has identified any (Plant 1997).

Another finding, confirmed in large-scale British and vast combined European data-set studies, is an association of alcohol consumption with a significant risk of reduced birth-weight (Waterson and Duffy 1992; Euromac 1992). The lowest level at which any independent effect has been discerned is a reported consumption of about one or two units of alcohol a day. Low birth-weight remains an important predictor of childhood mortality, morbidity and impaired later development (Barker 1994). What is important is that the social distribution of low birth-weight is strongly correlated with social class and has even been referred to as a metaphor for social disadvantage (Oakley 1989; Blackburn 1991). A social class gradient in infant mortality and morbidity is distinctive (Wilkinson 1996) and in the UK remains so even within ethnic groups (Balarajan and Raleigh 1990). But such complex interrelations between the cultural impact of ethnicity and that of socio-economic position need careful unpacking (Ahmad 1993). Gender influences add a further dimension (Payne 1991; Douglas 1992). However, despite these complexities, low birth-weight is now one of the indicators used in an annual report on poverty and social exclusion in the UK (Howarth and Street 1998).

In addition, whilst epidemiological studies can point to an independent alcohol effect, other factors such as diet and socio-economic status remain much more important than alcohol in determining the principal outcome of birth-weight (Plant 1985; Waterson and Duffy 1992). In reality, the adverse effects of alcohol are more likely to affect those women who are already very disadvantaged and thus be part of a constellation of adverse factors. Furthermore, in the US, where most cases have been identified, the incidence of FAS is associated with multiple deprivation (Bingol et al. 1988; Dorris 1989; Waterson and Murray-Lyon 1989c). But studies have shown that reduction of alcohol intake is beneficial to the offspring (Rosett et al. 1983; Halmesmaki 1988), which suggests that alcohol still remains a necessary and integral cause (Waterson and Murray-Lyon 1989).

Official health advice in the UK is for pregnant women either to abstain or to limit their intake to one or two units of alcohol once or twice a week to avoid any risk (Royal Colleges of Medicine 1995, Department of Health 1995). In the US, FAS has had a much higher public profile and total abstinence is stressed to avoid any influence whatever. Although potential dangers were highlighted in a report to the President and Congress in 1980, and again in 1991 in a report to the President's Committee on Mental Retardation, it was largely the press and media that promoted the issue during the 1980s. A government warning stating that women should not drink alcohol during pregnancy because of the risk to the foetus is now displayed on bottles, and in several states notices are also displayed in bars and restaurants (Waterson and Murray Lyon 1992). By 1984, Ernest Abel, a prominent researcher in the field, was able to ask whether FAS was a case of pre-natal child abuse. Court cases supporting foetal rights are not uncommon (*British Journal of Addiction* 1988), and today in some US states it is a legal requirement to report women who have used alcohol or illicit drugs in pregnancy to the child protection agencies (Chasnoff et al. 1990).

McNeil and Litt (1992) argue that much of this publicity stems from a best-selling book by Michael Dorris, *The Broken Cord* (1989). This is an account of his experience with his adopted Native American Indian son, who was diagnosed as suffering with FAS. However, as McNeil and Litt (1992) outline, the effect has not been to promote open dialogue of the relevant social and political conditions which underlie heavy female drinking, but rather to converge on a model of trying to reform 'guilty' mothers or to punish them. They maintain that in the US context there are five sources for this stance:

1. A media emphasis on images of the foetus as an innocent, autonomous being, easily damaged by its mother has promoted a distorted public awareness of foetal rights.
2. An increasing emphasis on maternal responsibilities during pregnancy and the extension of health care surveillance, even into the period before pregnancy as well as during pregnancy, have directed attention on maternal behaviour.
3. Women may have extended their roles, particularly in the workplace, over the last 20 years but their femininity is still in part measured by maternity. Although feminist scholars and the women's movement have worked to dilute this notion, it remains embedded deep within our culture (Abbott and Wallace 1996). The debate about drinking in pregnancy reflects predominantly male uncertainties about changing female identities, extending beyond motherhood. In this scenario, increased female drinking easily becomes viewed as the price for emancipation and, regardless of the circumstances, however desperate, in which drinking takes place, any drinking whilst pregnant, interpreted as a wilful act of violence against the defenceless unborn child. A parallel may be drawn with British history when maternal irresponsibility and ignorance were blamed for the poor physical condition of Boer War recruits, when the real cause was poverty (Lewis 1980).

4. In the US context, as already mentioned above, FAS is most common amongst deprived groups, especially inner-city ethnic groups and North American Indians. They argue that this leads to a belief that FAS belongs to marginalised groups, rapidly leading to stigmatisation and definition of 'at risk' groups who are somehow different from the moral majority, and in need of increased medical surveillance.

5. They argue that, as medical science progresses, the search for the perfect child has intensified. Middle-class parents in particular want to control their biological heritage and are willing to do whatever it takes, including ceasing alcohol consumption and expect all other groups to follow their example.

FAS is not curable, and that makes it susceptible to greater social significance, which easily promotes a view that all drinking in pregnancy is harmful, even though there is no research evidence which substantiates light drinking as harmful (Knupfer 1991; Behnke and Eyler 1993). Thus much of the medicalised discussion emphasising maternal blame has ignored the important questions: What provokes women's heavy drinking? And how do social inequalities structure maternal and child health, or indeed women's drinking?

Whilst there has been a far more muted response in Europe, aspects of those trends described by McNeill and Litt (1992) can be discerned. The debate about boundaries between foetal and maternal rights, increased medical surveillance in pregnancy and the search for the perfect child, all have their European counterparts. But, few cases of FAS have been diagnosed, and in England and Wales less than 2 per cent of women of childbearing age currently drink at sufficiently high levels to run any risk of FAS (GSO 1998). Whilst 'official' health advice is to reduce consumption to below 10 units a week during pregnancy, the clinical impact of drinking is severely confounded by socio-economic circumstances and is rarely obvious. However, some reduction in drinking during pregnancy during the 1990s has been reported in Europe as women have become more aware of the potential harmful effects (Ihlen et al. 1993).

What is more interesting is that although community surveys consistently point to a reduction in female consumption once they have dependent children (Breeze 1985; Goddard and Ikin 1988; GSO 1996), there has been no detailed examination of the changes which this transition brings to the everyday activity of drinking, or its importance for more general issues of non-problematic female drinking, or indeed whether this reported general decrease masks significant variations. It is the only time when women spontaneously reduce their alcohol consumption and men are encouraged to control female drinking, rather than vice-versa (Waterson and Murray-Lyon 1990a; Holmilla 1991). The birth of a first child remains a major turning point in many women's lifecycle (Allatt et al. 1986); indeed, the substantial changes and adjustments involved in becoming a mother have already been fully documented in a flurry of empirical research in the early 1980s (Graham and McKee 1980; Oakley 1980; Macintyre 1981; Boulton 1983). This book extends that focus by looking at changes in one everyday activity – drinking alcohol. It examines how socio-economic differences are reflected in women's drinking behaviour, noting that not all women reduce and for some the transition to motherhood may itself trigger alcohol problems.

## Double standards: male and female drinking

Having previously identified the need for a gendered understanding of women's drinking, it is important to realise that one notable omission in this interest is any comparable emphasis on the effect of alcohol on male reproductive capacity. It is well known that alcohol can have a deleterious effect on the male reproductive system, not to mention performance, and that paternal drinking may affect the foetus (Wilsnack 1985; Waterson and Duffy 1992). Even though similar drinking levels between partners have been reported in the UK and elsewhere (Waterson and Murray Lyon 1990, Hyssala et al. 1992; Bresnahan et al. 1992), consumption levels generally are significantly different and an indication of double standards between male and female drinking.

Social acceptability in terms of drinking behaviour does not begin on a level playing field. What is acceptable for men is less so for women. Such double standards begin in childhood. Boys are encouraged to drink at an earlier age than girls (Plant and Plant 1992; Lowe 1993; Fossey and Plant 1994). According to a survey of about 19,000 children aged between nine and 12 years, in the south-west of England, boys were almost one and a half times more likely than girls to have drunk alcohol in the previous week (Schools Health Unit 1997).

Attitudes towards women's drinking remain paradoxical. Women receive more approbation for drinking, yet their share of total consumption in European countries is only between one third and a fifth (Simpura 1995). Since 1978 the proportion of non-drinkers in the UK has remained at about 7 per cent for males and about 14 per cent for females (OPCS 1996). On every count they drink less than men and experience fewer alcohol related harms (Plant 1990; Goddard 1991; WHO 1992; Mills-Hopper 1992; Ferri 1993; McDonald 1994). For example, women account for only 5 per cent of all drink-driving offences and only 7 per cent of all drunkenness offences (Alcohol Concern 1996). In 1996 in England and Wales 2,754 male but only 1,730 female alcohol-related deaths were reported (ONS 1998). Similarly, national statistics estimate that only 4 per cent of women, but 8 per cent of men are problem drinkers (OPCS 1993).

Although women are drinking more in the UK, the US and Scandinavia (Helweg-Larson 1998), and the rates of drinkers versus non-drinkers are converging between younger men and women, particularly in those under 24 years of age, the overall rates for heavy drinkers are not (OPCS 1996). Amongst the drinking population men drink three times as much per head than women. Currently 28 per cent of men, but only 14 per cent of women consume more than the recommended 'safe' levels (21 units of alcohol a week for a man and 14 for a woman)(OPCS 1996). However, only 9 per cent of women were drinking at these levels in 1984 (the percentage for men has not changed). The numbers of women or men drinking at harmful levels (35+ and 50+ units a week) has not risen since 1984. These statistics suggest that although women's heavy drinking is increasing, any picture of a rising tide of female drinking is exaggerated. Men continue to be heavier drinkers.

Because women face formidable barriers to accessing treatment (Smith 1992; Thom and Green 1996) it is very difficult to gain reliable estimates of women's alcohol-related problems. Figures for admissions to Alcohol Treatment Units in the UK show that the ratio of female to male patients had declined from 1:3 in 1968 to 1:2 by 1980 (Beory and Merry 1986). One can presume that rates are now more or less equal as more women of child-bearing age are coming to the notice of the alcohol agencies (Waterson and Ettorre 1989; Smith 1992). Female rates of cirrhosis have increased by 16 per cent since 1980, but amongst men have increased by 50 per cent (OPCS 1992).

Despite this evidence that alcohol problems are predominantly a male issue, stereotypes are remarkably pervasive and persistent. Alcohol may be quoted as aiding male creativity but rarely that of women. For example, in one review Grant (1981) cites 40 writers who used alcohol as an aid to creativity. Only three are women. This may be no more than a reflection of societal recognition of male creative activity, but it is interesting that the positive aspects of alcohol use are rarely linked with women. Rather, societal views of alcohol serve to reinforce existing power imbalances between the sexes (Morgan 1987). In a similar vein, a more recent review of well-known twentieth-century artists, writers and composers was able to mention 31 men but only 3 women (Ludwig 1990). More commonly women are expected to moderate male consumption and to look after men with problems (Velleman et al. 1998; Holmilla et al. 1990). This remains true whether the drinking is to aid male creativity or not. Pubs remain predominantly male preserves (Hunt and Satterlee 1987). Unaccompanied women in pubs are still liable to be seen as sexually available and groups of women drinking together in public spaces may be subjected to male ridicule (Ettorre 1997).

Such public expressions of stigma are reflected in the early academic literature on women's drinking, dating from the late 1960s and the 1970s, which was predominantly derived from clinical populations (Clemmons 1985). The typical woman with a drink problem was portrayed as between 35 and 45 years old, probably divorced or separated, prone to drinking in isolation, depressed, sexually depraved and with a poorer prognosis than a man in a similar situation. No doubt, some of these indicators were found in some women. But further research in the 1980s showed that the reported telescoping of symptoms in women, and hidden drinking, was often no more than a natural reaction to hard situations, disapproval and difficult access to treatment (Dahlgren 1978; Vannicelli 1985; Ross et al. 1988; Thom 1986). However, these images became embedded in popular consciousness, reinforcing a gender-differentiated society. Women's fear of the stigma of being identified as having alcohol problems still remains a formidable barrier for many in seeking the treatment they need (Baily 1990; Smith 1992; Long and Mullen 1994)

This clinical literature drew attention to the female drinker's aberrations in 'normal' sex-role performance (Beckman 1978). The topic even merited a separate chapter in a review of alcohol and the family (Leland 1982). 'Life-events', a topical area of research at the time, were used to explain the onset of alcoholism in middle-aged women (Curlee 1969). Even these events, such as the 'empty nest syndrome' after the children had left, concentrated on incidents that disrupted a traditionally defined female identity rooted in husband and children (Lindbeck 1972; Corrigan 1980). Such interest in sex-role performance could almost be termed a dominant image, that is, a summary characterisation organised around a coherent perspective (Room 1974). Indeed sex-role disturbance has remained an important focus for clinical research on women's drinking problems until comparatively recently (Kroft and Leichner 1987; Sorell et al. 1993), and continues to feature in media coverage. Foster (1995

p. 135) quotes a *Guardian* headline of 3 December 1991: '*Drink peril faces women keeping up with the boys.*'

The absence of a similar organising concept based on a culturally defined sex-role in studies of male alcoholism, despite empirical evidence of equal pathology and problems, only serves to underline the greater stigmatisation and stereotyping of female drinking. It can only be the ideological usefulness of these stereotypes that explains their persistence. Stereotypes exist to order ideas, to express communal values and beliefs, and to maintain social boundaries, particularly where social categories are fluid.

Most people drink alcohol, so the ability to differentiate clearly those with a problem is reassuring (Fillmore 1985). This central concern with female sexuality is vital for, as Curlee (1969, p. 170) pointed out over 20 years ago:

> *Woman represents important symbols that are the bedrock of society. When angels fall, they fall disturbingly far. We would rather have them in their place, which is another way of saying that they define and make our place possible and ever more comfortable.*

Pregnant angels have even further to fall, and fall more heavily, which helps to explain why research and public attention have centred on women's drinking when they are pregnant. It also explains the lesser importance attached to women's drinking issues in general, why after decades of research we are not much further forward with a women-centred approach, (Ettorre 1997) why services remain underdeveloped (Waterson and Ettorre 1989) and why the field has remained remarkably static (Hands et al. 1995). This double standard is still influential. For instance, there are almost no in-depth accounts of how women use alcohol in the normal course of their lives. That is precisely the gap that this book goes some way towards filling.

## Changing drinking patterns and problems

Total consumption in the UK is lower than that in most European countries. In 1995 France and Germany had the highest per capita consumption levels of 11.9 and 11.2 litres of pure alcohol respectively, whereas for the UK it was only 7.2 litres. This was roughly the same level as Ireland and Greece. Within Europe only Sweden and Finland had lower rates. Outside Europe, UK rates are similar to Australia (7.7 litres), New Zealand (7.2 litres), the US (6.6 litres) and Canada (6.1

litres) (Brewers and Licensed Retailers Association 1997). However, since 1970 different European levels have been converging. Rates in France, Italy, Spain and Germany have fallen, whereas consumption has risen in the UK, Ireland, Denmark and Finland.

In order to understand women's current drinking patterns in the UK it is important to recognise that many of the foundations of current habits were established during the late 1960s and 1970s. Per capita consumption increased by 23 per cent between 1960 and 1969, and by a further 40 per cent between 1968 and 1974 (OHE 1981). Between 1963 and 1979, expenditure on alcohol doubled in real terms and by 1979 the nation was spending more on alcohol than on clothing or cars, that is approximately 8 per cent of consumer spending by 1979 (OHE 1981). This increase was related to a reduction in price, real prices having fallen by 50 per cent between 1949 and 1979. The cost of alcohol as a percentage of disposable income also fell during the same time (OHE 1981). The greatest percentage decrease was in the products most attractive to women who had become the primary marketing target for the industry (Shaw 1980). Indeed, new products such as cream liqueurs were created especially for this expanded female market.

Alcohol was more freely available. Purchase became easier following the 1961 Licensing Act which permitted the sale of alcohol during normal shopping hours. This was shortly followed by the abolition of retail price maintenance on alcohol in 1964, which was implemented in 1966–7 by the distillers and in 1970 by the brewers. Consequently, by the late 1970s more than half of all supermarkets were selling alcohol (Shaw 1980) with the corner shop trade well established by the 1990s (Edwards et al. 1994). Although the number of pubs decreased by 2 per cent between 1962 and 1975, the number of off-licences increased by 28 per cent. By 1980 25 per cent of male consumption and 39 per cent of female consumption was in the home (Wilson 1980). Also, licensing hours were extended in Scotland in 1976 and in England and Wales in 1988.

During the same period the trade tried to extend the image of the pub as a traditional male preserve to encourage the new female market. Increasing mass tourism during the 1960s encouraged more cosmopolitan drinking styles and preferences, which have been added on to existing patterns. Wine consumption increased by 240 per cent between 1962 and 1982, spirit consumption increased less spectacularly at 95 per cent, and beer consumption by only 22 per cent. Between 1967 and 1977 the real price of wine fell by 14 per cent and that of spirits by 21 per cent, but beer by only 4 per cent. Therefore, the greatest expansion occurred in precisely the end of the market where women were major purchasers, the fortified wines and table wine trades (Shaw 1980).

Although women's earnings remained lower than men's, their rate of increase during the 1970s was greater. Furthermore, women were coming into the labour market, particularly as part-time workers. In 1951 7.5 million women were employed. By 1986 the figure had risen to 9.4 million, representing some 45 per cent of the total workforce (McDowell 1989). As disposable income is closely linked to alcohol consumption levels (Harkin et al. 1995), an expansion of female drinking was hardly surprising.

After this rapid increase, overall consumption levels in the UK stabilised in the 1980s and have remained roughly the same since then (Department of Health 1995). Annual per capita consumption for the population over 15 was 9 litres of alcohol in 1980; in 1990 it was 9.3 litres. In 1981 spending on alcohol had decreased slightly to 7.3 per cent of total household expenditure. By 1989 it had dropped to 6.3 per cent and the average family spent £7 a week on alcohol which was consumed away from home (CSO 1991). Since then there have been some cultural changes in our drinking, for example the introduction of low alcohol drinks in the late 1980s, and designer drinks specifically directed at the female market in the 1990s. The *Guardian* (9 August 1997) quoted one manufacturer as having told a government enquiry:

> *Our main market is housewives. A lot drink during the day. With [this product] they can enjoy a quiet drink without their husbands knowing. The firm's purpose was to inject a little fun into the lives of women.*

£200,000,000 are spent every year advertising alcoholic drinks in the UK alone. With such commercial encouragement little wonder if women are drinking more. Whilst they still consume much less than men, in per capita terms per week this has risen from 5.4 units in 1992 to 6.3 units. Women under 24 years are the heaviest consumers, but as each cohort ages, older groups are also increasing their intake. Indeed consumption rates are rising in women over 65 as those who were in their twenties and thirties in the 1960s grow older (Ward and Goodman 1995).

Increased consumption during the 1960s and 1970s led to an increased rate of alcohol-related harms. In the UK population as a whole, cirrhosis death rates doubled between 1950 and 1979 (Royal College of Physicians 1987). Admissions to mental hospitals for alcohol misuse rose by 48 per cent between 1964 and 1969 and by 63 per cent between 1969 and 1974. Heavy alcohol use is associated with many mental health problems, and most markedly with depression. Alcohol has now become the third largest killer after cancer and heart disease. Alcohol Concern (a UK campaigning body) estimates that about 500,000 women in the UK are now dependent on alcohol. This is about twice the estimated numbers for illicit drug dependency. The costs of policing alcohol-related incidents and health costs are phenomenal. By 1992 Alcohol Concern reckoned that the total cost of alcohol-related harms, excluding unemployment and premature deaths, were in excess of £3 billion a year.

In modern capitalist societies drinking problems have been viewed as either moral, legal or health concerns. Governments have long been concerned with public control. This is why licensing laws were introduced during the First World War. However, increasing evidence over the last 20 years has shown that high alcohol consumption is linked with a wide range of health problems, including not only liver cirrhosis, but also heart disease, stroke, neurological problems and cancer. A public health perspective on drinking problems has emerged since the 1970s (Bunton 1990). Broadly speaking, it is now accepted that the level of alcohol-related problems, including mortality, is related to per capita consumption (Sales et al. 1989, Edwards et al. 1994). This whole population approach has been adopted by the World Health Organisation, which set a target of reducing alcohol consumption by 25 per cent in Europe from 1980 figures by the year 2000 (World Health Organisation 1991).

Clearly this overarching approach masks variations between groups. Quite how this affects female drinking is unclear, given that most alcohol harm stems from male drinking. But the effect has been for prevention activities to be directed at the whole population, not just those identified as problem drinkers. In addition, opinion has shifted from viewing alcohol problems as some sort of disease, to seeing drinking as a learned activity (Heather et al. 1989), in which anybody might be susceptible to drinking heavily (Orford 1985). Longitudinal studies have shown that very heavy drinkers of both sexes can spontaneously reduce their drinking as their circumstances change (Valliant and Milofsky 1982; Taylor et al. 1985; Smart 1994; Maslin et al. 1998). Furthermore, it has been recognised that harms can arise from quite different patterns of drinking. Intoxication, dependency and heavy regular drinking create different problems, and the social, psychological and physical implications for women are not the same as men (Royal College of General Practitioners 1986). For example, men are more likely to be become drunk and involved in public disorder, criminal activities and accidents.

Table 1.1   Female and male drinking risk levels

|  | Women's weekly intake | Men's weekly intake |
|---|---|---|
| No / low risk | 0–14 units of alcohol | 0–21 units of alcohol |
| Increased risk | 15–35 units of alcohol | 22–50 units of alcohol |
| Harmful | > 35 units of alcohol | > 50 units of alcohol |

Government response to this rise in alcohol harms has been to try to reduce overall consumption by decreasing demand rather than by restricting supply (Tether and Robertson 1986). The latter would have antagonised the powerful drinks industry, decreased government revenue and increased unemployment (Baggott 1990). Instead, in an era of cuts in public expenditure the government seized on the cheaper alternative of decreasing demand by encouraging health education. 'Prevention and Health: Drinking Sensibly' (DHSS 1981) and other health education material (Health Education Council 1984) which emphasised 'safe' levels of drinking were produced. Since then, the principal effect has been the creation of a new category of problem drinker, the 'heavy drinker' (Royal Colleges 1995, Department of Health 1995). These are drinkers whose consumption levels could be described as putting themselves at some potential physical risk, as defined by epidemiological studies, but who are unlikely to be defined as alcohol-dependent or suffering other alcohol-related harms.

In the UK the Government White Paper 'The Health of the Nation', published in 1992, determined sensible drinking limits as 14 units for women and 21 for men. These were the limits below which health damage was unlikely. This resulted in a graded system to risks of health-related alcohol harms (see Table 1.1).

When the Royal Colleges of Medicine reviewed recommended limits in 1995 they saw no reason to make any changes (Royal Colleges 1995). But in 1996, the government chose to recommend daily rather than weekly limits. Men were advised to drink no more than 3–4 units a day and women no more then 2–3 units (Department of Health 1995).

These different levels for men and women are because women are more susceptible than men to physical damage from alcohol, due to differences in body make-up and hormonal balance (Jones and Jones 1976). Liver cirrhosis also occurs in women after a shorter duration of heavy drinking than in men, and at lower levels of consumption (Saunders et al. 1981; Dunne 1988). More recent evidence suggests there is also a link with breast cancer (Alcohol Concern 1999).

By the late 1980s about 1.5 million people in the UK were estimated to be drinking harmfully and a further 7 million exceeding recommended 'safe' levels (Alcohol Concern 1990). Currently 14 per cent of women, but 27 per cent of men are above these limits (OPCS 1996). But the increase has been greatest amongst women. In 1984 only 9 per cent were drinking more than the suggested levels, but by 1993 this had risen to 11 per cent. In other words, this is an enormous 50 per cent increase, in just over a decade. Government strategy to reduce women's consumption has singularly failed. Targets set by the UK government to reduce this percentage to 7 per cent by 2005 look increasingly unrealistic (Department of Health 1992), as do European targets for reduced consumption (WHO 1993).

However, such an individualistic approach as exemplified by the British strategic document 'The Health of the Nation' ignores the social context of health promoting behaviours and influences, such as income levels, which are known to be linked with health status (Wilkinson 1996). It is all too easy for those who exceed recommended limits and take the 'risk' to be seen, as Douglas (1994) has put it, as the 'new sinners, culpable and blameworthy'. However, in the UK the Labour government's approach to public health seems to be signalling a greater acceptance of inequalities of health status being due not only to individual behaviours, but also to social and economic issues, such as poverty, unemployment and environmental harms. Interestingly, these are linked together as influencing the individual's state of mind, levels of optimism and sense of control, all of which are more likely to promote health-seeking behaviour (Department of Health 1998).

## The structure of this book

To date, most studies of health behaviours have concentrated on the links with social deprivation, looking at those groups who are least likely to have a sense of control over their lives or to be optimistic. There are few studies where explicit links have been made with socially advantaged groups (Calnan 1987; Backett 1992; Calnan and Williams 1992). However, in the UK the group of women who drink most are professional women or those working in managerial positions, who are working full-time (Prescott Clarke and Primetesta 1997). Both Burrows and Nettleton (1995) in their analysis of data from the General Household Survey and Savage et al.'s (1992) lifestyle research note that although middle-class people are often the most health-conscious, a substantial minority are also very indulgent in terms of their food and drink. Consequently this book, uniquely, looks at women's responses to drinking alcohol from the perspectives of both social disadvantage and social advantage.

I will also be regarding women's drinking as a normal and pleasurable part of daily life, and seeking to understand the ways women use alcohol in the context of their material and social situations. By so doing, I shall be emphasising how women's drinking at whatever level is most usually a rational choice when viewed from their perspectives. Although at times drinking may be potentially health-damaging, my predominant emphasis is on women's constructive and autonomous response to their lives, as they balance one risk against another. This is moving on from the individualistic approach to health behaviours, which I criticised earlier, which seek to make women feel guilty about their heavy drinking and totally responsible for creating any attendant problems. In my model, thinking about and taking account of their social positions, understanding their contexts and how they make sense of them are basic to understanding how women respond and behave.

The lack of previous work in this area has made an exploratory and 'broad-brush' approach necessary. I have been concerned to identify some possible explanations for women's differential drinking patterns. Thus, the strength of the book, in that it is broad-ranging, also creates limitations. I have been concerned to gain an overview rather than carry out a detailed investigation of individual influences such as friendship patterns on drinking behaviour. Such a study could provide the basis of a book alone. My emphasis on contextualising interlocking themes, seeing how they fit together, is a valuable step in itself. After all, women live their lives and create social roles within interlocking arenas of partnerships, children, work, family, friends and leisure. The balance and interaction between these varied aspects of women's lives are the stuff of this book.

Previous writing about women's drinking has called for research which looks at specific stages in women's life-cycles (Gomberg 1994; Thom 1997). The women who speak in this book were all in twenties to forties. They were all at a particular stage in their lives, starting to build their families. This is the stage in their life-cycle that the book is concerned with. To that end, I will not be looking specifically at issues for younger women, except as these recall their experiences, nor will issues relating to older women feature.

Whilst some of the women were identified as 'heavy drinkers', exceeding official limits, others were not. Only two women whose stories do not appear until chapter 8 were identified as problem drinkers at any stage. So, the emphasis, unlike much of the existing literature, is on everyday drinking, not the sort that concerns the treatment centres. As Hands et al. (1995) have said, there is a need to fill the present gap between clinical literature on the one hand and large-scale population surveys on the other. In policy terms it is nonsensical to base prevention efforts on what we know about problem drinking without looking at the other side of the coin, that is, how does harmless drinking escalate and become a problem? Very few people develop problems overnight and for most enjoying a drink is a pleasurable part of their lifestyle. This book offers some pointers by exploring how 62 women managed normal and heavy drinking. Their experience is then reviewed in the light of two women's accounts of their problem drinking.

The following chapter develops some of the themes already introduced. It introduces the notion of differentially structured access to drinking, by reviewing previous research. Women with higher incomes, certain sorts of occupations and social contacts not only have the material possibilities of enjoying their drinking more frequently than other women, but they are also more likely to move in social circles where female drinking is the norm. Drinking to 'drown your sorrows' is a well-known lay concept, but there is an element of truth in it. We know little about how women do this in fact. Most literature concentrates on personal difficulties, paying little attention to how these are socially structured. The chapter concludes with an explanation of how this book takes that into account and balances drinking as a response to opportunities and difficulties.

The third and fourth chapters introduce the 60 women from the main study whose stories provide the basis of this book. First, they give their understandings of why there are differences of drinking habits between women. Second, they give an overview of their own drinking career.

Chapter 5 looks in detail at the importance of understanding how occupation influences drinking patterns. Not only does it largely structure general material and social inequalities, but different sorts of occupation also create specific opportunities for drinking. For some women the way their domestic and work roles interact can create difficulties. Chapter 6 largely looks at how social opportunities to drink are developed by interactions between social advantage, personal attitudes, different drinking cultures, social networks and leisure interests. Chapter 7 addresses the theme of drinking associated with stress.

Chapter 8 draws the previous five chapters together, suggesting socially differentiated pathways to different drinking customs. These are further explored in the light of how two women not in the main study developed problems with their drinking. Chapter 9 moves on to consider the implications of these stories for appropriate health care practice. How can pleasures be balanced against potential hazards? The women themselves give their views of current practice. The final chapter questions how fair shares of the pleasures and protection from harms can be maximised.

# 2
# What Encourages Women to Drink?

In the previous chapter I explored some of the general questions surrounding women's drinking. Where do ideas about mother's ruin come from? Why should motherhood and drinking be linked together? Does society view women's drinking in a different way from the way it sees men's drinking? Finally, I looked at how changing consumption patterns in society at large, coupled with changing perspectives on alcohol-related harms, had made both drinking for pleasure and its potential risks or harms part of everyday life for the majority of us.

At this point it is useful to explore a little more the ambiguous nature of alcohol use and abuse, that is both sides of the same coin. In order to do this I shall be drawing very heavily on previous work by Ettorre (1997), who very usefully distinguishes between what she terms positive and negative drinking. In this she is not implying any moral connotations or value judgements about the drinkers themselves. Rather, she focuses on:

> women's use of alcohol as being experienced either negatively or positively . . . from the viewpoint of the women . . . When women experience problems with their use of alcohol, this inevitably leads to disapproval, negative feelings and discontent within themselves. They may also find themselves judged harshly by others. Here disapproval becomes the key issue . . . This places a double burden on women who experience problems with alcohol. Not only do they suffer from disapproval and scorn, but also appear to have failed as women. (Ettorre 1997, p. 6)

This clearly reminds us of the discussion of double standards between male and female drinking in the previous chapter. Positive drinking, on the other hand, is primarily for enjoyment, relaxation and pleasure. It can oil the wheels of social interaction and keep conversation going. Women who drink positively do not need to drink excessively to make themselves feel OK, acceptable or good. Their drinking is controlled, even if not consciously, and getting to know their own appropriate boundaries is part of the process by which women develop positive drinking (Ettorre 1997). Appropriate boundaries or limits are of course different for each individual, according to their circumstances:

> *A woman involved in negative drinking may experience multiple problems with her use of alcohol. She is likely to be unable to control her drinking, and this loss of control inevitably causes difficulties in her life. She needs to drink in excess to feel the effects of alcohol, but in the end these effects make her feel bad physically, psychologically or emotionally.* (Ettorre 1997, p. 10)

Often this means using alcohol to 'kill' painful intolerable feelings. As Ettorre (1997) notes, the social situations in which negative drinking occurs may be very similar to those in which positive drinking occurs, but the motivation and effects are quite different. For those who are drinking positively drinking enhances their lives; for those who are drinking negatively it appears to offer a way of managing stresses and difficult feelings, but can also create problems of its own.

Of course, many of us use alcohol to relieve temporary difficult feelings, for example, the 'I need a drink' response on getting home after a frustrating day, or on being told shocking news, or in order to get through some short-term difficulties. In many situations that is a consciously chosen and constructive way of coping. Sometimes it may also go alongside looking for alternative ways of changing the underlying situation so that relief is not so necessary. We should not fall into the trap of thinking that all drinking to cope with difficulties is necessarily negative drinking. On the other hand, it can be the first step (as can excessive positive drinking), towards negative drinking and I shall return to this theme.

This chapter first looks at factors that are more likely to promote positive drinking for pleasure – practical opportunities and alcohol-positive cultures. I then turn to examine the potential influence of difficulties and disappointments that might trigger drinking. However, whilst the former are more probably linked with positive drinking and the latter with negative drinking, in the context of women's lives this is more complex as we have seen, and both positive and negative implications will be considered in each section. In a more theoretical way I outline the way in which this book links these two themes to issues of social advantage and disadvantage. As I have already mentioned, community surveys have linked women's heavier drinking with social advantage, except for younger women (under 24) (Harrison and Gardiner 1999), but there has been no study of how this operates at a more detailed level. The following chapters do exactly that by recounting 60 women's experience in detail.

In looking at why women drink and why some women drink more than others, I am relying heavily on what previous research has suggested. At this point it is worth remembering that much of the literature on women's drinking derives from clinical studies of identified problem drinkers, rather than from women's experience in general. Much of it is male-dominated, reflecting male perspectives rather than giving voice to women's lives (Vanicelli and Nash 1984). In other words, it reflects the double standard outlined in the previous chapter. Samples are often unrepresentative, mirroring the admission criteria of the units where studies were carried out rather than the full range of alcohol problems or drinking styles in the community (Thom 1997). Whilst in the UK national community drinking patterns surveys provide an alternative source of information (Breeze 1985, Goddard and Ikin 1988, ONS 1998), these involve very large samples and lack detailed analysis. Nevertheless, they not only provide a context of current understanding, but are also a useful source for developing further models and ideas. What follows goes as far as possible towards synthesising existing empirical data, attempting to put forward an alternative to the perspective outlined in the previous chapter that heavy drinking in women, particularly as they become mothers, is due to individual ignorance, irresponsibility or faulty sex-role performance. I move away from this problem-focused and denigrating approach, trying to adopt what Ettorre (1997) has called a woman-sensitive approach, that is respecting women's perspectives and taking their situations seriously.

Broadly speaking, there are two main explanatory emphases which account for heavy drinking in both academic texts, whether sociological or psychological, and popular conceptions. One is to do with opportunity and encouragement, the other is about drinking to counteract difficulties of many sorts – the lay concept of drinking to 'drown your sorrows'.

Very recent work with heavy drinkers, both men and women, who had not received treatment for their drinking, or been defined as problem drinkers, confirms both sets of ideas. An individual's employment, financial, family or health status and interpersonal relationships often overlap to create situations which offer or inhibit drinking opportunities. On the other hand, exactly the same types of influences can form a constellation of difficulties, which make a person feel stressed, depressed or negative in some way and drinking can offer relief (Maslin et al. 1998). It is precisely these interlocking features and how they shape drinking which are the subject of this book

Of course, the balances and checks change during an individual's life. Robinson's (1976) early work on the shift from drinking to alcoholism is useful in helping to understand this. He argued that an individual's drinking pattern emerges as a result of the interplay between the factors shaping their lives. For example, it is unlikely that women consider their drinking behaviour in isolation from other aspects of their daily life. Although their behaviour will change during their lifetime, as with any other learned behaviour what goes before will shape what comes after. As I outlined in the first chapter, drinking behaviour is a learned social behaviour, and, like any social behaviour, once it is established it will acquire an influence of its own and become part of the context which will affect future drinking behaviour. In this way past responses to these different influences which have created specific drinking patterns influence present ones. Thus an individual develops their drinking career or pathway (Gomberg 1994). In other words, an individual's drinking profile follows a negotiated 'career' pathway as drinking opportunities and constraints emerge and as difficulties giving rise to certain negative emotions are negotiated, all shaping a 'drinking career'.

## Employment opportunities

We have seen how alcohol became more easily obtainable in the UK after the 1970s and how consumption rose. This clearly demonstrates that at a societal level, ease of access and increased intake are linked. The argument that follows extends this approach and looks at how ease of access is distributed among women of childbearing age.

As mentioned in chapter 1, it is well established that women with pre-school children are less likely to feature among the higher consumers in any community survey of drinking levels (Goddard and Itkin 1988; ONS 1998). The heavier female drinkers tend to be young (under 25), unmarried, without any dependent children and in regular employment (Breeze 1985; ONS 1998). The usual explanation is that when women have children they stop working, withdraw from the labour market, lose their independent income and, because of increased domestic responsibilities, have little leisure time. All these factors combine to reduce the opportunities for drinking. But not all women give up work at the birth of their first child. So, is this general picture true for them?

Interestingly, prospective studies of pregnant women in this country and North America have generally supported this picture. They have profiled heavier drinkers as being older, of higher social status and without dependent children (Streissguth et al. 1983; Heller et al. 1988). Following the argument above, these are precisely the women who have the opportunity to drink, but they also have social advantages. In addition, because they are older, their earning potential will probably have risen and they will have had more time to accumulate wealth.

We also know that higher income groups spend more on alcohol (Blaxter 1990). Women from professional/managerial households, who on the whole have higher incomes than other groups, drink more than other groups (Breeze 1985; Goddard and Ikin 1988; Goddard 1991; Marmot et al. 1991; Marmot 1997; ONS 1998). So this raises the question: does social advantage or disadvantage affect the general picture that women with children are less likely to be higher consumers? Is this picture true of all women?

There is now considerable evidence that working women are likely to be heavier drinkers than those who are not working (Breeze 1985; Cox et al. 1987; Shore 1992). Apart from an independent income, employment may also bring them into contact with drinking companions. Indeed, there is evidence that social contact with work friends is greater among drinkers than non-drinkers (Breeze 1985). Furthermore, entertaining may be part of the job itself. In general, these influences seem to be strongest on women who work full-time. In 1994 in the UK 20 per cent of all women who were working full-time, but only 12 per cent of those working part-time and 11 per cent of those who were not working were exceeding the recommended guidelines (GSO 1998). We do not know whether this pattern is true for all women with dependent children, or whether the type of job has any impact.

However, the influence of employment on women's drinking behaviour seems to be becoming more important, whether they are mothers or not. In the UK women now outnumber men in the workplace for the first time in fifty years (GSO 1997). Women with children are also more likely to be working. In 1950 only 13 per cent of women with a child under the age of five were working. This had risen to 28 per cent by 1983, thus coinciding with the expansion of the alcohol market. In the mid-1980s, 7 per cent of women who had at least one pre-school child were in full-time work and a further 20 per cent were in part-time work (Martin and Roberts 1984). In 1983 both parents were earning in

52 per cent of households where there was at least on pre-school child. In 1990 it was 64 per cent and 11 per cent of mothers were working full-time (ONS 1998). Throughout Europe it is now commonplace that most mothers will participate in the labour market (British and European Social Attitudes Survey 1998). Women's employment is so central to material support for families that it is estimated that if all married women with dependent children gave up work, then four times more families than currently would be living in poverty (Glendenning and Millar 1987).

Returning to the influence of social advantage, the higher the level of the occupation the more common it is for women to continue working, thus reinforcing income differentials (Martin 1986). Those with higher incomes may well be able to afford to continue drinking, even when they have children.

The type of job itself may actually encourage drinking. Alcohol-related mortality rates vary widely between male occupations (Plant 1979, Slattery 1986). High-risk occupations have some of the following characteristics:

- alcohol freely available
- encouragement to drink
- frequent absence from home
- little close supervision
- high stress and responsibility
- very high or low rates of pay
- colleagues may collude in heavy drinking

Finally, it may be that certain occupations recruit those with a predisposition to heavy drinking (Plant 1981). The evidence on women's jobs is less conclusive (Breeze 1985; Shore 1992; Wilsnack and Wilsnack 1992), but as women continue to participate more in the labour market and enter previously male-dominated jobs then it is reasonable to suppose that some of these occupational influences will emerge. Employment type is almost certainly an important consideration in explaining differential access to drinking.

To summarise, it seems that income, social position, employment status and employment type may all help in explaining differentials in drinking behaviour. But, drinking companions acquired through employment are not the only social contacts that affect women's drinking. The next section examines the influence of drinking companions and cultures in promoting positive drinking norms.

## Shared drinking norms

Childhood family cultures influence adult drinking patterns (Fossey and Plant 1994; Orford 1985; Maslin 1998). Enabling families to provide children with appropriate norms and models of drinking is a recurrent theme in health promotion literature on preventing alcohol-related harms (Orford 1985). However, the evidence as to how this occurs is conflicting.

We know that the stage of family life-cycle development influences drinking behaviour. For example, in general, people at the stage of family formation tend to moderate their consumption (Power and Estaugh 1990), but as already mentioned we do not know if this true for all families regardless of socio-economic position. Do all women moderate their consumption when they start their families?

Evidence from community surveys, clinical literature on women with alcohol problems and studies on the sociology of friendship notes that drinking norms are similar between friends and within families (Weiner et al. 1983; Jerome 1984; Wilsnack et al. 1984; Bingol 1988; Waterson et al. 1990). In other words, higher-consuming women seem to associate with heavier drinking companions. Unfortunately, none of these studies sheds much light on which social processes achieve these similarities of behaviour or establish common drinking cultures. Bourdieu's notion of 'habitus' may be useful here. He suggests that social groupings develop a culture of habits or unthinking actions, which become part of their everyday life. Groups have different patterns of habitus (Bourdieu 1984). Breeze (1985) found that heavier drinkers were more likely to have leisure activities that can be combined with drinking. If we think of drinking as a taken-for-granted, everyday occurrence in this way then similarities of drinking patterns between companions is no more than a reflection of their shared habitus, or way of life.

Similarly, community surveys and specific studies of drinking patterns amongst pregnant women have noted that marital partners often have similar drinking patterns (Weiner et al. 1983; Black 1983; Wilsnack et al. 1984; Bingol 1988; Shore and Batt 1991; Wilsnack 1994). Indeed, several classical studies and reviews of married male alcoholics (Schukitt 1972, Orford and Edwards 1977) note the presence of a heavy drinking spouse.

Family cultures and, to a lesser extent, friendship patterns are influenced by religious and ethnic context. Anthropologists have paid considerable attention to the regulatory effect of culture and religion on drinking in primitive societies but there has been less interest in current

European cultures (Douglas 1987). However, there is evidence that certain religious groupings such as Catholics drink more than Jews and nonconformist Protestant groups, who, if they drink at all, are likely to be light drinkers (Jolly and Orford 1983). Although alcohol is prohibited by certain religions such as Islam and Hinduism, recent empirical evidence suggests that some ethnic minority women do drink, but on the whole they remain light drinkers (Waterson and Murray-Lyon 1989d).

Curiously (or as might be expected in view of the previous discussion on double standards), one factor barely figures in the literature and that is women drinking for enjoyment. After all, the time-honoured reason for drinking is to fall under the influence, or at least to take pleasure from it. Many women like the taste, enjoy alcohol with meals and use it to celebrate (Ettorre 1997). A study of friendship patterns amongst a group of middle-class older women by Jerome (1984) amply illustrates this point. The group met frequently to entertain each other with meals and drinking, thus providing a leisure activity and a source of companionship. Unfortunately, studies which look beyond partners and families are rare (Holmila 1994). But, there is some suggestion that the influence of female peers is important in shaping that ways women drink (Taylor and Wang 1988).

Moving on from shared norms which might promote drinking, what about those that might limit it? The most obvious are those that emphasise potential harms. During the 1980s government policy was to use health education to encourage individuals to moderate their drinking. It was hoped that an emphasis on 'safe' levels of consumption would restrict the social acceptability of heavy drinking. There has been little detailed study of the anticipated changes in acceptability. But evidence shows that the public do not see drinking as a major health concern (Blaxter 1990), and remain confused about what levels of intake are recommended and the relative strengths of different drinks (Anderson and Wallace 1988; Department of Health 1997).

While we have no detailed evidence about the impact of health education on women's drinking in general, except that the proportion who are drinking above recommended limits is increasing, we do know that many women reduce their alcohol intake during pregnancy. But rather than a measured response to specific health advice, this is more likely to be out of deference to taboos against drinking whilst pregnant, or because of a generalised sense of responsibility to prevent any harm to their child (Plant 1985; Sulaiman et al. 1988). Direct action as a result of health education is less likely, because we do know that specific knowledge about 'safe' levels is not influential (Minor and Van Dort 1982; Megberg et al. 1986).

More generally, there is now a considerable body of literature on lay perceptions of health and the causes of illness. Building on this we realise that middle-class women tend to hold views that are congruent with those of health professionals. They are more easily convinced of the validity of knowledge and advice generated from epidemiological studies (Calnan 1987, 1996). For example, Blaxter (1990) found in her national survey of health that it was primarily middle-class people who knew about the health risks of drinking, even if they did not rate it as a major problem. Other lifestyle and consumption research has shown that middle-class groups are more likely to try to promote healthy living through diet and exercise (Savage et al. 1992). Less advantaged women sometimes regard health promotion messages as taking all the fun out of life (Cornwall 1984), and are far less likely to incorporate healthy living activities into their daily lives. Indeed it may be precisely their socio-economic position which makes it much more difficult for them to do so (Blackburn 1994; Savage et al. 1992).

Although we might expect to find that the influence of official moderating advice would be strongest amongst middle-class women, this leaves us with a difficulty. It is precisely this group who, according to general research on lay beliefs about health, are most likely to heed health care advice who are also more likely to be the heaviest drinkers (ONS 1998). Savage et al. (1992) offer an explanation by suggesting that there is a sub-grouping of middle-class people who are not only high consumers of activities linked with healthy living, but who also consume food and drink to excess.

Pulling the threads so far together, the research literature suggests that heavier drinking women are more likely to:

- have a high income
- live in a professional/managerial household
- be employed – particularly in an occupation associated with heavy drinking,
- move in a social milieu where heavy drinking is a shared norm
- enjoy it
- have leisure pursuits which involve drinking
- be sceptical about official advice to restrict drinking.

The next section considers drinking to relieve stress or negativity, the other main theme identified in the literature.

## Material and social stresses

Alcohol has sedative properties, but whether it really helps to reduce tension is debatable (De Boer et al. 1993). Nevertheless, it remains a common assumption that it can help people feel more able to cope. In a study of stress among 1,008 executives, when asked about ways to reduce stress 54 per cent said they had an alcoholic drink (Hartz et al. 1990). There is some evidence that women who are heavier drinkers in the community may be more likely to think that it can lift depression (Breeze 1985). This belief has been confirmed in a study of women who were dependent on alcohol (Long and Mullen 1994). But it is simplistic to presume that women use alcohol to counteract all psychological difficulties, or that all individuals with such difficulties use it in that way.

Using alcohol to cope with difficulties where there were few other alternatives can start when women are young. One woman, quoted in a recent study of heavy drinkers, described how she started drinking to enable her to sleep when her parents were fighting. She had learnt this technique from her parents, who used alcohol to help them cope with their own conflicts and difficulties (Ferrins Brown et al. 1998). People learn to use alcohol, often by binge drinking, to manage their own difficulties. In Ferrins Brown's study, such binging was episodic, and in contrast to that of many of their parents, a short-term expedient only. Furthermore, it seems more likely that those who are already accustomed to drinking and who have ready access to alcohol would be much more prone to drink to counteract negative feelings.

General stress, both social and psychological, is frequently cited as a cause of heavy drinking. But stress is difficult to define and even more difficult to measure (Pollock 1988). Objective indices of deprivation or difficulty can be constructed, but evaluation of the differential impact on individuals depends on their context. For example, the numbers of other simultaneous difficulties and the resources of the individual to meet such demands are important.

Whilst community surveys indicate that heavy drinking is most commonly found in socially advantaged groups, there is no clear class association with problem drinking amongst women (Burrows and Nettleton 1995). How accurate these estimates for problem drinking are is questionable. There is a little empirical work available about whether heavy drinkers in the community report more stress than those who drink less heavily. Breeze (1985) found that heavy drinkers complained more that 'things were getting on top of them', of losing confidence, that nobody understood them, that life had no purpose, and of feeling miserable or depressed. Feeling shy in company, anxious or nervy, irritable, touchy or worried about the future were also more commonly reported by the heavier drinkers in that study. This is in keeping with reports that women drink when they need to increase their self-confidence, to aid interpersonal contact, decision-making or in executing some particularly demanding action (Johnson 1982). Certainly many of the older clinical reviews, from both the US and UK, have frequently suggested that female alcoholics are often depressed, intimating that their drinking began to counteract those feelings before it became a problem in its own right (Corrigan 1980; Cooke and Allan 1983). Data from an American community survey confirms this association (Midanik 1983). Women with alcohol problems often claim their drinking offered respite from feelings of low self-esteem and self-image and being lonely (Long and Mullen 1994; Thom 1994). However, whilst these studies note an association, they do not explore in detail what social circumstances might give rise to the sorts of feelings that women would seek to dispel through drinking. The question of whether there are specific sorts of difficulties that were linked with heavier drinking and how the women viewed them is rarely asked.

As I go on to outline some of the disparate studies which link difficulties, both social and psychological, with heavy drinking I shall explore links between a woman's social situation and her feelings of unease or distress. It is very important to remember that the availability of both material and social support can ease feeling miserable, or being lonely and depressed and indeed protect women from mental illness (Barnes and Maple 1992). After all, Brown and Harris as long ago as 1978 demonstrated how working-class women were more prone to depression. As compared with their middle-class peers they were the group who had less access to material supports and were also least likely to have confiding relationships. The presence of close confidantes and social support networks is known to be protective. So social networks may on the one hand encourage drinking, but at the same time protect against mental distress.

Turning to relevant previous research, North American studies carried out in deprived inner city areas found that although drinking in excess of prescribed limits was greatest amongst women who were socially privileged, the very heaviest drinkers were women who had multiple social problems (Weiner et al. 1983; Stephens 1985). Similarly, one of the British prospective studies indicated a small pocket of very heavy drinkers with major social difficulties (Heller et al. 1988). Furthermore, several British studies reported that women who smoked during their

pregnancies were more likely to drink more than was officially suggested (Waterson and Duffy 1992). Oakley (1989) has described smoking as a sign of deprivation. Recent work by Graham (1995) suggests
that in the last decade when income differentials have increased and
smoking rates in general have fallen, this association is becoming more
pronounced  Certainly national survey data on drinking suggest that
whilst women in lower social classes as a whole are light drinkers, there
is a subgroup who drink very heavily (Harrison and Gardiner 1999;
Marmot 1997) and it may be this group that were being identified.

Looking at this from the other side of the coin, we know that material
resources give security. If finances are sufficient, other practical supports, such as domestic help, childcare and transport, can be purchased.
Women still take primary responsibility for housework and childcare,
even if working (Borchorst 1990; Brannen and Moss 1991; British and
European Attitudes Survey 1998). This is in spite of an apparent trend
towards greater father participation (Lewis and O'Brien 1987). It is now
over thirty years, since it was recognised that combining employment
with housework and childcare is difficult (Gavron 1966). Women who
can afford to, buy in help and have a material buffer against stress
arising from the complex demands of childcare, particularly if they are
also working. Mothers living on a very low income with no domestic
help or practical supports are likely to experience the greatest difficulties in caring for a child, both on a practical and on an emotional level.
Their social contacts are more likely to be home-centred, due to lack of
income to purchase time or transport. Their leisure is much more likely
to be more limited than that of more affluent women. Furthermore, if
they live in deprived areas where crime rates are high, they may be
frightened to leave their homes or to travel on public transport (Green
et al. 1990). At first, it might be imagined that, as with smoking (Graham
1998), having a drink at home would be an accessible pleasure, and this
could explain the association between major social problems, smoking
and drinking. But social norms of drinking amongst British working-
class people have traditionally been less encouraging of drinking at
home, especially by women, than amongst middle-class people. This
may be different for the subgroups of women with extreme social problems who were identified as very heavy drinkers in both the US and UK
studies mentioned earlier.

A woman's network of family and close friends not only strengthens
her sense of identity, but is a vital source of practical and emotional
support (Oakley and Rajan 1991; O'Connor 1991; Franks 1992). This
support can guard against ill-health and psychological difficulties, by

acting as a first-line defence and resource in the face of sudden difficulties (Brown and Harris 1989), including post-natal depression (Oakley 1980). The quality of this support is important. Being sure of help in a crisis and 'being there' may be just as important as frequent contact (Brannen and Moss 1988). Those with limited social networks and who lack a confidante are most likely to experience the greatest difficulties and be most vulnerable in the face of sudden life changes, including the transition to motherhood (Oakley 1992). Situations where women are faced with a demanding baby, involving increased practical and emotional demands, as well as having to continue to meet the dependency needs of her partner are likely to test these supports.

There is now increasing evidence to show that material and social support interact. In a study of women's confidantes outside marriage, O'Connor (1991) found that those who experienced marital and financial insecurity were also least likely to have a confidante. Oakley and Rajan (1991) compared social support amongst middle-class and working-class mothers with young children. They found that the working-class mothers were less involved with their families and were more socially isolated in terms of friends. They were also less likely to receive any practical or emotional support from their male partner.

Existing data connecting these factors with drinking are sparse. Breeze (1985) found that the heaviest drinkers were least likely to have a confidante. An examination of this interplay between material and social support and its effect on mental wellbeing would seem to be important if we are to understand women's drinking behaviour as they build their families.

Physical difficulties, in particular those relating to gynaecological or obstetric concerns, have featured large in the clinical literature on women's drinking problems (Wilsnack 1985). Long and Mullen (1994) note that women may use alcohol simply to cope with sex and reduce their inhibitions. Becoming pregnant and giving birth unavoidably involve physical changes, frequently accompanied by discomfort. These have already been documented (Graham and McKee 1980) and do not need repeating here, but the point that such stresses need to be examined with regard to drinking is important. Moreover a recent survey of over 11,000 women shows that the physical effects can be long-term (MacArthur 1990).

For those who work after child birth, trying to combine domestic and employment demands can lead to role strain and work overload, with their attendant time pressures and fatigue (Shaw 1980). Women's employment is still considered something to be accommodated to domestic requirements (Brannen and Moss 1991). Indeed, female alcoholics have often recorded their guilt at not being a 'proper' mother who is at home with the children (Vollicer et al. 1981). The literature suggests that there is not a straightforward relationship between combining work and home roles and alcohol consumption (Shoer and Batt 1991; Wilsnack and Wilsnack 1992). As Doyal (1995) has pointed out, the question is probably: what work by whom? Evidence suggests that for women who have small children, part-time work is better for their health than full time work (Bartley et al. 1992). This relationship is particularly true for women in the lowest socio-economic groups, suggesting that the demands of full-time work, low income and childcare are more stressful than part-time work, high income and childcare. Furthermore, those with least control over their working environments are likely to find employment most stressful (Doyal 1996).

Women with higher status occupations are less inclined to subscribe to the traditional view that 'a woman's place is in the home' (Martin and Roberts 1984; Brannen and Moss 1991). They often derive intrinsic rewards from their work itself. In addition, they are more likely to be able to control their working arrangements. Given that they are more likely to carry on working after having children, they are also likely to have more material resources, enabling them to purchase domestic help. Women with lower-status jobs do not have the same advantages. If they also hold traditional views about women with children and are only working for financial reasons, then they may well find work less rewarding and frustrating (Martin 1986).

Thus we begin to develop a possible picture of a woman who uses alcohol to counteract feelings of stress and discomfort. She is prone to psychological difficulties, not well supported, materially or socially, finds her domestic and employment roles both demanding and unsatisfying, and is less able to purchase material help and support than those who are more affluent.

## Difficulties and dissatisfactions

This section looks at the influence of sudden difficulties and the potential discrepancies between what women expected it would be like as they began to build their families and the reality. Contrasts between romantic ideas of pregnancy and motherhood that characterise popular literature and media portrayals and reality are vast (Littlewood and McHugh 1997). At its most developed, the institution of motherhood is portrayed as the crown of womanhood (Oakley 1980), but for women themselves, having children can constitute an intellectual as well as a social crisis (Busfield 1974). Those who give up employment lose status and income and can become isolated (Oakley 1974). Many women find that the experience of motherhood does not measure up to their expectations. Or they may love their children, but not childcare, yet believe that society equates maternal love with maternal childcare. In the face of this dissonance they can feel inadequate, isolated and have little sense of themselves as women or mothers (Doyal 1995).

This is another way of looking at the sex-role conflict, which, as noted in the first chapter, has been such a dominant preoccupation in much of the clinical literature and popular conceptions about women's drinking. Some of those clinical studies used fairly simplistic psychological tests to demonstrate conflict between unconscious femininity and conscious masculinity (or vice versa) (Leland 1982). The direction of such conflicts still remains unclear (Kroft and Leichner 1987), but what is important is that these studies presume that drinking diminishes the psychic pain associated with conflict between conscious and unconscious processes (Wilsnack 1973). That sense of dissonance or conflict could equally well apply to conscious discrepancies between experience and hopes and desires – the sort of internal pain that all too readily can lead to negative drinking. To date few researchers have explored how women use alcohol to cope with the pain of difference between what they see as society's expectations of them as women and as mothers, and their actual daily experience (Ettorre 1997). There is some tangential evidence that amongst housewives with identified alcohol problems, the severity of their alcohol problem may be related to the degree of dissatisfaction with their domestic role (Farid et al. 1989). If the discrepancy and consequent disappointment are marked, then drinking to dispel feelings of dissatisfaction seems very plausible. Could this mechanism also apply to experiences of becoming a mother and starting to build a family?

Most women are unhappy about some aspect of their pregnancy (Zajicek 1981) and worry about the well-being of their child (Kumar and Robson 1984). However, the experience of pregnancy and giving birth is commonly linked with depression (Oakley 1980; Littlewood and McHugh 1997; Nicolson 1998). There is considerable disagreement about the causation (Richards 1991, Doyal 1995), but that is not the focus here. It is noteworthy that several of the factors already listed, such as financial and housing insecurity, little social support, a poor relationship with a partner and disappointment with childcare do seem to be implicated (Oakley 1980; Richards 1991; Nicolson 1998). As Doyal (1995) notes, for women as a whole, social deprivation is linked with depression and it seems reasonable to suppose this is likely also to apply particularly to new mothers. Such depression is itself a departure from an idealised view of motherhood, and this could lead to increased disappointment and reduced self-esteem, thus probably increasing the depression as well as increasing propensity to seek comfort – so establishing a truly vicious circle.

On a practical note, whilst there are a few references to alcohol in breast-milk which conclude that its effect on the child is negligible (Little 1989), there are also a few which detail women's drinking patterns in the post-natal period. These suggest that consumption may increase from what it was prior to pregnancy, mainly because of health professionals encouraging drinking to aid to relaxation (Davidson 1981). Although the overwhelming impression from community surveys is that the birth of children marks a downturn in drinking for most women, we do not know if this is universal. Given that post-natal depression is very common (Richards 1991; Pitt 1991) and that depression is linked with women's drinking problems, even if there are few references to post-natal. depression as such (Curlee 1969, Long and Mullen 1994), then such health visitor practices seem very questionable. Moreover, as Littlewood and McHugh (1997) point out, post-natal depression is very often not recognised, because women feel it is a stigmatised condition and not one to admit readily to. In this sense, stigmatisation, as with all female alcohol problems, may mean women are reluctant to seek help.

There is now a considerable body of literature demonstrating that 'life-events', or significant changes in individual's lives, such as a major role transformation, a marked change in health, domestic or social status or environment, are associated with a wide range of physical and psychological difficulties (Brown and Harris 1989). This body of research is riddled with methodological difficulties, but the consensus is that whilst they may be important in explaining the onset of alcohol problems data on women are sparse (Gorman and Peters 1990).

In one sample of 132 women, heavy drinking was not linked with life-events but was with depression (Cooke and Allan 1984), but in another study, Thom (1986) found that 50 per cent of her sample of women in treatment for alcohol problems reported that significant life-events had precipitated their heavy drinking. One criticism of her study is that heavy female drinking is highly stigmatised and some women may try to reduce their sense of stigma by ascribing their problems to a specific cause or life-event, beyond their control. However, for the purposes of my argument, it is important to note that it was often a life-event connected to their ability to relate to others or to carry out their expected roles as wives or mothers that precipitated them into treatment (Thom 1986).

Further support for the importance of life-events which undermine women's roles as partners, comes from studies of women identified as problem drinkers, which frequently mention partnership breakdown, whether through separation, divorce or death (Power and Estaugh 1990; Wilsnack 1994; Long and Mullen 1994). Similarly, changes such as a miscarriage, the death of a child, a child being placed on the 'at risk register' because abuse is suspected, hysterectomy, menopause, all of which are related to reproductive or mothering performance, also often feature (Long and Mullen 1994).

Breeze (1985) found that the very heavy drinkers in her community survey were slightly more likely then the rest of the sample to have recently separated, changed partners or to be worried about a relationship with a partner. This is in keeping with many other studies, which have drawn attention to higher consumption levels amongst divorced and separated women (Wilson 1980; Goddard and Ikin 1988; Heller et al. 1988; Goddard 1991). Indeed, although young women tend to be high consumers, having earning potential and few domestic responsibilities, those that are separated, divorced or widowed do seem to be noticeably at increased risk of heavy drinking in community samples (ONS 1998). A recent US longitudinal study of 2,085 people, born in 1946 has found that divorced women, whether they remarry or not, are prone to heavy drinking as they seek to overcome the major trauma involved. Predominantly, they seek relief at home in secret drinking (Gomberg 1994).

Breeze (1985) also found that illnesses, accidents, losing a job, moving to a new area or bereavement were not more common amongst heavy drinkers. So, it does seem that it is occurrences where women's dependency on their partners was threatened that were most significant. In addition, it is noticeable that the life-events mentioned in the Thom (1986) study, which included divorce, separation, diagnosis of infertility and the birth of a handicapped child, related to women's ability to perform the traditional female roles of partner and mother. The only exception was bereavement of people other than partners or children. Given that life-events are clearly linked with depression and that depression can be associated with heavy drinking, it seems that more attention should be given to those events which threaten women's self-esteem associated with female role performance.

Early family influences can socialise children into particular drinking cultures by inculcating images of appropriate and inappropriate drinking.

Early exposure to parental drinking problems and associated potential neglect, abuse or disharmony may in some cases make women vulnerable to mental health problems later in life (Bifulco and Moran 1998). Furthermore, there is increasing evidence which suggests that childhood stresses such as maltreatment, or loss of parent through separation, divorce or death, are linked to an increased propensity to heavier drinking (Long and Mullen 1994; Burghes 1994). Some of such childhood experiences may, of course, themselves be alcohol-related in origin.

To summarise, it seems that some heavier drinkers are likely to show more signs of psychological distress, be less satisfied with their experience of pregnancy and motherhood, and have been exposed to more life-events, particularly those that threaten a sense of self-esteem linked with gender roles, than lighter drinkers. Those who because of material position are unable to purchase practical support are likely to be especially vulnerable to negative drinking.

## Developing a social perspective

So far, I have argued that heavier drinkers have more opportunity and possibilities for drinking, and may also be subject to more stresses and difficulties, which might encourage them to seek psychological relief. It stands to reason that if these difficulties are cumulative, then difficulties will be compounded and individuals even more likely to turn to drink, if that is a useful coping device for them. The degree to which they do this will also depend on what other coping strategies, particularly social support they have access to.

It is important to note that much of the literature simply describes an association between many of the factors we have been looking at and higher alcohol consumption, and does not go into the nature of the relationship, that is quite how one influences the other. Nor does the literature always distinguish between positive and negative drinking, a point I shall return to in later chapters. But to remind ourselves of the points covered, these influences were:

- social class
- income levels
- employment – status and type
- a shared positive attitudes towards drinking
- liking and enjoying alcohol personally
- leisure activities involving drinking
- a sceptical attitude towards official advice about safe levels

- a belief that drinking helps with negative feelings
- psychological difficulties
- limited material supports
- limited social supports
- ill health
- employment difficulties
- disappointment with the role of mother
- 'life-events', particularly those that threaten the roles of partner and mother

Whilst this reads rather like a shopping list of potential influences, each has been linked with heavier drinking in women of this age group. What has been largely missing to date is any systematic attempt to explore how women react to these different opportunities or difficulties which might encourage drinking, as they negotiate their daily lives. When we turn to the women's experience in the following chapters then we begin to see how each factor is linked to drinking behaviour. Of course, for the women no one factor could be taken in complete isolation from each other. Their lives were complex and full. For each woman these varying factors were experienced in a unique constellation. As I said in the first chapter, the aim of this book is to look at the interactions of these different influences and seek to understand how women negotiated them and created their own drinking pattern.

I have been arguing that social advantage is an important dimension to our understanding of women's drinking. In fact as I have gone through each potential influence I have frequently noted how it is influenced by socio-economic circumstances that women find themselves in. This is of particular importance in a context where economic inequality and unemployment have been increasing over the past two decades (Brown and Scase 1991). One way of approaching these differences is to look at the effects of social stratification. This could be done in a number of ways, but in the literature this has traditionally been indicated by the Registrar General's system of classification of social class based on the occupation of the male head of household (OPCS 1980). Class, as so defined, is only one way of trying to measure structural influence on groups and individuals. Sociologists have been only too aware that concepts such as class, however measured in practice, are broad working definitions only, indicating a range of social experiences, possibilities and expectations. But using some class measure does offer a gateway to explore inequality, by indicating in general terms an individual's material circumstances and command over resources, as it reflects income, education, prestige and status, employment conditions, power and patterns of consumption (Marsh 1986; Reid 1989; Crompton 1998). My concern when looking at women's drinking is to find a way of comparing broad groupings who share roughly similar levels of material resources and life-styles and using a class measure however crude offers this possibility.

Moreover, the use of social class as a concept is well established in analysis of health status, perceptions of health and usage of health care facilities (Macintyre 1986; Doyle 1995; Marmot 1996). It is quite clearly linked with exposure to health risk, and associated morbidity and mortality (Townsend et al. 1988; Davey Smith et al. 1991; Wilkinson 1996; Drever and Whitehead 1997; Acheson 1998). Class differentials in morbidity and mortality are clear (Arber 1990; Bartley et al. 1992; MacRan et al. 1994) and demonstrate the impact of increasing inequality (Phillimore et al. 1994). This link holds true for women (Blackburn 1991). As I noted in the first chapter, although the similarities of women's experiences have been rightly stressed, particularly in reproductive contexts (Graham and Oakley 1981), differences in access to material goods are important divisions and create major differences in experience (Oakley and Rajan 1991; Oakley 1992; Graham 1993; Doyal 1995). However, as Graham (1998) points out, those who are most deprived are those who frequently do not figure in analysis by social class. They are the unemployed or unoccupied.

Since the Black Report on health inequalities (Townsend et al. 1988) was first published there has been considerable controversy over the explanation of this link. A number of reviews of the competing explanations are now available (Blane 1985; Macintyre 1986; Carr-Hill 1987; Davey Smith et al. 1991). Cultural behaviour and material circumstances are closely linked, as a number of studies have shown (Marsh and McKay 1994). For example, women's smoking behaviour, which in the long term damages their health, often reflects women's efforts to cope with their level of material deprivation (Graham 1995). Behaviours that promote health are more widespread amongst people in good material circumstances than amongst those in more deprived circumstances (Blaxter 1990).

Despite this, social class remains a composite and ambiguous measure. Quite how it affects the distribution and genesis of ill health remains unclear. In that sense it remains a more descriptive than explanatory concept. Furthermore, it is well accepted that there are major problems in using the Registrar's system. These have been subject to continuing discussion on both theoretical and practical grounds for many years and in 2001 a new system will be introduced in UK government statistics.

Problems with the classification are especially pronounced for women (Abbott and Sapsford 1987). The existing measure is based on the occupation of the (generally male) head of household, and thus assumes that all members of the household share the same class. But as Pahl (1989, 1990) pointed out some time ago, wealth is not necessarily evenly distributed between husbands and wives. The measure also assumes that occupation rather than education, consumption, lifestyle, income or assets is the most important factor in stratification. It ignores an individual's stage in the life-cycle, chosen economic inactivity and unemployment. It fails to deal with the position of dual-earning households, which have increased dramatically, in number. In situations where the woman is working and the man is not, or in dual-career families, the man's occupation still takes precedence even where the woman's occupation has a higher status (MacRae 1986).

Feminist analysis has noted that gender is ignored, and has criticised the assumption that the family or household rather than the individual is the appropriate unit of stratification, and that a woman's position is changed dramatically when or if she lives with a man (Delphy 1981). Even if women are classified by their own employment, this presumes equality of access to employment between the sexes. In reality, this is not the case, for example the manual/non-manual divide is less important for women, particularly in areas where new technology is rapidly expanding. In addition, the problem of how to stratify women who have no direct relationship with the means of production except that gained through a man persists (Crompton 1998). To summarise the feminist critique, female dependency, the institutions of marriage and the family are emphasised, and much of women's work, particularly caring work, which is not directly related to the labour market ignored.

Despite methodological and theoretical obstacles, much of the continuing interest in the question has involved attempts to resolve these difficulties (Prandy 1990; Erikson and Goldthorpe 1992; Bartley et al. 1996). These are reviewed by Arber (1997) and include the individual classification of women, systems where the dominant occupation of a household is measured, and combined approaches where both male and female occupations in a household are analysed. Interestingly, the results of attempts at joint classification have proved to be less divergent from a traditional system than had been supposed (Graetz 1991).

Despite this debate and recent attention to alternative stratification measures such as consumption (Warde 1990) no generally accepted alternative is yet in common usage (Oakley and Rajan 1991) which would permit comparison with other studies. Until the fundamental problem facing feminist theorists of linking gender with the means of production, in other words of linking the private sphere with the public, is resolved, researchers will continue to use generally available systems. After all, despite the shortcomings, social class has frequently been used by feminist researchers as an analytical tool. Important examples include Oakley's studies of housework, the transition to motherhood and of social support (Oakley 1974, 1980, 1992; Oakley and Rajan 1991).

My account in this book of women's drinking experiences, whilst highlighting their very different material positions, does not attempt to discuss stratification in detail, nor does it suggest alternative systems. What I am concerned with is some means of examining the impact of social advantage on women's drinking. I compare the experiences of 30 middle-class professional managerial women with 30 other less advantaged women. To that pragmatic end I used a simplified version of the Registrar General's system of social class when I was recruiting them to my study. The way I did this is described in detail in the next chapter.

## Conclusion

In conclusion, this chapter has argued that a woman's drinking pattern at any one time will be due to the differential impact of two types of influence: those to do with opportunity and encouragement to drink, and those relating to difficulties where drinking may be used as a coping mechanism. I have explored those two groups of influences in detail and argued strongly that each is linked to socio-economic position. A woman who has many social advantages will experience life very differently from one who does not have the same advantages. Consequently, the ways in which women balance and negotiate these types of influence in the context of their daily lives will differ and the resulting drinking styles are likely to be different.

I have also argued that drinking, like any other learned behaviour, has a history and develops over time. In this way past drinking patterns influence current ones, which will in turn influence future ones, as they fashion women's drinking stories. We look in detail at the course of these stories in chapter 4. Before looking at women's experience in detail, I was interested to see how far the women themselves agreed with what the researchers said. The next chapter looks at how they accounted for women's different drinking patterns.

# 3
# Women Account for Drinking Differences

There were two main sources for this book. The first was material gained from 60 interviews with women, all of whom had a young child. None of them was identified as a problem drinker, but some were heavy drinkers (defined as drinking more than officially defined levels). Their comments provide the basis for this and the next four chapters. Second, I use two case studies of women who had been heavy drinkers prior to having a child, but who had developed recognisable problems when their child was very young. We hear their voices in chapter 8. Why combine a survey with case studies? In essence this was because case studies permit exploration of individual biographies in much greater detail than is possible in a larger survey (Stake 1995). This is an unusual approach to take when studying drinking behaviour (Velleman et al. 1998). But, by using this more detailed biographical approach, I was able to flesh out more fully how their experience as identified problem drinkers mirrored that of the heavy drinkers in the main sample, none of whom identified herself as in need of specific help.

My general purpose when talking to the 60 women was to get a sense of how their lives had changed after they became mothers, and in particular how behaviours which might be associated with health had been affected. Drinking alcohol was approached as an example of an everyday health-related behaviour, which had probably altered over the last few years, reflecting the changes in their lives. But before we talked of their personal experience, I was interested to know how far they subscribed to the dominant viewpoints on women's drinking described in the previous chapter. How did they explain why some women drank more than others? Did they offer an alternative view drawing on their experiences of employment, participation in social networks and the stresses, strains and pleasures of everyday life. What did they regard as heavy drinking? How did they view drink-related problems? Their reflections form the basis of this chapter.

The first section of this chapter describes how all the women were chosen to talk about their drinking. I then give an overview of what it was like talking to them. The remainder of the chapter recounts how they viewed women's drinking behaviour in general. They talked about changes in what was seen to be acceptable for women, what they thought about drinking problems, how they viewed women who were drinking too much, and how they accounted for women's drinking problems. The concluding section compares their views with the arguments I was developing in the previous chapter.

## Introducing the women

The 60 women, whose views and experiences provide the main material for this book, were recruited from a larger more representative sample of women booking into a central London antenatal clinic expecting their first child. By the time I talked to them they were aged between 20 and 44, all with a first child of about 20 months old. Thus they had had time to settle into the necessary changes in daily life that being a parent entails. Those who were planning to return to work, resuming some of their previous lifestyle, had done so. Six had further children and eleven were pregnant again. Others were planning future pregnancies.

Members of ethnic minorities were excluded, mainly on pragmatic rather than theoretical grounds. They were few in number at the selected hospital. As in other UK studies (Bhatt and Dickinson 1992; Ettorre 1992), a large proportion (41 per cent) of them did not drink. Ethnicity and religion, especially in Islamic traditions, are major factors for not drinking. In cultural groupings where prohibitions exist they are generally applied more strongly to women than men (Mullen 1994). However, there is little UK research on drinking amongst ethnic groups and even less on ethnic minority women (Harrison et al. 1996). This is in marked contrast to the US research literature which pinpoints very heavy drinking amongst black women coupled with social deprivation (Herd 1988; Herd and Grube 1993; Vega 1993) and markedly different drinking norms between black and white groups.

I wanted to talk to some women who had been drinking lightly and some who drank more heavily, before they had a child, that is who embarked on the major change that is most linked with a reduction in women's consumption generally. So I selected two groups of 30 women, based on what they had told antenatal clinic staff about their drinking levels before they became pregnant. Half had kept below the 'official' limits and half had been drinking more (for details of these limits see chapter 1). But how could I be sure that what they reported in the clinic was at all accurate? It is well established that community surveys of drinking, which use self-report methods (for example, the General Household Survey) account for probably only about 50 per cent of the total amount of alcohol consumed, as indicated by Customs and Excise statistics (Wilson 1980; Royal College of Psychiatrists 1986). Such statistics are themselves underestimates of total consumption and do not account for home production or duty-free imports. Certainly, community surveys report only a very small number of very heavy drinkers. Indeed, one survey of female drinking had to recruit a supple-mentary sample of heavy drinkers, because they were inadequately represented in the original sample (Breeze 1985). In addition, some studies suggest that women are far less likely to underestimate their consumption than men (Cooke and Allan 1983; Cutler et al. 1988). Ernhardt et al. (1988) noted that women questioned about drinking during pregnancy five years later reported higher rates than when questioned during pregnancy, a probable explanation being that if their offspring was healthy, they felt more able to confess to higher intake levels than they would have before such assurances. So, it is almost certainly safe to assume that the levels of drinking these women described, if inaccurate at all, were more likely to err on the side of caution. For my purposes of comparing heavy with light drinkers, this crude division was fine.

As the previous chapter showed, professional women are most likely to be heavy drinkers. It also showed the theme of social advantage, as demonstrated by the major differences between the lives of professional women and non-professional women, featuring throughout the discus-sion of factors linked with consumption. Thus this theme of relative social advantage and disadvantage seemed fundamental and I wanted to look in more detail at the effect of this key variable. So as with drinking level I selected two groups of 30 women. Half were from professional or managerial households, and half were not. Whilst recognising the criti-cisms I outlined in the previous chapter about traditional measures of social class, on pragmatic grounds I defined the women's social class according to the occupation of the generally male head of household. In fact, any resulting distortion was probably minimal, for as chapter 5 shows, when the status of the women and their partners were compared they were remarkably similar.

**Table 3.1    The four groups**

| | |
|---|---|
| Heavy drinking professionals | Light drinking professionals |
| Heavy drinking non-professionals | Light drinking non-professionals |

Putting these two main groups together created four in total (see Table 3.1). By selecting 15 heavy drinking professionals, 15 light drinking professionals, 15 heavy drinking non-professionals and 15 light drinking non-professionals, I was able to explore differences in both drinking levels and the impact of social advantage.

The two women whose stories are used in chapter 8 were approached through an alcohol treatment service, which offered specific help for women. I asked for volunteers with similar characteristics to the main group, that is women with young children, but whose drinking problems came to a head after the birth of their children. In keeping with the overall sampling frame, Geraldine was a professional woman and Sophie was not.

Full details about these women, are given by drinking group in Table 3.2. Their names have been disguised but their current occupations are shown. Working part-time is denoted by 'p/t'. For those who gave up work after having their child their previous occupation is pre-fixed by 'ex'. In the few cases, where women were not working beforehand they are described as being 'at home' and their last occupation placed in brackets. Those women who were pregnant again are indicated by (*) and those who already had a further child by (**).

## Talking to them about drinking

Obtaining accurate information about sensitive issues is difficult enough (Brannen 1988; Lee 1993), talking about a highly stigmatised topic such as female drinking is even more difficult. In practice it was easier than anticipated. Although the 60 were selected randomly, refusal to be interviewed was a very minor problem. Most respondents agreed to be interviewed very willingly. This seemed to be indicative not only of their desire to be helpful, a traditional female trait, but also of their need to talk about their experience, and have it recognised and valued. As Karen complained when I did talk to her:

*'It's all baby, baby, never how are you?'*

Table 3.2   The sixty women

| Name | Age | Occupation | Partner's occupation |
|------|-----|-----------|---------------------|
| **Heavy drinking professionals** | | | |
| Bernadette | 36 | Accounts director – advertising agency | Musician |
| Chris* | 31 | Primary school teacher (p/t) | Musician |
| Claire | 33 | At home (ex-secretary) | Oil executive |
| Donna | 33 | Proofreader | Teacher |
| Emma | 34 | Ex-translator | Airline pilot |
| Fiona* | 32 | Publisher | Solicitor |
| Gillian* | 33 | Ex-stockbroker | Lloyds insurance broker |
| Lee | 36 | At home (ex-art buyer in advertising agency) | Advertising executive |
| Lynn | 31 | Ex-computer programmer | Computer programmer |
| Margaret | 36 | Nursing tutor (p/t) | Marketing executive |
| Maureen | 36 | Psychotherapist (p/t) | College lecturer |
| Patience | 30 | Secretary (p/t) | Chartered accountant |
| Phyllis** | 33 | Shop owner | Property developer |
| Ros | 32 | Ex-secondary school teacher | Bank executive |
| Stella* | 31 | Further education lecturer | Social worker |
| **Heavy drinking non-professionals** | | | |
| Andrea | 25 | Ex-clerk | – |
| Anne** | 22 | Ex-hairdresser | Butcher |
| Caroline | 24 | At home (ex-secretary) | Taxi driver |
| Christine | 26 | Personnel officer | Decorator |
| Diana | 20 | Ex-hairdresser | – |
| Eliza | 25 | Ex-hairdresser | Unemployed (long-term) |
| Eva | 42 | At home | – |
| Jane** | 29 | Ex-secretary | Removals man |
| Jill | 31 | At home (ex-dancer) | Decorator (recently laid off) |
| Joy | 44 | Make-up artist | – |
| Karen** | 32 | Ex-housing worker | Gardener |
| Linda | 30 | Factory worker (p/t) | Carpenter/joiner |
| Moira | 29 | Ex-cashier | Shop assistant |
| Sandra | 33 | Nursing assistant (p/t) | Film technician |
| Vivienne | 26 | Shop assistant (p/t) | – |
| **Light drinking professionals** | | | |
| Anna | 36 | Ex-missionary | Missionary |
| Eileen* | 37 | Art lecturer (p/t) | Secondary school teacher |
| Elaine | 39 | Ex-secretary | Civil engineer |
| Elizabeth | 28 | Picture restorer (p/t) | Solicitor |
| Janet | 37 | Ex-nursing sister | Chartered accountant |
| Lesley | 33 | Secondary school teacher | Architect |

| Liz* | 32 | Ex-clerk | Electronics design engineer |
|---|---|---|---|
| Mandy* | 33 | Lecturer in higher education | Solicitor |
| Marie* | 31 | Accountant (p/t) | Management accountant |
| Mary | 34 | Actress (p/t) | Chartered accountant |
| May** | 28 | At home (ex-nursery nurse) | Primary schoolteacher |
| Meg | 30 | Administrator | Chartered accountant |
| Miranda | 29 | Speech therapist | Town planner |
| Sally | 36 | Photographic librarian (p/t) | Photographic librarian |
| Susan | 37 | Voluntary sector consultant (p/t) | Television researcher |

**Light drinking non-professionals**

| Carol | 27 | Ex-shop assistant | Shop assistant |
|---|---|---|---|
| Frances* | 24 | Shop assistant (p/t) | Milkman |
| Helen | 27 | Computer data preparation clerk (p/t) | Technician |
| Jan | 30 | Secondary school teacher (p/t) | Milkman |
| Joan | 22 | Ex-shop assistant | Packer |
| Josephine | 31 | Security officer | Security officer |
| Judith* | 35 | Ex-secretary | Labourer |
| Louise | 27 | Bank clerk | – |
| Marion | 30 | Gardener (p/t) | Student |
| Mildred | 28 | Ex-secretary | Unemployed |
| Monica | 31 | Sale representative | Taxi driver |
| Rosemary | 29 | Ex-clerk | Policeman |
| Ruth* | 20 | At home (never worked) | – |
| Sheila | 39 | Ex-clerical worker | Electrician |
| Veronica | 22 | Ex-shop assistant | Carpet cleaner |

Once telephone or personal contact was made, only two mothers refused. I was surprised that several women spontaneously telephoned or wrote to express their interest immediately after receiving the introductory letter I sent them, long before I had time to contact them to arrange an interview. Many others telephoned to rearrange letter appointments.

I was welcomed warmly. At almost all of the 60 interviews, I was immediately offered some form of hospitality, usually in the form of tea or coffee, but sometimes alcohol, or on one occasion when I was suffering with a cough, medicine. As this was usually produced before we talked, it provided an informal start to interaction, allowing time for introductions to the child, or other family members and pets. It was a period of mutual assessment. Offering hospitality was not only a sign of welcome, but also a means of establishing that I was a guest allowed in their house on their terms. Although they might temporarily cede control to me for

the duration of the interview, thus was dependent on appropriate behaviour on my part, and would automatically be returned to them as soon
as the formal part of the interview was completed. This need to be in
control was to be expected but was all the more pertinent when we
were discussing something that was potentially very sensitive. They
needed to be sure that I would not be judgmental, whatever they said.

I was struck by how frequently the women thanked me at the end of
an interview when I was thinking that it should have been me thanking
them, rather than the reciprocal thanks that became customary. On
reflection, I realised that the interview had been a time when their stories
were told and heard. Not their child's story, but theirs. Returning to my
previous point that for these women the fact that somebody was interested in them, and their experiences, rather than the child was important,
it was clear that I was interested in them as women, rather than as how
they performed as either partner or mother. The thanks I received were
an indication of how rare such an opportunity was for them. Regardless
of material advantage, they could all feel isolated. Many also made it
quite clear to their partners that I had come to interview them, and was
not, as they put it, very interested in fathers. Such almost possessive
attitudes were another indication of their desire for individual attention.
It was their time to review their experiences. I was privileged to hear
their stories. Overall, I felt honoured to be party to their experiences, and
surprised by their willingness to talk and share confidences.

Once we had started to talk, the women restricted any interruptions,
often dealing with the child's demands while continuing to talk. Such
ability to cope with a dual agenda is well developed in mothers of small
children, and in this situation the child was relegated to second place. On
occasions when the child was unhappy with this arrangement, explanations for their seemingly uncooperative behaviour were made, for
example, the child had had a bad night, or some other disruptive experience. Very occasionally, it was almost as if the women felt I was judging
their competence as mothers by their child's behaviour. They were
sometimes considerably embarrassed by retaliatory behaviour from the
child, such as turning up the radio, tormenting the family pet, or fiddling
with my tape-recorder or briefcase. However, most of the children were,
fortunately, quite content to regard me as yet another diversionary entertainment, kindly provided by their mothers for their amusement.

Telephone calls were cut short, and other interruptions minimised
and apologised for. Only crises and the exceptional were deemed to be
legitimate interruptions. For example, some unexpected visitors came
to the house of an artist I was interviewing, with the purpose of buying

some of her work. As they were only in London for one day this seemed to be a reasonable interruption, but lengthy apologies and justifications were still given.

In presenting their stories, all the women speak for themselves as much as possible. The analysis is primarily qualitative, sometimes drawing out the differences, but sometimes drawing out the similarities between the four groups. Some tables are used to give an overview. The two case studies feed off the picture of the heavy drinkers that I develop in the following chapters.

## Their ideas about why drinking has increased

Amongst the 60 women, regardless of group, there was an overall awareness that women in general were drinking more than they used to do. Most thought this was a reflection of social changes, which had increased the availability of alcohol while at the same time making it more acceptable for women to drink. As Emma, a heavy drinking professional, noted:

> *'It's so easy to pick it up. You can pick up your bottle of wine with your baked beans at the supermarket.'*

Marie, a light drinking professional, had a similar view:

> *'It's more freely available and more acceptable for women to drink.'*

Several individuals, from the heavy drinking professional group especially, suggested that for many women, drinking had become commonplace and an expected part of the daily social round, as indeed it had, for many of them. As Monica, another light but this time non-professional drinker, put it:

> *'Women are drinking more as it's more acceptable for them to go out and into pubs or bars these days.'*

Changing employment patterns figured large in their explanations for the changes in women's drinking habits. For Liz, a light drinking professional, the reasons were that more women were going out to work and therefore had access to an independent disposable income, and many households now have dual incomes, which increases overall resources. She commented:

*'Heavy drinking's quite usual where there's two good incomes. They can afford one or more bottles of wine a day.'*

Marie similarly saw part of the explanation being women's earnings. Many others also drew attention to the decrease in the real price of alcohol and that as more women were working they had their own disposable income to purchase it with. As Elaine, a light drinking professional, said:

*'There's more money coming in. Yuppies expect to have a bottle of wine every evening. The women work to pay for the extras and to keep up the life-style.'*

Notions of increased spending power and social acceptability were common. Lesley, a light drinking professional, noted:

*'Social people who go out a lot and who can afford it, now drink more.'*

For many the impact of employment was not limited to providing income, fundamental as it was. Rather, going to work offered opportunities and sometimes expectations to drink. It also provided a context for socialising which could be linked with drinking:

*'A lot of women who are working go drinking at lunchtimes and after work. Many mums go back to work now. That's why women in general are drinking more.'* (Anne, a heavy drinking non-professional)

Additional explanations such as women who were involved in entertaining a lot, either because of their own or their husband's job and therefore able to, and encouraged to drink, were also cited as reasons for women drinking more.

Interestingly, many were aware of younger women drinking heavily:

*'It's more common for youngsters. They're into all those fancy cocktails.'* (Emma, a heavy drinking professional)

*'The older women follow the younger ones. It goes in generations. The younger ones are earning more and drinking more. They go out and pack it in.'* (Judith, a light drinking non-professional)

Such generational changes were made more obvious in comparison with their parents:

*'It's a generational thing. Young people are drinking more but my parents' generation haven't changed. My parents have one bottle of whisky a year and the occasional bottle of wine when we go to see them.'* (Margaret, a heavy drinking professional)

These women were certainly aware of the major changes in women's drinking patterns. The explanations they offered were remarkably similar to those theoretical ones we explored in the previous chapter. For them, the increased availability of alcohol and greater public acceptance of female drinking not only provided an increased potential for women to enjoy alcohol but also exposed them more to potential problems. Drinking was seen as having two sides. For example, 80 per cent (which included all but one of the heavy drinkers) considered that drinking alcohol really did help people relax. It was after all a socially acceptable avenue. As Monica, a light drinking non-professional claimed:

*'Some women under stress or who are on their own drink a lot. It calms them down and they find it relaxing.'*

Similarly, two professional women, Lee, a heavy drinker, and Eileen, a light drinker, both thought some women who were very unsure of themselves used it to boost their confidence and give them 'Dutch courage'. Indeed, for most of the 60, limited use to moderate minor mood swings, to give oneself 'a lift' or calm 'frazzled nerves' was quite acceptable.

## Their knowledge about problem drinking

Whilst these women thought it was generally acceptable now for women to drink more, almost all of them, when asked why people are encouraged to moderate their drinking, mentioned serious health risks, social problems and accidents:

*'It can create awful financial problems.'* (Emma, a heavy drinking professional)

They were aware of an apparently all-encompassing list of potentially dire consequences arising from heavy drinking, affecting physical well-being, mental well-being, family relationships, sexual relationships, ability to care for children, and being able to work:

*'It affects your performance at work and family relationships.'* (Marie, a light drinking professional)

In other words, it could ruin your whole life. And worst of all, potentially,

*'Anybody can become a heavy drinker, there's no set pattern. It's quite common.'* (Andrea, a heavy drinking non-professional)

Women from all four groups were only too conscious of potential physical dangers:

*'It's a health risk. Once your liver's gone, you've gone.'* (Emma, a heavy drinking professional)

*''My friend's husband died two months ago. He drank all the time. He really was a heavy drinker. He had a heart murmur as a child. It got worse. His liver gave up. Then everything else went. It shakes you up, when you see what can happen.'* (Anne, a heavy drinking non-professional)

*'Alcohol is a killer. It all builds up in your body and slowly rots you. You can't suddenly start repairing yourself.'* (Liz, a light drinking professional)

*'Illnesses come to light after drinking. It's bad for the system.'* (Judith, a light non-professional drinker)

But for the women such effects were largely invisible. Real problems began when signs and symptoms could no longer be hidden or swept aside. Potential dangers might be lurking, but problems only began when they were obvious, especially to other people:

*'There's something really distasteful about people who drink a lot. Their faces and bodies become bloated and they get that heavy jowly look.'* (Eva, a heavy drinking non-professional)

Some physical changes can be hidden, but behavioural changes are more obvious. It was behaviour which transgressed social norms, rather than serious consequences alone that seemed to denote problem drinking. According to their view heavy drinking could quite clearly be distinguished from problem drinking. As Janet, a light drinking professional, said:

*'I've seen people drink four doubles of an evening. They never looked bad, and it never affected their behaviour.'*

Indeed, Claire, a heavy drinking professional, who in early mother-hood was drinking 27 units of alcohol a week, was able to comment, in all seriousness:

*'I've never had any difficulties with alcohol.'*

This intake borders on that associated with potential liver damage in women. She claimed she had never been aware that her behaviour had got out of control, that she had been rowdy, suggestive, obscene or offensive, all those characteristics associated with heavy drinking women I discussed in chapters 1 and 2. Problem drinking, whilst being regarded as something very unpleasant, sometimes associated with physical problems, was always denoted by changed behaviour which infringed established social norms and upset other people. Physical effects however serious were not 'real problem drinking'. This contrast was graphically described by Meg, a light drinking professional:

*'I knew somebody who nearly died of alcohol pancreatitis. She'd start drinking in the morning and functioned like that during the day. Then she got drunk in the evening. That was when the problems started. She'd get out of hand and be offensive. It was embarrassing.'*

Similarly, Gillian, a heavy drinking professional, remarked:

*'People who drink a lot become difficult. It's very unattractive.'*

Problem drinkers' behaviour was considered to be a serious issue, distasteful and most concerning of all, out of control. At this point, it is worth noting Eva, a heavy drinking non-professional's comment about her own quite considerable regular drinking. She described her drinking as follows:

*'I'm addicted in a controllable way.'*

These women had little sense of heavy drinking in terms of consump-tion levels, that is, the ways in which official health advice is couched. For them it was the outcomes rather than consumption which signified potential problems. As far as they were concerned drinking was either within visible, sociably acceptable bounds or it was beyond them. Being beyond them meant what they called problem drinking, which was distasteful:

> *'It's not a very endearing thing. I had a friend at college who went most peculiar after she'd started drinking. It was embarrassing.'* (Lee, a heavy drinking professional)

All drinking problems are subject to some stigma. British community surveys repeatedly illustrate that the term 'alcoholic' is used in a pejorative sense to refer to a person physically, psychologically and socially deteriorated, a member of a deviant minority group, or somebody whose essence is tainted (Breeze 1985). But, as we saw in the first chapter, special censure is reserved for women who have problems with their drinking (Smith 1992).

## Views on women with alcohol problems

Why should changed behaviour be so subject to censure? Ettorre (1997) has written about the acceptable and unacceptable faces of dependency. Culturally sanctioned dependency for women consists of dependency on, and subordination to, men, and certainly not dependency on a bottle. Heavy drinking might threaten their ability to perform domestic roles and reliability for others to depend on. As we shall see, this double standard of more negative views of heavy female drinking compared to those of men with similar problems operates at the level of popular thinking, in professional attitudes as well as in more academic writing (Smith 1992). Women with alcohol problems have consistently received more disapprobation then men (Thom 1986; Waterson and Ettorre 1989; Ettorre 1997). Corrigan (1980) has drawn attention to the low self-esteem women problem drinkers have, and how they often perceive themselves in a worse light than men with similar problems. In one survey carried out twenty years ago, only 18 per cent thought that the effects of alcohol problems would be the same in both sexes. Women with an alcohol problem were seen to be more sexually available and this was deemed more morally disgusting than male violence (Cartwright et al. 1978). Although attitudes towards female drinking have liberalised, a more recent community survey carried out in Scotland ten years ago confirmed these findings (Dzaldowski et al. 1988). As we have seen, it is now more common for women to drink in public and to drink more heavily, but the double standard outlined in chapter 1 is still alive:

*'It's pretty vulgar if a woman gets drunk. It's worse for a woman. I went to a pretty Victorian school and it wasn't considered the thing to do.'* (Marie, a light drinking professional)

Eva, a heavy drinking non-professional, was even more scathing in her views:

*'The sight of a woman drunk is worse than a man.'*

For Ruth, a light drinking non-professional:

*'Women look more disgusting than men when they've got drinking problems.'*

They were equally censorious of women who drank above recommended limits in pregnancy:

*'I've seen pregnant women knocking it back at a rate of half a pint of spirits a day and it looks awful'.* (Christine, a heavy drinking non-professional)

*'Such women are wilful, wanting to prove a point.'* (Rosemary, a light drinking non-professional)

Joy, a heavy drinking non-professional, drew a parallel with pregnant drug addicts, whom she regarded as totally undesirable group:

*'We all know what heroin addicts do. They force the baby to withdraw as soon as it is born. Drinking's the same.'*

As Marie, a light drinking professional, explained:

*'It stunts adults' growth so it must affect the baby. They don't ask to be born, so you owe it to them to give them the best start possible. Those women who refuse to give up need a crutch, a prop or a safety valve. It's a way of getting rid of frustrations. Giving up has to do with will-power.'*

Similarly:

*'Those who drink heavily when they are pregnant are selfish and take the attitude that the baby must fit in with me because nothing's going to change.'* (Miranda, a light drinking professional)

Clearly they were referring to situations where drinking was no longer controlled or regular and had got out of hand. This was not what 'official guidance' called heavy drinking, that is, consuming more than a certain amount. After all, all 30 heavy drinkers had exceeded 'official guidance' before having their child and they certainly did not view themselves as problem drinkers.

Interestingly, these women proved to be surprisingly traditional in their views, ascribing a double standard to male and female problem drinking. For them female problem drinking was deeply disturbing and much more shocking than male problem drinking. In this they followed a well-established tradition in the older clinical literature and popular culture. Empirical work done in the 1970s when much of the original research literature on women's drinking was being written, demonstrates gender-differentiated clinical models in practice, expecting men to be more assertive, outgoing and independent and women to be more submissive, withdrawn and dependent (Broverman et al. 1970). Following from this, it is easy to see why female drinking in public would have been construed as a very unfeminine activity, showing signs of independence and flouting established norms of behaviour (Litman 1978), rather than quiet female depression (Carob 1987). Notions of female drinking as more pathological also come to light in a study of people with similar stages of alcohol-related liver disease, where it was more common for women than men to have received psychiatric treatment in the past (Saunders et al. 1985).

Similar views of women with drink problems are echoed in popular culture. In films, women with drink problems are often seen as inherently more depraved than men with similar problems and with a poorer outlook for overcoming their problems (Harwin and Otto 1979). Drinking is frequently linked to a lack of sexual inhibition, as in the film *The Graduate*, where Mrs Robinson drinks before indulging in sex with her daughter's boyfriend (Winick 1983). Such women are seen as betraying and debasing the fundamental nature of their feminine identity, whereas male alcoholics are frequently endowed with semi-heroic qualities as they battle with their dependency (Chalfant 1973). Such images obviously remain remarkably durable in the public mind (Edgar and Knight 1995), even being assimilated into these women's consciousness.

## How difficulties arise

Despite their disapproval, and conviction that women with real alcohol problems were somehow qualitatively different from themselves, the women in the study did offer some suggestion as to how difficulties might arise. Quite logically, these women imagined that where a framework of drinking to relax or alter mood was established, even if the desired effect was temporary, turning to drink for comfort or relief from more serious difficulties would be quite understandable. Not surprisingly, notions of blocking out pain or distressing feelings were most frequently suggested as explanations for problem drinking. For example, Linda, a heavy drinking non-professional, described her mother's drinking, explaining it as follows:

*'She drinks quite heavily. It's her only comfort. She's been abused by men.'*

Mildred, a light drinking non-professional, described how her mother started to drink quite a lot more around the time of the menopause. There were a few such references to women of their mothers' generation, but on the whole these women referred mainly to women of their own age. Perhaps they were imagining themselves in similar, but other shoes to their own.

Prolonged drinking to seek relief from difficulties was their most usual explanation for problem drinking. Like Marion, a light drinking non-professional, suggested, many of them were aware that:

*'It could happen to anybody under stress.'*

Other women had more specific stresses in mind, which are very reminiscent of some of the factors which were looked at in the previous chapter:

*'Slightly manic women who may be depressed, but live very busy lives often use it to keep going and block out the depression.'* (Maureen, a heavy drinking professional)

*'Women who aren't happy may drink more. The pressures of work or family can be strenuous. It's not uncommon to drink to relieve pressures and alleviate the problem by becoming less aware. It's an escape.'* (Judith, a light drinking non-professional)

*'Some women drink too much – like somebody who has lost her husband. Take an older woman who's depressed. She'll look to it for relief and comfort and maybe a little happiness'.* (Anne, a heavy drinking non-professional)

Despite some cynicism about television commonly showing women drinking because they are bored, several mothers thought this was realistic, particularly if alcohol is readily available and they are feeling lonely and frustrated with their child. As Ros, a heavy drinking professional, reflected:

> *'My sort of person who's at home, with time on their hands, with the whisky bottle there, could easily take to drinking.'*

Marie, a light drinking professional agreed:

> *'I know people who have reached for the gin bottle at 11.00 am when they got so bored or felt like hitting their kid. That's no good.'*

Most of the stressful situations described were domestic:

> *'Those who can't put up with what's going on around them, where the men and the kids are giving them trouble might turn to drink.'* (Veronica, a light drinking non-professional)

Some of the women drew attention to women finding themselves in male-dominated work settings and feeling obliged to demonstrate that they can compete with the men, including their drinking performance. Perhaps they were drawing on their own experience. Gillian, a heavy drinking professional, thought women with personal difficulties were especially susceptible in these types of situations:

> *'If one's stable and got a good job one might drink for pleasure but it's normally limited. It's when you need to fall back on something for support that the problems start.'*

The themes of support and being valued featured frequently, whether the difficulties mentioned were domestic or employment-related. Where women might not have enough support, their self-esteem was likely to be undermined. In such circumstances, the women I interviewed had the notion that many problems arose when women attempted to seek comfort and support from their drinking. The physiological effects they sought would be to relax, feel better, more in control, more loveable and more desirable.

Most of the difficulties mentioned placed little importance on material conditions. Those difficulties that were mentioned were viewed in terms of their psychological and emotional impacts. Jill, a heavy drinking non-professional, summarised this perspective:

*'Single parents are more likely to be lonely or depressed. They and women who get trouble from their husbands could turn to drink for comfort. It's a release for those with bad marriages. It's worse if you've no job and are living in crummy conditions.'*

Her picture is one of women having to provide for their children, not receiving sufficient emotional support, and like so many women in such situations unable to exert any control over their material environment (Graham 1998).

Emma, a heavy drinking professional, was convinced that loneliness was at the root of drinking problems:

*'For some, it's to do with unemployment, stress and insecurity. They need friendship and social contact, so go into a pub or wheel a trolley round the local supermarket, and pick up their alcohol.'*

Clearly they did not think that the addictive properties of alcohol could be held totally responsible. In fact, the different reasons they linked with very heavy drinking such as stress, psychological discomfort, boredom, loneliness, bereavement are reminiscent of the discussion of drinking to counteract difficulties and disappointments in the previous chapter. Whilst they recognised that wider social changes had created more opportunities for women to drink, these alone did not account for the development of women's problem drinking. After all many of them availed themselves of these avenues.

Although these women widely recognised the potentially difficult outcomes of using alcohol as some sort of emotional pain killer, or what might be termed symptom relief drinking or drinking to cope, very few saw it as the first step towards dependency for women. Veronica, a light drinking non-professional, was one of the few to mention addiction:

*'You become addicted to it and you don't feel yourself.'*

Whilst they were less aware of what factors promoted men to become heavy drinkers in the first place, they were very sure of the power of addiction once drinking had become established. Once addicted, the man qualitatively changed, stopping was virtually impossible and certainly beyond mere will power. These were 'real' alcohol problems:

*'I remember seeing men, down-and-outs, drinking in the graveyard when I was 17 or 18. It's so degrading and nobody gives a damn. They just become*

*flotsam. Some of them had good brains. You'd think they'd have had more sense and stop before they got addicted.'* (Anne, a heavy drinking non-professional)

*'My step-father was an alcoholic. It's a drug. Once it takes hold you can't stop. That's when your problems start.'* (Eva, a heavy drinking non-professional)

*'I had a girlfriend whose father had an alcohol problem. It destroyed her parents' marriage. He died from drinking. It's very sad watching somebody who had been distinguished just destroying himself. There was nothing anybody could do. It didn't matter how much you reasoned with him when he was sober. Their characters change and they become quite different from what they would be normally. It's a very slow poison.'* (Marie, a light drinking professional)

In many ways their comments about women who drank heavily in pregnancy were reminiscent of the way they described men with 'real' alcohol problems. Explanations involving social opportunity for drinking or those relating to difficulties, whether material or emotional, became markedly less popular as explanations for heavy drinking among pregnant women. Only three of them had mentioned addiction in the general context of women's heavy drinking. This was in marked contrast to the 26 who cited addiction as the main reason why pregnant women drank heavily. For these women drinking to excess whilst pregnant was deemed not only exceedingly undesirable but incomprehensible. The previous tolerance and understanding shown to women who drank heavily rapidly evaporated. These women were morally inferior, irresponsible, incapable or weak-willed:

*'Those women who refuse to give up need a crutch, a prop or a safety valve. It's a way of getting rid of frustrations. They are weak-willed.'* (Marie, a light drinking professional)

*'Those women who are unaware and ignorant of the dangers, those that don't care about the dangers, and those with certain types of personalities like manic depressives or weak characters, might be more at risk of drinking too much. It's because they're addicted in an uncontrollable way.'* (Eva, a heavy drinking non-professional)

*'Spirits are certainly out. They filter through and rot the baby and pickle it. Those who don't stop are addicted.'* (Liz, a light drinking professional)

*'Some women don't go off it when they're pregnant. It's to do with under-
lying tension or the opposite. If you're feeling magnificent you think you
can do what you like and get away with it.'* (Emma, a heavy drinking
professional)

This is very reminiscent of some of the comments in the alcohol literature, about damage to the unborn child being the ultimate female crime
(Gomberg 1979). For these women to think about such drinking was
deeply disturbing to their strongly held images of motherhood, recognising that women carry a heavy burden of responsibility for the well-
being of their unborn children. They could not understand how those
who persisted in drinking heavily could be 'good' mothers. Curiously
enough, they hardly touched on the implicit explanation in much of
the alcohol and pregnancy intervention literature that such drinking,
like smoking in pregnancy, was due to ignorance (Waterson and Murray-
Lyon 1990b). Such interpretations take us back to the discussion of
faulty sex-role performance, outlined in chapter 2, which was, and
apparently still is, certainly for these women, a dominant explanation
for excessive drinking in pregnancy.

Their view with its emphasis on two main types of drinkers, ordinary
(including those drinking well over official limits) and 'real' problem
drinkers, where drinking is out of control, is reminiscent of the disease
concept of alcohol problems outlined in chapter 1. As an earlier study
of public perceptions of alcohol problems found, it seems that this
model, with its emphasis on the deadly properties of alcohol, in spite of
scientific evidence to the contrary, has barely been extinguished from
the lay mind (Crawford and Heather 1985). For just under half of these
women, who were so understanding of what they viewed as heavy
drinking in normal circumstances, the concept of addiction seemed a
very plausible explanation of a behaviour which so appeared to trans-
gress their expectations of what motherhood entailed. It offered a less
overtly critical explanation than simple irresponsibility.

Such an explanatory theory postulated that serious drinking, which
originally started to relieve worries and distress or to calm down, could
eventually escalate out of control. Thus, as in their explanations of 'real'
problem drinking, alcohol took over. Such women were no longer
responsible. Blame could be transferred to 'the bottle'. The predicament
of the individuals concerned was viewed as more serious and hopeless
as control and power over their drinking was deemed to be in 'the
bottle'. The women drew a clear distinction between normal drinking
(even if exceeding recommended limits), including drinking to cope,

and 'real' problem drinking. They did not suggest any progression between them. However, there was more than a hint in their replies that they considered drinking to relieve psychological discomfort indicated the start of potential dependency, down the slippery slope to addiction and 'real' problem drinking.

Certainly, whilst as chapter 1 indicated, the literature notes that in the social context of a generally increased consumption, problems also increase, it rarely directly links increased opportunity to drink with the development of harms at an individual level. This is a theme we will return to in later chapters.

## Conclusion

In terms of their ideas, described in this chapter, there were few differences between the four groups. Not surprisingly, both groups of heavy drinkers were more interested in the topic of drinking, changed social attitudes towards women drinking, why some women drank more than others and the pleasures associated with drinking. However, both drinking groups had strong views about what constituted an alcohol problem and how problems developed. Despite the differences in how interesting the topic was, there was great unanimity amongst their opinions. This was in spite of their widely contrasting social positions, experience and drinking patterns.

These women were well aware of increased drinking and drinking problems among women in general. They ascribed this to falling prices, greater availability and greater social acceptability. But, when asked why some women drank more than others, they cited personal difficulties. In such circumstances it was quite understandable for a woman to seek relief in a bottle.

They made clear distinctions between normal drinking, however heavy, and 'real' problem drinking, where behaviour became inappropriate and drinking went out of control. Hovering on the borders of dependency, even if usually in response to difficulties, was dangerous territory and they were reluctant to imagine this, probably because they were only too aware of the great stigma attached to women who drink too much. With 'real' problem drinking their interpretations changed dramatically and the blame was shifted to the addictive properties of alcohol itself. This type of explanation accounted for the characteristic behavioural abnormalities or changed physical appearance associated with problem drinking. It was also a way of creating social distance and barriers between those who indulged in such 'real' problem drinking and those who did not. This was particularly apparent in the way they described women who drank very heavily in pregnancy. That was due to addiction. It was too threatening to think the unthinkable, as Andrea, a heavy drinking non-professional did, that:

*'Anybody can become a heavy drinker, there's no set pattern.'*

It could be them. How was that to be squared with their notions of maternal responsibility? The notion of addiction provided a comfortable barrier. In their eyes, either you were addicted and therefore a problem drinker, or you were not and therefore OK. Whilst some of this group might have admitted to being heavy drinkers, as indeed some were in terms of risking physical damage, they certainly did not identify themselves as problem drinkers, or even potential problem drinkers.

The next chapter moves on to look at these women's personal experiences of drinking. They tell their drinking stories, charting their drinking careers. How they linked their general explanations of changes in the acceptability of female drinking, reasons for heavy drinking and the potential drift into problem status, outlined here, will be followed up in the succeeding chapters.

# 4
# Drinking Careers

In this chapter eight women tell their drinking stories in detail, from their earliest encounters with alcohol, through youthful extravagances, into adulthood and then parenthood. They speak for themselves. In our conversations, the topic of drinking alcohol was approached as an example of an everyday behaviour, which had probably altered over the last few years, reflecting the changes in their lives.

Two women were selected from each of the four groups of drinkers – heavy drinking professionals, heavy drinking non-professionals, light drinking professionals and light drinking non-professionals, described in chapter 3 (see Tables 3.1 and 3.2). I chose these eight women in particular, not because they were more articulate, or their experience more colourful than any of the other women, but because their experiences were characteristic of their group. Each group had a distinctive drinking pattern, which they retained throughout the period I was interested in. Whilst the drinking stories of these eight form the main plot, I use other women's experiences from the same groups to amplify some points.

For them, telling their story was a way of making sense of their experience and communicating it to others, first me and then you, the reader. I asked them to recall their drinking history, with a special emphasis on the last few years. Research studies asking women about their experiences of pregnancy and childbirth have illustrated that women are well able to recall such major events accurately. Blaxter and Paterson (1982), when interviewing grandmothers in Aberdeen, were surprised to find how clearly they remembered events from twenty years before, when interview data were checked against medical records. Similarly, retrospective interviewing about alcohol consumption has also been shown to generate surprisingly accurate information (Edwards et al. 1973; Streiss-guth et al. 1977). No doubt what is remembered indicates its significance for the individual (Moss and Goldstein 1979). We all reassess the past in the light of subsequent experience (Stimpson and Webb 1975). But all these women were well able to provide quite detailed and full information about their drinking careers to date.

## Emma and Margaret: heavy drinking professionals

The first pair were Emma and Margaret (as noted in chapter 3, these names are pseudonyms). Emma was a 34-year-old, former translator, married to an airline pilot, also 34 years old. Margaret was a 36-year-old nursing tutor, married to a 38-year-old marketing executive.

Emma had always been a fairly heavy drinker. She recounted how she started drinking as a student:

> *'I studied Russian at university. It was a vodka-oriented course and after studying in the USSR I'd think nothing of drinking half a bottle a day. You didn't get a hangover. It was a question of who got under the table first.'*

Indeed, she remembered telephoning Alcoholics Anonymous after an especially heavy party, telling them about her drinking and being told she was an alcoholic who needed treatment. Her reaction was defiant:

> *'Just to show them, I gave it up completely for six weeks.'*

These experiences of heavy drinking as a student were typical of the heavy professional drinkers. She explained it as a time when she was able and expected to drink a great deal. There was the opportunity, encouragement from her peers and freedom from other responsibilities. She had never drunk so much since:

> *'It'd dropped off a bit anyway after I left university.'*

Getting into work encouraged her to drink fairly heavily:

> *'Once I was earning I took it up again, drinking wine.'*

Many women in this group recalled particular heavy drinking times in their late twenties, or even in their thirties. Unlike the more youthful student excesses already recounted this was more regular and frequent. Usually, it was connected to their type of work. For example, Ros, who was working in the City, and Phyllis, who was running a wine bar at the time, felt that they should drink with customers. For others, going for a drink after work-related meetings was a routine part of life:

*'We'd be in the pub every night after work with colleagues. It was some-thing that was very work-related. At the weekend I could get through eight double vodkas in a night. I'd also got a taste for wine. I could drink more than my friends were able to.'* (Donna)

Emma continued drinking heavily and regularly, well into her thirties:

*'I was still quite a heavy drinker when I met my husband. We went out a lot to the theatre or for dinner. That involved drinking. At home we'd always have a bottle with the evening meal.'*

For this group, the prospect of pregnancy meant change. As Fiona, foresaw:

*'I knew things were never going to be the same, in more ways than one.'*

Most of them cut down:

*'I thought to myself that I'd got the rest of my life and I could live for a year with less. It'd save money anyway.'* (Chris)

Once pregnant Emma too cut down:

*'While I was pregnant I cut down, drinking a lot on social occasions only. I remember we celebrated her arrival in a rather alcoholic fashion.'*

But, despite these general modifications to drinking profiles, those who were heavy consumers before pregnancy continued to be so during their pregnancies. These women were the most likely to celebrate the new arrival with a bottle. They were also the only ones to say they made an immediate return to previous drinking habits, that is, drinking above recommended limits. Indeed, all members of this group had returned to something like their previous levels by the time they had stopped breast-feeding. A few were drinking as much as 30 or 40 units of alcohol a week.

*'When I was pregnant and couldn't drink or smoke I thought that the party was over. I now realise that it's only partly over.'* (Maureen)

Emma did likewise:

> '*While I was breast-feeding I tried very hard and only had one glass of wine a day. It was a real pleasure. It was a large glass. Once I stopped feeding her, we really celebrated in style.*'

Getting back to being able to drink as she put it 'normally' and certainly regularly was real relief, as it was for Donna:

> '*I thought "great I can drink again. We can have a bottle of wine again in the evenings".*'

Now that her child was a toddler Emma thought of alcohol in this way:

> '*Now it's my reward and I like it. I'd like us to drink a bottle a day like we used to but getting blotto is irresponsible. I've got to think of her. I've got to get up and face the next day. Still, it does help me to relax. I have a large glass of wine when she's gone to bed and another with my meal. We'll drink a bit more at weekends. There's always the whisky bottle if I'm desperate.*'

Margaret's experience was different. Having always been a fairly big drinker since student days, she started drinking much more in her early thirties during a marital break-up. However that changed:

> '*After meeting my second husband that sort of drinking stopped. We still drank fairly heavily. We were both working and sociable. I got used to drinking a lot. I could appear sober and still drive the car. After ten drinks or so I never fell about the place or was sick.*'

She cut down when they were planning to have a child.

> '*I went to a lecture on the Fetal Alcohol Syndrome and that put me off a bit. I limited myself to two glasses of wine a day while I was carrying her. We celebrated her arrival in style with a bottle of bubbly. I certainly had more than one glass of wine when I was breast-feeding. It helped get her to sleep.*'

Very few women actually craved for alcohol, like Stella, who said she had drunk it by the bottle while she was pregnant. Those heavy drinkers who had given up, initially because of nausea and vomiting,

gladly returned to their previous consumption once they felt physically better. In this way, daily life was returned to its customary routines
and an air of normality resumed. After all, drinking was a part of their
daily round in a way it was not for light drinkers. They, not the light
drinkers, used it to structure their lives both objectively and symbol-
ically. Quite understandably, they were especially upset when their
physical state interfered with their usual routines. This desire to get
back to normality is very similar to the way Murcott (1988) describes
the changes in eating habits that accompany pregnancy and how most
women try to return to familiar habits as soon as they can. As Lynn
said:

> *'I cut it out last time, but I don't think it was necessary. Next time I'd
> drink a bit.'*

Indeed, several women who had either given up or cut down drastically
while they were pregnant felt that it had been a rather unnecessary and
unrewarding effort.

Over a year and a half after becoming a mother, Margaret described
her drinking thus:

> *'These days, we do most of our drinking at home, either together, or with
> family and friends. It's mainly wine with a meal. Those wine boxes are a
> bit lethal aren't they? Sometimes we'll have sherry and I do like a whisky
> or a G and T. It relaxes me. Yes, I do occasionally have a drink if I'm on
> my own, but I wouldn't if I was alone with her. We try to get out together
> once a week to the theatre or for a meal. We always go for a drink then and
> have a bottle with our meal. I get out quite a lot on my own too. I've
> noticed that if I'm meeting other people in the morning, say at a group,
> I get offered sherry, wine or coffee. I mean the sorts of groups that I got into
> since I gave up work. For example, I go to a group for working mothers once
> a month on a Saturday. At 11.00 am the wine comes out. Everybody takes
> a bottle and we get pissed, but there's a moral code against drinking if
> you're breast-feeding.'*

Regular drinking integrated into the daily routine was a conspicuous
feature amongst these drinkers. The ways in which this group described
their drinking were strikingly reminiscent of accounts of smoking and
poverty, previously detailed by Graham (1987). For this group, a drink
marked a shift into 'adult' time at the end of the day, when their child
had gone to bed. It was a legitimate reward for the day's activities:

*'It's an off-duty thing. You put your feet up. It's a time when we can chat.'* (Lee)

They would pour themselves a drink whether they were alone, with their partner or with friends. Typically, Chris said that at the end of a day when she felt tired she would pour a drink, justifying it to herself by saying:

*'I've earned this. I'd then follow it up with a second because, the first went down rather well.'*

Stella mentioned having a glass of wine before her evening meal:

*'It's a habit and a reward. It marks the beginning of my time.'*

Bernadette also used alcohol as reward:

*'Once he's [her child] gone to bed the first thing I do is to sit down and have a drink. I've earned it and it relaxes me before my husband gets home.'*

For them, drinking was one of the ways they structured their lives. For this reason they were understandably anxious to return to usual patterns as soon as possible either during pregnancy or after giving birth. For them daily wine-drinking supplemented by spirits was the norm – a sign of stability. They regularly had a drink in the early evening after the child had gone to bed and followed this up by opening a bottle of wine with the evening meal. This pattern was augmented by drinking at lunchtimes at weekends and more irregularly as social occasions occurred. This was not the case for the heavy drinking non-professionals as the next section demonstrates.

## Anne and Eva: heavy drinking non-professionals

Anne was 22 years old and married to a 28-year-old butcher. She had worked as a hairdresser before becoming a mother. Eighteen months after the birth of her first child she had a second child, so by the time of the interview she had two children. Eva was very different, but representative of a small group of heavy drinkers, who all seemed to have known 'better' days as children if not as younger women. I will talk in detail about this group in chapter 5. Eva was 20 years older than Anne and was not married. She was not working but talked of various short-lived jobs in the past. She employed a resident nanny to help her look after her son, used private medical facilities on occasion, and talked of eating at famous London restaurants with other members of her family.

Anne remembered starting to drink when she was a teenager. This early drinking was characterised by a search for a good time, going to clubs and discos, and enjoying the luxury of being able to spend her Saturday earnings by going out with friends. Her consumption reached a peak in her early twenties. She was working by then:

> *'During the week we'd only drink in the evenings after work, never at lunch times. I'd only have four drinks of an evening than, but at weekends it'd be eight or more vodkas. We'd be out until 4.00 in the morning regularly. I'd be drunk. I could hold it, but I'd not get up the next morning.'*

She accounted for her teenage drinking as originally being part of a teenage rebellion. Converting her first earnings into a liquid currency was no more than a symbol of emancipation from parental control. After her initial teenage rebellion Anne had also found peer support and companionship an important encouragement to have

> *'...a fling. I really enjoyed it.'*

For the women in this group, drinking was something you did when you went out socialising, an activity quite separate from work. Christine's experience was common:

> *'I could manage a couple of bottles of wine in an evening, when we went out with friends.'*

When Anne became pregnant for the first time she was in her early twenties:

> *'I suppose you should give up drink when you're pregnant. I knew smoking was bad and it had to be one or the other. I gave up drink, unless we went to a party, because it was easier. I didn't go off it. We just went out less. I thought that if I packed up smoking altogether I'd be more stressed and thought that'd affect the baby more, but I managed to cut down from 15 to 10. At the end I was back to normal. I was bored being stuck in all day.'*

Cutting down by going out less was usual for these women:

*'We didn't go out, so I didn't drink. If we went out, I wanted to drink.'*
(Jill)

While most cut down a bit, as a group they still drank considerably more then the light drinkers. Some changed their drink. Joy for example opted for Guinness, in the belief it was better for her.

For those who had a second child, experiences were not necessarily the same in the two pregnancies. Karen described how she had been forced to cut down the first time because she was feeling very sick in the early stages. When she found that she was not being sick the second time round, she was relieved to be able to drink more. Andrea reasoned that she had drunk during her first pregnancy and her child was all right, so there was no reason not to drink during the second pregnancy.

These perceptions indicate how hard these women found it to accept health advice, founded on concepts of a statistical risk of harm, which seems to have no real impact, at least not in their experience. It is not surprising that many of them, particularly the heavy drinkers, felt that cutting down their drinking had been an unnecessary deprivation of something they enjoyed. Why should they deny themselves something that seemed to pose no obviously relevant risk? Whilst they had been willing to condemn those who drank to excess when they were pregnant, their drinking seemed to them to be far removed from the sort of out-of-control drinking that horrified them. They had felt justified in continuing or resuming their drinking during their pregnancies because they were convinced that their behaviour was not irresponsible, and certainly not verging on what they saw as problem drinking.

All of those who had cut down waited until completing breast-feeding before increasing at all, many of them taking a long time to achieve previous levels. Some even maintained the decreased levels of their pregnancy permanently:

*'Before he arrived I could physically manage to drink much more.'* (Christine)

This was very different from the experience of the heavy drinking professionals, who got back into regular heavy drinking as soon as possible. But by the time I was interviewing them ten were back to consuming more than the recommended weekly levels for women (14 units a week). They were the ones who could get out regularly. This group habitually concentrated their drinking into a few days at the weekend when they went out. On the whole, their drinking took place outside the home. However a few, like Moira, began to drink at home after the child's arrival. Such changes in leisure patterns will be discussed more fully in chapter 6. Drinking at home was only permissible when there was company and on such occasions tended to be heavy. This prompted Karen to say she would only drink at home if she knew somebody was looking after the children and that they were unlikely to wake up. Most importantly, regular nights out at a club or pub were very significant opportunities for drinking. For example, Jane played in a darts team on Friday nights. For the group as a whole, celebrations of one sort or another and parties figured strongly in their social calendar. When out drinking, in contrast to the heavy drinking professionals, they placed less emphasis on wines and preferred beer and spirits.

Returning to Anne, once she had children, life was rather different:

> *'I could cope with drinking when I was working. I could take time off. I'd only got myself to worry about, but when you've got kids they've got to come first. We go out for meals with old friends occasionally, or to the pub. I last had a drink at Christmas and New Year. That's over a month ago now. Drink doesn't relax me, on its own. I need to go out to be merry. Drinking's part of going out for me. It doesn't feel right drinking at home.'*

Eva's story was unique, but as I have already said, many features of it were typical of a small subgroup of heavier drinkers whose upbringing had been more middle-class. She also talked of drinking a lot earlier in her life, in her mid-twenties, also emphasising the influence of her peers, which in her case were the people she was living with who were following a very bohemian lifestyle centred on music and drink. Looking back, she recounted how she drank a great deal in her mid-twenties.

> *'I hit the bottle hard. We would start at 6.30 pm, eat late, go to a club and drink until 5.00 am. I had a hangover most days. We got up at about 1 pm.'*

Later on this changed:

> *'All that really heavy drinking dropped off by the time I was 30. I was mixing with different sorts of people by then. I still drank quite a lot though.'*

This heavy drinking, non-professional group were most conscious of their previous heavy drinking. As they matured, their excesses may have been curbed, but they still settled for a heavy drinking style. For example, Eva's phase of excessive drinking was over by her late twenties and she settled into simply being a heavy drinker, justifying it by saying, in a memorable phrase:

> *'I'm addicted in a controllable sort of way.'*

Pregnancy meant changes:

> *'It was different before I was pregnant. I was going out more. I could afford a hangover. At first when I discovered I was pregnant I kept on drinking very heavily, because I didn't intend to keep it. After deciding to go through with it things changed. I went off gin. I'd drink white wine and Perrier water, because I went off red wine as well. I guess it was about half a bottle of wine a day. It helped me to sleep. After all, the French women drink all the way through their pregnancies. In the hospital after he was born a friend brought in a couple of bottles of wine. I started to drink a glass with lunch. The staff didn't seem to mind. By the time I got home I was sick of white wine. I was back on gin within the month.'*

She was still drinking a fair amount by the time we talked:

> *'These days at 7.30 pm, before eating, out comes the ice. It's my treat and I find it relaxing. It's what we've always done in my family. I do the same whether I'm on my own or with other people. I always have three double gin and tonics of an evening. I buy two bottles of gin and two bottles of wine a week, but I'll only have wine if somebody else is there. If I'm feeling rich I'll buy a bottle of whisky. I never run out of those things. I enjoy it. Drinking is a drug. It gets difficult to stop taking it. I'm addicted in a controllable sort of way. I don't allow it until after 7.30 pm however desperate I feel. I do drink alone whether I'm at home or out. If I'm out and it's my drinks time I'm careful that I've got my supply with me. I never drink because I'm depressed. It's not that sort of thing with me.'*

As mentioned earlier, Eva was one of an important subgroup of heavy drinking non-professionals. The other three who were also daily drinkers were Joy, Karen and Christine. These four were slightly older then the rest of their group. Although not specifically asked about their childhood or parental occupation, they indicated that they had been brought up in Professional households and that they had retained some of that lifestyle. Joy, for example, would always have a drink on getting home from work as well as wine with her meal. She described her routine saying:

*'It's my reward, a little perk and a wind-down.'*

Whilst this was a common response for some heavy drinkers, light drinkers never viewed it in such a way, as the next section shows.

## Marie and Liz: light drinking professionals

Marie was a 31-year-old, part-time accountant, married to a management accountant aged 47. Liz, a 32-year-old woman, was no longer working. Prior to having a child she had worked as a clerk. Her husband was 33-years-old and employed as an electronics design engineer. Both women were pregnant again.

Drinking careers seemed to take a different course for these light drinkers. Marie remembered heavy drinking in her early twenties, when she had just started work:

*'There was one holiday when I was about 22 I went away with two medical students. We drank one and a half bottles of spirits a day between us. I was pacing along with the boys. In those days, I could drink four doubles without even thinking about it. I didn't notice. I never had a hangover. I never drank more than I wanted to. It was always a matter of principle not to go over the top.'*

However, once she had been working for a while she was less keen on drinking a lot:

*'By the time I reached my late twenties I still drank anything except beer, but only in small quantities. I don't know why it changed. You grow out of some things don't you? I'd never really liked it that much anyway.'*

By the time she married three years previously:

*'I'd drink occasionally. We'd drink when people came in or sometimes I'd have a whisky and soda before a meal and wine with it. I never did drink alone. That's a rule easily kept, as I've never found that it helps me to relax. I know other people say it helps, but I saw what it did to a friend of mine. Problems can crop up very easily.'*

Her consumption levels had already dropped off by her mid-twenties, and marriage at 28 confirmed her role as a light drinker. During her pregnancy, she was violently sick and tired:

*'It never entered my head to drink any more than it entered my head that I shouldn't. I never thought about it. I don't think I could have faced it. Anyway, I didn't miss it. I didn't drink again at all until I'd finished breast-feeding and then it was only the odd drink.'*

Since then:

*'If people come in I might drink. Being pregnant again has made no difference. I couldn't drink like I did when I was young now and I wouldn't want to, whether I was pregnant or not.'*

Liz also started her drinking career by drinking heavily in her mid-twenties:

*'I drank heavily eight years ago. I could go right through a bottle of Martini by 3.00 am. I had no mortgage. I was around the arts scene and the person I was living with drank heavily. He was an artist and couldn't work unless he'd had a lot to drink. After we split up I drank a lot less.'*

Such periods of excess generally ended as circumstances changed. They either met a new partner or 'settled down', like Marie. For Liz it was when, aged 27, she left the heavy drinking man she had been living with for four years and changed her work. When she was working she liked to

*'. . . go and sit in a pub, but I'd never drink very much. I was always worried about getting up in the morning and I wasn't that bothered about actually drinking anyway.'*

For this group drinking with colleagues after work or as part of their working life did not seem to figure as much as for the heavy drinking professionals.

In pregnancy, Liz said:

*'I didn't cut down, but when I was breast-feeding I took to drinking Guinness as a tonic. It was my one treat of the day. I'd have it while waiting for my husband to come home. I stopped it when I finished feeding him.'*

Liz was not alone in changing her type of drink. Several women in this group did so; for example, Miranda drank Italian red wine produced by relatives, because of its iron content. Several others gave up drinking completely. Nobody returned to their previous levels until after breast-feeding and several maintained their decreases permanently:

*'It's not made any difference. I didn't drink much before and I still don't.'*
(Elizabeth)

By the time we were talking:

*'I'll have the odd glass of wine with a meal. That's all. It's always with somebody else. I'd never drink alone. I'm pregnant again, but that really hasn't made any difference. We're both light drinkers. My husband has a can or two of lager a week at home. He doesn't go to the pub.'*

By contrast with the heavy drinking professionals, there was no regular pattern to drinking amongst this group. For them daily drinking was an exception, rather than the rule. Drinking was consequently less ritualised. Mary was the only one who frequently had a glass of wine in the early evening as a reward for the day's efforts. Likewise, alcoholic accompaniment to meals at home was both irregular and infrequent. Sally was one of the very few who routinely had a glass of wine with her evening meal a few times a week. This group tended to confine their use to times when they were out visiting, or when friends came to see them. Even so, they still drank less on such occasions than their more adventurous heavy drinking sisters. They also tended to limit themselves to drinking wine whereas their heavy counterparts consumed a variety of drinks, with more emphasis on spirits.

## Judith and Monica: light drinking non-professionals

Judith, who was 35 years old, had worked as a secretary. She was married to a 33-year-old labourer. By the time of the interview she was pregnant again. Monica was a 31-year-old sales representative married to a 32-year-old cab driver.

Judith was introduced to the impact of heavy drinking at a very early age, as she recalled:

*'My father always found it hard to control his drinking. He wasn't really aware of it. By my age he was really dependent on it. That put me off.'*

But,

*'I still managed to drink a lot when I was working as an air hostess in my early twenties. After a flight I'd think nothing of having four whiskys or five Martinis, just for starters.'*

The combination of memories of her father's problematic drinking, changing her job and illness served to encourage her to be a light drinker:

> *'I got hepatitis eight years ago and I had to give it up for a while, but by
> that time I wasn't a heavy drinker anyway.'*

Although she returned to drinking later, her intake remained low:

> *'We'd go out once a week or so. I'd drink a couple of vodkas. When he [her
> child] was on the way I thought it'd be better to be safe than sorry. I didn't
> want an alcoholic baby. So I cut down.'*

Now she had a small child:

> *'We are not into the habit. Our lifestyle's different now. We hardly ever go
> out. I had half a glass of beer with a neighbour six days ago. I'd never
> drink alone and certainly not in the house. I don't find it relaxes me, but I
> think other people find that it does.'*

In many ways Monica's experience was similar. She talked of when
she was 17 or 18:

> *'We went out a lot. I could drink a hell of a lot more then, not that I
> wanted to get drunk. I did it to get a high. I'd drink anything, cherry
> brandy, vodka. You name it, I drank it.'*

Half of both groups of non-professionals, regardless of recent drinking
levels, had launched into serious drinking as teenagers, consuming large
quantities of lager, fortified wines such as martinis, and spirits especially
vodka. This fits with the national picture of young working-class women
drinking very heavily indeed. A number cited heavy drinking in their
early twenties:

> *'When I was about 22 or 23, we were out at the pub, or at a club or disco,
> almost every evening. We'd drink at lunchtime as well. In an evening I'd
> have eight white wine and sodas. I'd be so ill afterwards. It was my biggest
> problem. It went down too easily. I wished I could drink more slowly, but I
> couldn't.'* (Jill, a heavy drinking non-professional)

For all of them such times of very intense drinking were intrinsically
linked with having a good time with friends. These women viewed it as

the natural outcome of a time in their lives when as young adults they had no financial or domestic responsibilities and were spending a good deal of their time in the company of other heavy drinkers. Such youthful experimenting has reported elsewhere (Plant and Plant 1992).

For Monica, getting married was a turning point:

> *'I slowed up an awful lot after settling down when I was 24. My mother was a light drinker and I started taking after her then. We'd go out several nights a week to the pub but would always be home by 10.00.p.m. I'd have two glasses of wine and soda. Never any more.'*

Once through these early stages, for the subsequent lighter drinkers their drinking styles seemed to settle. For many, like Monica, 'settling down' was the turning point. Mildred, a light drinking non-professional put it thus:

> *'When we were 16 to 18 we drank ourselves sick. I met my husband when I was 18 and he wasn't a big drinker. After that, I enjoyed it but I'd stop. I no longer wanted to feel terrible for the sake of it.'*

This retreat from youthful teenage or student extravagances was common to all groups. Some moved away from their college friends or workmates. Some had health problems, which required them to cut down. For some their social life altered and there were no longer the same opportunities or encouragement to drink. For these lighter drinkers alcohol itself was not important to them, the circumstances surrounding their drinking had been more so.

Like many in this group, Monica gave up drinking completely when she was pregnant:

> *'I had orange and soda when we went out.'*

For these light drinkers becoming pregnant and having a child often made little difference to their drinking. For those who had cut down, nobody increased to their pre-existing light level until after breast-feeding and many hardly drank at all:

> *'I didn't drink much before her, but I drink even less now.'* (Josephine )

By the time we were talking, Monica described her pattern as follows:

*'I have the very occasional can of lager indoors with friends. I've never drunk alone. It can help me to relax but only if I'm in the right mood. If I'm depressed it only makes it worse. I drink very little. Last week was a bit different. We went overboard. We went to the pub with my brother as it was his birthday and we also went out for a meal as it was my birthday later in the week.'*

In this group, drinking had become a very restricted activity, taking place when intermittently visiting the pub at weekends, going to parties, or when out with friends or relatives:

*'We don't drink indoors much and we don't go out much now. I've never drunk much and there's no opportunity now.'* (Frances)

Nobody mentioned daily drinking and there were almost no references to drinking at home. Only one mentioned occasionally buying a bottle of wine at the weekends. They had fewer celebrations than the heavy drinking non-professionals. A sharp decline in going out socially and strong taboos against drinking at home had made opportunities for drinking almost non-existent for them. Sheila summed it up:

*'Drinking's something for high days and holidays only.'*

## Linking stories

These stories have served to outline the broad generalities of these women's very varied drinking experiences. They clearly point out that the basic differences between the heavy and light drinkers, which are heightened by differing socio-economic circumstances. Although all four types of drinking patterns were modified when the women became pregnant, these distinctions were still maintained despite these changes. Most significantly, the higher consumers remained the higher consumers at all stages.

Their stories demonstrated the development of four distinctive forms. These women did have obvious drinking careers, with continuous changes in drinking level and style. Their drinking profiles at any one time were noticeably influenced by what had gone before. Therefore, at any one stage the ways that these women changed their drinking depended on what their drinking had been like before. Research on younger people has also demonstrated similar continuity of drinking careers (Ghodsian and Power 1987).

Most of these women, regardless of their later drinking levels, recalled phases of consistently extravagant drinking. For the non-professional groups this was linked with rebellious drinking in their teens and first years of paid work. They could afford to drink, were very sociable and had no domestic responsibilities. For the most part, this had subsided by the time they reached their mid-twenties. On the other hand, the professional groups recalled times when they were students, and in their first years of paid work.

Once the stage of youthful experimentation had subsided, patterns became more stable. The light drinkers displayed remarkably little interest. The heavy ones modified their exuberance to become what I termed in chapter 1 'heavy drinkers', offending nobody but possibly damaging themselves, as they regularly exceeded officially suggested limits. However, the heavy drinking professional group had a very divergent drinking style from the heavy drinking non-professionals. They may have been consuming roughly similar amounts, but the way they did so was markedly different.

Despite the almost universal changes of drinking practices during pregnancy, higher consumers tended to remain so throughout, as did the lower consumers. Groups retained elements of their previous drinking styles throughout. However, the experiences of drinking careers were very different for women from different levels of material advantage, even if they had been drinking at similar levels before becoming pregnant. It was the heavy drinking professionals not the heavy drinking non-professionals, who were most able to return to their previous styles after giving birth. Regular drinking, often at home, was an integral part of their daily existence, whereas the heavy drinking non-professionals concentrated their drinking into the few times when they were able to go out drinking. Although both remained heavier drinkers in comparison to both lighter groups, the professional group was able to draw on their socio-economic advantages to easily maintain their previous intake levels. It was harder for the non-professionals. This nicely illustrates the influence of social advantage and the next three chapters will explore these implications as they affected links between work, social activity and stress and these women's drinking.

# 5
# Occupational Hazards

Why bother with looking at occupation? As we have seen in chapter 4, the women themselves referred to how going out to work offered them opportunities to socialise and particularly for the professional group it seemed that the type of work itself encouraged heavier drinking. Second, we saw that there were distinctive class differences in drinking patterns and style, even amongst women who were drinking roughly the same amount. Notions of class are, of course, based on occupational differences. In addition, as we saw in chapter 2, previous large-scale surveys of drinking behaviour over the last decade have repeatedly drawn attention to major differences linked with socio-economic position, as defined by occupation. On the whole women over the age of 24, from professional or managerial backgrounds report drinking more than other women (Breeze 1985; Goddard and Ikin 1988; Heller et al. 1988; Waterson and Murray Lyon 1989a; ONS 1998). Certainly, this earlier work demonstrated that the link with social class held, irrespective of the presence of dependent children or age. In addition, secondary analysis of large data-sets such as the British General Household Survey indicates that class and gender together are strong indicators of different tastes in alcohol (Bunton and Burrows 1995). Third, whilst there is much emphasis on lifestyle in popular culture today, in that individuals are able to choose and create their social identities to an unprecedented degree (Featherstone 1991; Bunton and Burrows 1995), people choose what they can afford (Warde 1992).

Blaxter (1990), in her study of health and lifestyles, comments on the limited room for manoeuvre that most people have. Her conclusion was that voluntary adoption of healthier lifestyles was an option only in more favourable circumstances. Thus most health promotion activities exacerbate existing inequalities, as those who can afford to adopt healthier lifestyles. Paradoxically, as Nettleton and Bunton (1995) note, most social research into health-related habits has concentrated only on those who are disadvantaged.

Chapter 4 demonstrated that having some disposable income for the first time and few other demands on their finances was often mentioned by women in all groups as a reason for youthful drinking. In chapter 3 several of them suggested that households with a high income, prob- ably based on two salaries, would be more able to purchase alcohol and domestic help, thus releasing time for leisure activities, which might involve drinking. Further evidence of the importance of income comes from the fact that in earlier work women who were less advantaged mentioned cost as a reason for reducing their drinking when they were pregnant (Waterson and Murray Lyon 1989b).

Despite the difficulties of using a measure of social class to classify women, the divisions between the 30 professional households and the 30 non-professionals reflected distinct social differences. The nature of these material and social differences form an important background. Social class was assigned on the basis of the employment of the head of household using the Registrar General's classification (OPCS 1980). Head of household status referred to the male occupation when the women were married or living with their partner, and female when the women were single. All the professional women were living with part- ners, whereas seven of the non-professional women had no partner. I have deliberately named the non-professional group in that way, because it included households that would have been classified as social classes III (non-manual and manual), IV, V and those who would not have been classifiable, according to standard procedure (OPCS 1980).

Interestingly, hardly any women would have been classified differ- ently if the social class classification had been based on the woman's employment status either before or after the birth. Where both part- ners were working there was a marked similarity between the occupa- tional statuses. Similar findings are reported in another smaller sample of mothers of young children (Brannen and Moss 1991). There were only two women, Patience and Claire (both secretaries) who, according to their own occupation, would have been put in the non-professional group, but because of their partners occupation (accountant and oil executive respectively), were classified as professional. In addition, there were three cross-class families, as defined by MacRae (1988), where the women would have been classified as professional but the male head of household occupation was non-professional. These were:

Christine, a personnel officer married to a painter and decorator, Sandra, a nurse married to a film technician, and Jan, a teacher married to a milkman. Following my scheme they were all categorised as non-professional.

Relationships to the labour market will be approached in several ways in this chapter. First, I will illustrate how heavy drinking is likely to be much more common amongst professional women. This is primarily linked with income and wealth, permitting the purchase alcohol or leisure. Second, the women's experiences of employment and different occupations will be used to illustrate that although employment, as opposed to unemployment, is not linked with different drinking patterns, the type of work frequently is. Finally, the women weigh up the pros and cons of their occupational situations, assessing them against what they would ideally have liked.

## Material and social support

The professional women were considerably more materially advantaged than the non-professionals. Average income was more than twice as high in the professional groups as in the two non-professional groups. Not only were overall income levels higher for the professional groups, but several of the non-professionals were dependent on benefits and had to cope with all the attendant insecurities.

Average age in both the professional groups was higher at 33 years than in the non-professional groups where it was 28 years. Similarly, partners were slightly older in the professional groups. So, not only was their earning potential higher, but they had also had more time to increase their earning power and accumulate wealth. Women in the professional groups were more likely to be graduates or have professional qualifications. They were also more likely to be studying for further professional qualifications than their non-professional counterparts. Again, this might have increased their earning power. Nine women were currently studying, all except one for a recognised qualification. These included a Diploma in Nursing, a psychotherapy qualification, a PhD, an MA dissertation, an RSA typing course and Open University courses. Only one was in the heavy drinking non-professional group and one in the light drinking non-professional group.

Part of this material disparity was achieved not only through having jobs and more highly paid jobs, but also through dual-incomes. Ten households in each of the professional groups were dual-income. This compares with three in the heavy drinking non-professional group and five in the light drinking non-professional group. Women in these two non-professional groups were most likely to have given up work after the birth, so the income differentials between the non-professionals and the professional women were immediately widened. This class discrepancy in returning to work after the birth of children has been reported in earlier surveys (Martin 1986; Brannen and Moss 1991). At the time of interview about a third of the non-professionals were working, as compared with two-thirds of the professional women. The non-professional mothers, regardless of drinking group, were more likely to think of returning to work when the child was at full-time nursery class or had started school. Interestingly, the three non-professional women with middle-class occupations (Christine, Jan and Sandra), had already returned to work. Whether this class discrepancy was due to different class norms about who should look after children or lack of suitable part-time employment remunerative enough to make it worth their while is not my main concern here. The importance is that for these women, losing their source of independent income made finances even more strained for quite a long time, and of necessity they concentrated on maintaining daily life, rather then purchasing luxury items or leisure.

These differences were clearly reflected in how the women perceived their financial position. When asked how they managed on their income, it was noticeable that the professional women were much more comfortable. Eight in each of these two groups were able to manage with some to spare. This contrasted with four in the heavy drinking non-professional group and only two in the light drinking non-professional group. It was the professional group that was much more likely to say they could quite easily manage financially. Presumably they had disposable resources to spend on alcohol if they wished, whereas the non-professionals had more difficulty. Fifteen (half heavy and half light drinkers) of the 20 women who said they found it hard to make ends meet came from the two non-professional groups. Many of these non-professional women said they depended on their parents for financial help. The implications of such financial constraints are described by Eliza, a heavy drinking non-professional:

> 'All the baby's stuff had to be second-hand. It was impossible to buy every-thing social security said she should have with the £100 they give you. I couldn't even afford second-hand stuff.'

Table 5.1   Indicators of material resources

| Indicator | Heavy drinking professionals | Light drinking professionals | Heavy drinking non-professionals | Light drinking non-professionals | Totals |
|---|---|---|---|---|---|
| **Housing tenure** | | | | | |
| Owner-occupiers | 15 | 14 | 7 | 9 | 45 |
| Private rental | – | 1 | 5 | 1 | 7 |
| Council rental | – | – | 3 | 1 | 4 |
| Other rental | – | – | – | 4 | 4 |
| Totals | 15 | 15 | 15 | 15 | 60 |
| **Housing type** | | | | | |
| Whole house | 14 | 12 | 5 | 6 | 37 |
| Self-contained flat | 1 | 3 | 9 | 9 | 22 |
| Rooms | – | – | 1 | – | 1 |
| Totals | 15 | 15 | 15 | 15 | 60 |
| **Car ownership** | | | | | |
| Own | 11 | 11 | 5 | 5 | 32 |
| Shared | 1 | 2 | – | 1 | 4 |
| None | 3 | 2 | 10 | 9 | 24 |
| Totals | 15 | 15 | 15 | 15 | 60 |
| **Regular paid help with child and/or housework** | | | | | |
| Live in help | 3 | – | 2 | – | 5 |
| Help with housework | 7 | 5 | – | – | 12 |
| Help with child | 5 | 7 | 3 | 2 | 17 |
| None | – | 3 | 10 | 13 | 26 |
| Totals | 15 | 15 | 15 | 15 | 60 |

Mildred, a light drinking non-professional, whose husband had been unemployed for three years, told how:

> 'We were short of money. I couldn't go and buy what I wanted for her or do for her what I wanted. I kept bursting into tears.'

It was hardly unexpected that drinking would be greatest where income levels were highest and lowest where neither partner was earning. One point to note is that within each social stratum income levels were slightly higher in the two heavy drinking groups. However, this was not necessarily due to whether the mothers worked or not. Their partners may have been better paid.

These differentials were evidenced in differences in material resources between the groups, as shown in Table 5.1. As might have been expected, home ownership, and larger and better dwellings, were commonplace for the professional women. Several of them had moved recently as they upgraded from one owner-occupied dwelling to a larger one. The non-professionals were much more likely to have housing problems. During their pregnancies, two women, one from each of the non-professional groups, had had to live with relatives, and another had been homeless. By the time I was interviewing them, the heavy drinking non-professional group seemed particularly vulnerable. Four women in this group had major housing problems. Jill, a heavy drinking non-professional, was threatened with eviction from privately rented accommodation; Jane, also a heavy drinking non-professional, had only one bedroom for a family of four; Vivienne and Eliza, both heavy drinking non-professionals, had severe problems with damp. Mildred, a light drinking non-professional, also had problems with damp.

Only four women in each professional group did not have access to a car. This was not because they could not afford them, but because they either did not see the need for a car if they lived very near a tube station or they did not drive. By contrast ten women in each of the non-professional groups were without their own transport, with little likelihood of being able to afford it in the near future. Only one said it was because she did not drive. As noted in chapter 2, being reliant on public transport complicates daily life, creating its own pressures especially for parents of small children (Hamilton and Jenkins 1989; Pearson 1993).

The use of paid domestic help was usual for the professional women. Indeed, three of these households employed live-in help. Three were also able to afford nannies or maternity nurses when the women returned home with a new baby. The two non-professional households who employed live-in help came from the hybrid group of four women, who, whilst classified as non-professional in terms of their current status, had apparently known 'better days'. I surmised that private income paid for this help.

The two professional groups were very much more materially and socially advantaged than the non-professional groups. The impact of structural and practical disadvantage was clearly greatest for the non-professional groups. In the course of interviewing I was forcibly struck by the range of lifestyles and differences in access to material wealth, as well as education and employment. I had planned this and expected it, given that I was interested in pinpointing such differences. I was, however, still surprised by the reality. For example, in two interviews with middle-class women the au pairs were intermittently present. These were two young women in their early twenties. Their presence in the household seemed to be one of hearing all, seeing all and saying nothing. Although pleasant towards me, they never volunteered any information, and quietly got on with taking the child out or whatever they were supposed to be doing. As far as the mothers were concerned they hardly seemed to notice that the nanny was there, so taken for granted were they. As Margaret, a heavy drinking professional wryly remarked:

*'Women need to train for the marathon before looking after a baby.'*

In terms of practical help with childcare and housework, non-professional mothers were further disadvantaged once the initial period of homecoming from the hospital had passed. At that time almost all the women had extra help. In the majority of cases (60 per cent) partners took time off work to help with the new baby. This was frequently supplemented by help from mothers or mothers-in-law, particularly where there was either no partner or where he was unable to help. However, those first few days of enhanced support quickly passed and all mothers quickly assumed overall responsibility for childcare. For the non-professionals without the means to purchase domestic help it was a heavy load.

For almost all of them the experience of childcare in the early days was one of adjusting to constant demands. Even though there were very often difficulties with specific aspects of childcare such as feeding, these experiences were equally common to all groups. Similarly, there were no differences as to when the child started sleeping through the night. A good third of women (11 non-professional women but only eight professional women) were initially disappointed with caring for their child. In this context, it is worth remembering that women in the professional groups were much more likely to be employed. Childcare may well be more enjoyable if it is not a full-time occupation (Brannen and Moss 1991) and if you have practical help, especially live-in help. Twice as many middle-class women used paid help with childcare; the non-professionals had to rely on relatives.

When speaking about their current feelings towards childcare, reactions were either strongly negative or very positive. Negative responses emphasised tiredness, boredom and the stress of meeting continuous demands. Those who were more positive enjoyed watching their child grow and demonstrate an increased awareness and understanding of the world. They liked playing with them and enjoyed their company. In all, five women in each of the non-professional groups as compared with only three in each of the professional groups stressed the negative aspects. These non-professional women were more socially disadvantaged, received less practical support and were more likely to be disappointed with their experiences of motherhood.

By the time of the interview, partners were the most usual source of help with childcare in all groups. Those in the professional groups were not only markedly more likely than those in the non-professional groups to be involved in the first place, but more likely to do so without being asked. Graham and McKee (1980) also report that higher-status fathers were more involved with domestic work. Overall, in comparison with the professional mothers, the non-professionals were less likely to be supported by more than one type of help. In fact, if they got any help at all they were doing well.

Although many women were employed outside the home, all but Vivienne, a heavy drinking non-professional, who lived with her mother, took overall responsibility for the housework as well. Such allocations of responsibility have been reported by other researchers (Nicolson 1998). Whether this was by force of circumstance or by choice was not always clear, for many of them seemed to follow Karen, a heavy drinking non-professional, who reckoned:

> *'You can't rely on men doing things in the home. They just don't see the dirt. It's easier to do it yourself.'*

Once again there were clear differences between the social strata. Of course, as we have already noted, three middle-class households had live-in help and three-quarters of them had paid help. The non-professionals had no paid help and had to cope single-handed. As with childcare, non-professional partners although no less helpful overall than middle-class partners, were again less spontaneous in offering help. Sharing housework as a matter of routine occurred only in middle-class households. Apart from different gender norms, the non-professional women were less likely to be in paid work and they may have been more reticent to ask their partners for help, which may partly explain why more of them had to cope single-handed.

In terms of alcohol consumption, the important points from this section are the income differentials, which not only permitted the purchase of alcohol, but accommodation which offered more space for entertaining, and the purchase of domestic help and transport released time for leisure. In addition, material advantage shields women from difficulties and stresses. The middle-class women were better supported on a practical level. We must also remember that four of the non-professional women, but only two middle-class women, had more than one child.

## Paid work

> *'I wouldn't mind working and mixing with other people more. I'd like the money and I will go back when he's older.'* (Joan, a light drinking non-professional)

> *'I'd never cope with looking after a little one and the housework. I don't think it's fair on them if you work.'* (Caroline, a heavy drinking non-professional)

Having established the very different material circumstances of the professionals and the non-professionals, this section moves on to look at how roles outside the home through employment or education influenced opportunities for drinking. Some of the theoretical literature, as noted in chapter 2, pointed out that women who worked were heavier drinkers than those who did not. The explanation for this seems to lie in the income differentials generated by working and the implications of the increased social contact that employment offers.

Prior to having a child, employment patterns were very similar in all groups. At that time seven women were not working. This included five non-professionals, including one single mother who had never worked. Almost all women were working full-time, that is 30 hours or more a week. Only seven were working part-time (less than 30 hours a week).

But, by the time I was talking to them, when their children were aged between one and two years, there were distinct differences. Most of those who had gone back to work after having their child returned to what they had been doing beforehand. Only a few women changed their jobs, generally to something of comparable status and income. For example, Stella, a heavy drinking professional, changed from school teaching to adult education. Marion, a light drinking non-professional, went from working in housing to being a gardener. Frances, a light drinking non-professional, who had been a canteen assistant, moved to shop work. Helen, another light drinking non-professional, went from being a receptionist to computer data preparation, and Donna, a heavy drinking professional, from selling life insurance to freelance proofreading, which was more easily combined with childcare. Susan, a light drinking professional, moved from community work in a local government setting to becoming a freelance community work consultant. The main benefit of these changes was that the jobs were more flexible and easily combined with childcare.

In all, only about half of the sixty were working, but this total comprised about two-thirds of each of the middle-class groups, and less than a third of each of the non-professional groups. Although more professional women were working, this was predominantly part-time. Whilst fewer non-professional women were working, those who were, were more likely to be working full time. This may be a reflection of the lack of suitable part-time work, but more probably of economic necessity: they needed the money. It is worth noting at this point that other evidence shows that whilst part-time work may be beneficial to the health of mothers with small children, full-time work is less so (Bartley et al. 1992). The professional households were able to maintain higher income levels without the women working full-time. However, the fact that the professional women continued working almost certainly substantially boosted household income differentials in comparison with the non-professional groups.

In addition, the professional women were not only more frequently combining motherhood with employment, but they were also more likely to be studying for further educational qualifications. In the two professional groups this was true for four and three individuals respectively, and for one individual in each of the non-professional groups. In effect, this meant that three women in each professional group and one non-professional woman were combining motherhood, employment and study.

The importance of drinking with work colleagues either after work or as part of the job was mentioned by many of them as they recounted their drinking stories in the previous chapter. Obviously, the non-professional women who gave up work no longer had access to those sorts of drinking companions. The situation was less changed for those professional women, who, regardless of drinking level, were less likely to give up work altogether. We will return to the importance of these social contacts in the next two chapters.

Professional households were wealthier, more professional women retained an independent income, as well as having more access to social activities, through their multiple roles, than the non-professional groups. This does make it easier to understand why in general women of higher social status report higher drinking levels in community surveys. But so far in this chapter, we have not explored why some non-professional women and some professional women were heavier drinkers than others. I now go on to look at the influence of the type of job, which does seem to offer some explanation.

Research on the social patterning of consumption indicates major linkages with lifestyles which are culture- and class-specific. For example, Savage et al. (1992) in their study of 'middle-class' lifestyles note that for high-earning middle-class people consumption practices are paradoxically linked with both health and physical fitness, but also with excess eating and drinking. They argue that lower incomes do not permit such indulgences. This would seem to be the case in this study. Furthermore it applies that within each socio-economic group the heavier drinking groups had slightly higher incomes.

In Savage et al.'s (1992) survey, professionals who were largely employed in the health, welfare and education sectors, where earnings are modest, demonstrated consumption patterns that were more ascetic then their peers working in private enterprise. Their culture and life-style not only reflected their 'expert' social knowledge of the self in society, including healthy behaviour, but also their social, cultural and professional isolation from the world of private enterprise. On the whole they rejected highly competitive individualism. This study sheds light on the way educational qualifications and professional and employment cultures together influence consumption patterns. Comparing the two middle-class groups, both partners in ten heavy drinking professional couples worked in the private sector, whereas this only applied to seven of the light drinking professional couples. Looking at this from the other side, in only two cases did both partners in a heavy drinking professional household work in the public sector, whereas this was the case for four light drinking professional couples.

As we saw in chapter 2, previous research on male drinking patterns suggested that heavier drinkers are more likely to be working in occupations where alcohol is freely available, drinking encouraged as part of the job, drinking with colleagues frequent and where there is a certain amount of job-associated stress or responsibility. Some of these women, when describing how they had drunk a lot in their late twenties, certainly drew attention to the opportunities for drinking that their employment had offered them then. So I expected that, in terms of past employment, there would be some slight differences between the heavy and light drinking groups. In fact, 17 women in the heavy drinking groups as compared with 13 in the light drinking groups had previously worked at one time or another in the performing arts, in a pub, hotel or in a bar, all occupations traditionally linked with a high consumption amongst men. This suggested that there might be some value in taking this line of reasoning further to look at current jobs.

A wider list of risk occupations, taken from Breeze's (1985) study, was used. The list included occupations where the standardised mortality rates from liver cirrhosis were well above average and where conditions of work such as irregular hours, absence from home, lack of close supervision and availability of alcohol on the job were considered likely to encourage drinking (Breeze 1985). This revised list, which included accountants and financial specialists, advertising, marketing and public relations, artistic occupations, occupations in entertainment and hotel industry, and health service occupations, was found to be more discriminating. Twelve women, of whom five were heavy drinking professionals and three were heavy drinking non-professionals, were currently working in these occupations. However, when I asked them about their current occupation, none of them drew attention to the fact that their type of employment *per se* offered more opportunities to drink than other employment, remaining apparently oblivious to these distinctions. Nobody claimed that drinking was expected as part of the job. What they described was a predominantly social activity at lunchtime or after work. There was no mention of using alcohol to counteract work or home pressures. But, it did seem that drinking associated with the working environment was more important for professional women. For a start more of them as a whole were working, and more of the professional heavier drinkers worked in the private sector, where drinking is more commonplace. One was working in advertising, three were in publishing and one in high finance, all of which are areas where one might suppose entertaining is commonplace. None of the light drinking professionals worked in advertising, publishing or high finance. One had been an actress, but none of the rest of them worked at all.

It will be remembered how both Liz, a light drinking professional, and Eva, a heavy drinking non-professional, talked of living with heavy drinking partners in the past, both of whom had worked in the entertainment industry (see chapter 4). Both women commented how that had encouraged their own drinking. In addition, Liz, Marie, another light drinking professional, and Mildred, a heavy drinking non-professional, had commented on how their drinking patterns had changed radically after they had met a new partner. So it is interesting to note that when the partner's current occupation was taken into account, although only professional women had partners working in defined risk occupations there was a clear trend for this to be more frequent in the heavy drinking professional group than the light drinking professional group. Ten heavy drinking professional women had partners who were working in risk occupations, whereas this was the case for only five of the light drinking professionals.

In three heavy drinking professional and two light drinking professional couples, both partners were currently employed in risk occupations. Prior to the arrival of the child this had been true for two heavy drinking professional couples and one light drinking professional couple. Consequently, in situations where both partners were employed in risk occupations the mother was more likely to be a heavy drinker. Inferring that they were also high consumers reinforces the finding from earlier studies (Waterson and Murray Lyon 1990a) that women who drank more often had partners who drank more and that drinking was often a shared activity. Where partners had private sector jobs such as a company executive, bank official or advertising executive entertaining at home was commonplace.

So although going out to work as opposed to not working was not linked with drinking levels the job type apparently was, especially for the professional groups. Partner's occupation also appeared to be key in developing shared drinking norms and patterns between couples. The next section looks at the interplay between the women's domestic roles and paid employment. To date the research literature has been equivocal on whether this has any association with drinking levels.

## Balancing roles

> *'I couldn't be a full-time mother 24 hours a day for 365 days a year. I need to be myself in my own right.'* (Bernadette, a heavy drinking professional)

> *'Men are more physically suited to be the hunters. Only women can have babies and they're more emotionally equipped to deal with them, so it's better they are at home.'* (Anne, a heavy drinking non-professional)

Although it was the professional mothers who were most likely to work, the concern here is about the balance of roles between working and motherhood. Regardless of which group the women belonged to, the realities of combining childcare with other demands presented problems. Some women in every group were dubious about their ability to be full-time mothers. As Phyllis, a heavy drinking professional, who owned a delicatessen shop, commented:

> *'It is best if a mother can bring up her own child, but you get tunnel vision. You need something else.'*

Monica, a light drinking non-professional, put it even more strongly:

> *'It's good to get away. I was tearing my hair out by five months.'*

There were clear status differences. It is well established that professional women are less likely to be satisfied with the role of housewife (Oakley 1974). Seven women in each of the professional groups, but only three in the two non-professional groups were concerned to maintain their independence and to develop their own careers. Mandy, a light drinking professional, a further education lecturer, was a case in point. She said:

> *'My job is mine and gives me social contact, but because I've had to become less ambitious it's become more boring now.'*

So it was not surprising that more of the professional women were working, predominantly for their own satisfaction, rather than out of economic necessity, though no doubt the income was useful. Employment, if satisfying and where individuals have some control over their working environments, promotes mental well-being (Blaxter 1990; Doyal 1995). Certainly, the trend here is that this was probably more true of the middle-class group.

Combining roles has its disadvantages as well as advantages. Irrespective of drinking level, 90 per cent of the professional women, who were the group more likely to be working, but only 60 per cent of the non-professional mothers, complained that they had no time for themselves. Margaret, a heavy drinking professional, a nursing tutor, summed it up:

> *'I'm either working or I'm at the beck and call of somebody small.'*

Ensuring continuity of childcare arrangements and coping with continuous tiredness were a continuous part of life, presenting major problems. As already described, it was the professional women who were trying to juggle work, sometimes studying, keep up with their friends and leisure interests and look after their children. Brannen and Moss (1991) have described this dual-earner lifestyle with its attendant personal pressures in detail. But did it impact on drinking? Maureen, a heavy drinking professional, suggested that some very busy women might use alcohol to keep going. Certainly these heavy drinking professional women appeared to be the busiest group. If any group might be tempted to use alcohol to keep going it was them. As will be described in more detail in the next chapter, they managed to keep up more leisure interests, see their families more regularly and go out more often in the evening than their light drinking professional counterparts. Despite material advantage and practical help their lives were complex and pressured. As Fiona, a heavy drinking professional, who worked in publishing, pointed out:

> *'I meet stimulating and interesting people during the week and she [her child] recharges my batteries at the weekend. But, we're [her partner and herself] both very pressured.'*

For those who were not working their situations were also double-edged. Gillian, another heavy drinking professional, an ex-stockbroker, recalled how she had always wanted children but did miss the stimulation and satisfaction of working. Ros, also a heavy drinking professional and an ex-teacher, explained her position thus:

> *'I'm here with him and that's important. I can do all the domestic work as well. But, I do miss the contact with a variety of people. I tend to see standard middle-class people, people who are my mirror image. It's less stimulating. Sometimes, I feel left out.'*

Women in the two non-professional groups who had given up work missed the company, but not work for its own sake. They particularly missed the money. However, heavy drinking non-professionals were no more likely than light drinking non-professionals to complain of greater difficulty in terms of either combining work and childcare or opting for full-time childcare.

I wondered how their actual experiences measured up to their expectations or ideals and whether this would yield differences between the drinking groups. As chapter 1 emphasised, sex roles have become a dominant theme in much of the earlier literature on women's drinking. Chapter 2 suggested that a revised form of this might be worth exploring further, particularly in connection with events or circumstances which might threaten a woman's view of herself as fulfilling what she saw as an appropriate gender role.

When these women were asked whether traditional gender roles (with the man being the principal breadwinner) were natural, many of them, regardless of personal aspirations or desires, were quite pragmatic. The higher earning capacity of their male partners simply meant that anything other than their partner working full-time was not a realistic option. As Lynn, a heavy drinking professional, explained:

> *'He'd be quite happy to stay at home and look after the kids, if I could earn as much as him.'*

As the previous discussion implied and other research has confirmed (Doyal 1995), the two non-professional groups were inclined to be more traditional in their views, Mildred, a light drinking non-professional, for example, declared:

> *'That's the way it's always been. You expect them to provide.'*

Indeed, several of these non-professional women who were currently working said they did so only because they needed the money, otherwise they would rather be at home. Predictably, the professional women were more inclined to reject Mildred's assumption, being less traditional in their views. Only three of them accepted that it was natural that the man should be the breadwinner, and 12 of them categorically rejected the assumption. The non-professional women had the opposite response. Fifteen of them agreed with the traditional view. Only five rejected it outright. The other 25 women (15 professional and ten non-professionals) were more pragmatic, rejecting any concepts of naturalness, adopting a more practical line, which gave maximum economic advantage with as much personal satisfaction as possible. Certainly this pragmatic line was in touch with reality, for as Wilkinson (1994) has concluded, there will be no returning to the traditional male role as sole breadwinner in the context of present labour markets.

When asked how the reality of their situation compared with their ideal, about 50 per cent of them were more than satisfied with their situation. Such levels of satisfaction have been previously reported in other studies of mothers of young children (Boulton 1983). Looking at the group who felt their reality was not compatible with their ideal, as in another earlier study more non-professional women (17) than professional women (14) found that their reality was incompatible with their ideal (Brannen and Moss 1991). Their main source of dissatisfaction was their partner's failure to provide financially for them. This meant that they had to work, and were unable to live out the traditional role which they so wanted. Those without partners, such as Andrea, Diana and Vivienne, all heavy drinking non-professionals, and Louise, a light drinking non-professional, who were all in their twenties, were particularly

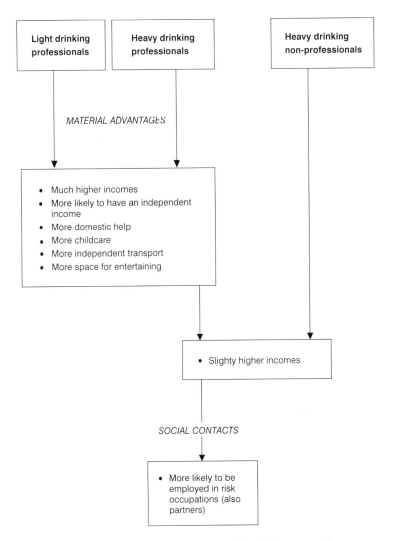

Figure 5.1   **Material advantages and social oportunities**

bitter about having to work. Those such as Eliza, a heavy drinking non-professional, and Mildred, a light drinking non-professional, whose partners had been unemployed for a long time, complained about their partner's inadequate support. In less advantaged families it is has been traditional and more usual that the male's obligation to be in paid work is seen as binding, whereas for the women it is a matter of choice (Jordan et al. 1992). However, as we have seen, those norms were breaking down. For a few, like Monica, a light drinking non-professional, or Christine, a heavy drinking non-professional, paid employment involved an element of positive choice, either because they needed something to contrast with childcare, or because they enjoyed their work.

Levels of general satisfaction were not linked with drinking levels at all. Heavy drinkers within each social grouping were no more likely to be dissatisfied than light drinkers. These sorts of dissatisfaction clearly did not lead to drinking. However, the middle-class women were frequently discontented with their employment situations, but in a rather different way. Their expectations, looking to it as a source of self-fulfilment as well as for income, were hard to meet. If working, they either wanted a more stimulating job or to cut down to part-time work. If not working, they wanted a part-time job so that they had something that was theirs. As Ros, a heavy drinking professional, put it:

> *'I'd like to be less dependent on my husband, so that it's not always Mrs X or wives are invited. I'd like an identity of my own.'*

None the less, it is significant that there was really little difference between the two professional groups in terms of the degree of dissatisfaction. For these women dissatisfaction with this aspect of their lives did not seem to have been linked with high drinking rates.

## Conclusion

In this chapter we have seen that these women were exposed to different drinking opportunities and possibilities. The professional women, by virtue of their material position, had higher incomes and more chance of an independent income. They had greater means to purchase alcohol if they wished. They had more time flexibility, due to their ability to purchase domestic and childcare help, and access to independent transport. Even though more of them were working, which meant juggling activities, this combination still left them more possibilities for socialising, either with work colleagues or through pursuing their own leisure interests. They also had more physical space for entertaining at home. Their possibilities for drinking were enhanced, if they chose to do so. These points are summarised in Figure 5.1.

Interestingly, within each social status group, the heavy drinkers were slightly better off, and so were marginally more advantaged than their peers. The influence of occupational type was most pronounced amongst

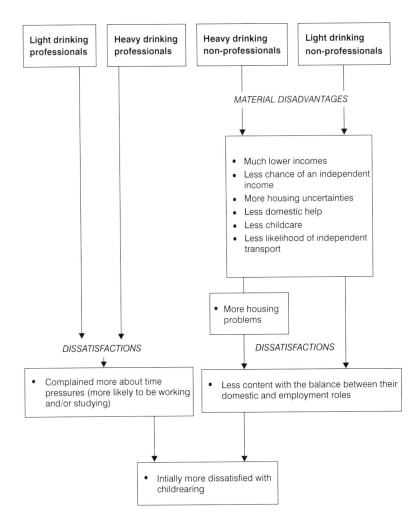

**Figure 5.2  Material disadvantages and dissatisfactions**

the middle-class women, where more were working. In the heavy drinking professional group, the women themselves were most likely to be
working in occupations linked with higher drinking, and to have partners
who worked in alcohol risk occupations. For them material advantages
and opportunity coalesced with social opportunities. It was easier for
them to drink heavily and expected.

The discussion of contact with drinking companions at work leads us
to consider the influence of other drinking companions – family, friends

and partners. I will develop the theme of drinking opportunities in the next chapter. We will also consider personal preferences, whether alcohol was something they saw as enjoyable, life enhancing or an irrelevance.

This chapter has also begun to shed light on the possibilities of drinking to cope with stresses. The non-professional groups were more obviously materially disadvantaged, creating a potentially more stressful background than for their professional sisters. The heavy drinking non-professional group had specific housing issues (see Figure 5.2).

In terms of expressed dissatisfactions both heavy drinking groups were initially more disappointed with childcare (Figure 5.2). As more interaction with their children became more possible, this abated. In general, both non-professional groups were more likely to be unhappy with their employment situations, generally because economic necessity required them to work when they would much rather not. Amongst the professional groups there was only one area of greater stress, and that was lack of time.

Returning to the question put at the beginning of this chapter – why bother with occupation? – we can see that by looking at it more closely we are beginning to see that the professional women had far greater material and social opportunities than the non-professionals for heavy drinking. This was pronounced for the heavy drinking professional group. Conversely, if any groups were more likely to be encouraged to drink because of material or social stress, then it would be the non-professionals, particularly the heavy drinking non-professional group. Chapter 6 looks mainly at how social cultures, norms and contacts structure drinking opportunities. Chapter 7 investigates the likelihood of drinking to drown sorrows. However, both themes arise in each chapter: they are not entirely separate.

# 6
# Social Circles

The women themselves pointed out the importance of drinking companions in their social circles as they recounted their experiences, and in chapter 5 we looked at how workplaces sometimes provided drinking companions. In this chapter we concentrate on drinking as a recreational activity. Although some of the women did drink alone, their main emphasis, as they themselves recounted in chapter 4, was on drinking as a commonplace and frequently taken-for-granted social activity. This was governed by all sorts of assumptions about appropriate behaviour and reciprocity. Drinking was an integral part of leisure. As Allan (1996) has emphasised, such social contacts, which include friendship systems as well as kin networks, are embedded within the organisation of social life. Whilst face-to-face contact with all relatives and close friends has dropped in the last decade (McGlone et al. 1996), such contacts remain the stuff of socialising. After all, many of these women suggested that drinking was a positive thing to do with other people, giving cohesion to relationships.

Looking at the patterning of consumption practices in general, Bourdieu (1984) has suggested that they can be understood in terms of the underlying unarticulated preferences, or taken-for-granted choices. These differ between groups and serve to distinguish one group from another. He argues that certain consumption patterns allow individuals to identify with social groupings. In other words, these patterns acquire symbolic meaning. In this way, choosing a 'G and T', a lager and lime, Pimms, a designer drink or a half of stout not only indicates the social grouping of an individual, but often gives a clue to their age, as fashions change over time.

Families too have their styles, but studies of family influences on drinking patterns have been dominated by interest in the effects of problem drinking by one parent or other (Orford 1990). Other studies have looked at drinking in couples, but where one of the two is identified as a problem drinker (Velleman et al. 1998). This one-sided interest has led to the neglect of how family culture shapes adult drinking in a non-problematic way. A recent study of nine heavy drinking women (over 35 units a day), but who were not identified as problem drinkers, is very useful here (Ferrins Brown et al. 1998). Most of the women were employed. About half had professional or managerial jobs. Half were living with a partner.

This study has identified a great variety of drinking traditions in their families of origin. In all instances, drinking was part of the family cultures, creating a sense of identity and with attendant advantages and disadvantages, which they were very aware of. As children they observed these traditions. Sometimes they were included in what was going on, often by way of a treat either by simply being allowed to be there or being given alcohol. Their first independent encounters with alcohol as adults were to engage with what they had seen as the benefits: to feel good, grown up or included in what was going on.

For these nine women, their own patterns in adulthood, were intrinsically shaped by those early experiences. People whose parents drank alcohol with their meals tended to do the same when they were adults. Those whose parents preferred drinking in pubs did likewise. Above all, they tried to maximise the advantages and benefits, as they saw them. In addition, they tried to minimise the harms they had seen, such as parental heavy drinking to cope with difficulties. In other words, they made their own choices and tried to control or minimise negative outcomes. We will return to how they used alcohol to cope with difficulties in the next chapter. Where alcohol had been used to cement family relationships, this was continued and extended to friends in adult life. Their social life tended to revolve around drinking activities and was a primary reason for their very high levels of intake. This study gives useful pointers to understanding the social circles of these women.

Friendship is association by choice (Pahl 1996). In the late 1990s the majority of people's most satisfying social involvement was with kin, work contacts and friends. For many people, friends provide continuity in their lives, more so than siblings or other relatives. Friendship has become an essential part of contemporary intimacy as a pleasurable end in itself (Giddens 1992, p. 58). According to a British Household Panel Study, about 80 per cent of women are in contact with a close friend every week (Pahl 1996). However, this emphasis on friendship was not common to all 60 women I talked with, as this chapter will show. The influence of socio-economic position remains a strong influence on intimate relationships, constraining or enabling them (Jamieson 1998). Even if friends are the primary source of day-to-day practical help and as confidantes, Willmott (1987) has pointed out that relying on friends for support and practical help in a crisis is much more common for middle-class people. Forty years ago Bott (1959) pointed out that where marital roles were segregated, friendship networks were likewise segregated; where they were more joint then friendship networks were joint. Given the very different orientations between the professional women and the non-professionals towards who should be the breadwinner in the family and appropriate roles between partners, as described in the previous chapter, different friendship patterns between the two socio-economic groups seemed likely.

In addition, where both partners are working, even if one is working part-time, they are likely to spend much of their time travelling, collecting children, visiting elderly relatives, shopping and looking after the children's social lives. As the middle-class mothers I talked to demonstrated, they are likely to be time-challenged and harassed. Such people are going to be highly selective about how they spend any free time and who with.

This chapter looks at these women's social circles in detail, the importance they attached to drinking to be sociable, their changed patterns of socialising after having a child, and the influence of partners, family and friends in encouraging and facilitating drinking. Finally, I review their views on drinking alone.

## Drinking to be sociable

As they said in chapter 3, most of these women had viewed their drinking as part of their normal social activity. A previous large-scale survey of pregnant women had indicated that about 50 per cent claimed they drank solely for social reasons, but that the other 50 per cent recognised that their motives were more mixed, and included seeking relief from unpleasant emotions. Other work has indicated the heavier a drinker a woman is the more likely she is to report drinking for a variety of reasons (Waterson 1992). These women were given a list of possible reasons for drinking, and asked to rate each as to whether it was at all important to them. Three-quarters said they would drink to celebrate a social occasion and about half said they would drink to be sociable. Far fewer (about a third), thought they would drink to be polite. A similar proportion admitted to using alcohol to help them relax. Less than a third saw their drinking as a means of seeking relief from pressures by cheering them up, or helping them to reduce tension or forget their worries. I will return to this point in the next chapter.

For the most part, social encouragement or even pressure to drink heavily was commonly mentioned:

> *'There's nothing worse than remaining sober when everyone else isn't.'*
> (Linda, a heavy drinking non-professional)

But there were few differences between the groups in this respect. Most of the women in each group (68 per cent overall) had experienced situations in which they found themselves drinking more than they wanted, particularly when they had felt obliged to participate in round drinking as a gesture of goodwill and sociability. Only Susan, a light drinking professional, remembered feeling pressured to drink in order to keep up with male company, describing how in her early thirties she went to meetings and then to the pub afterwards:

> *'I went to "oil the works". It was a question of beer with the boys. I had to hold my own in a group that revolved around drinking. We drank at lunch time and in the evening. I was also getting over a relationship at the time which made things worse.'*

It is noteworthy, though, that when asked about how they had learned about alcohol problems, a majority (65 per cent) cited personal contacts. Both groups of heavy drinkers were more likely than the light drinkers to cite personal experience of somebody with a drinking problem. This suggested that they were more likely to move in social circles where serious drinking was more common than in the circles frequented by the light drinkers.

Several from the heavy drinking professional group especially suggested that, for many women, drinking had become commonplace and an expected part of the daily round, as indeed it had for many of them. As Claire, a 33-year-old woman who was at home and married to an oil company executive (aged 39), said:

> *'In my circle if women meet socially in the afternoon it's gone past the stage of having cups of tea. They open a bottle of wine these days.'*

Easy access to alcohol was important to this group. They all kept a constant supply of alcohol at home, whereas only eight or nine members of the other three groups did so. In those households it was more usual to buy it in just before a specific social occasion, such as Christmas, and consume it quickly, there and then. The reasons for this in the two non-professional groups became apparent when several of them described drinking at home as drinking 'indoors', drawing a clear distinction with drinking 'outdoors', that is, outside the home. For them, 'drinking indoors' was only respectable when there was company. As Veronica, a light drinking non-professional, explained:

'I wouldn't drink "indoors" unless somebody came round.'

For many of the heavy drinking non-professional group, like Anne, the fun was in going out. Drinking lost its appeal if done at home. It was the company, the environment and simply getting out that they enjoyed.

This goes some way to explaining why Wilson (1980), in his national survey of drinking patterns, found that middle-class people drank more at home than working-class people. In this study it explains why many of the heavy drinking non-professionals, in contrast to many of the heavy drinking professionals, maintained the decreases established when they were pregnant. They claimed that once they went out less, they had fewer opportunities to drink in their previously established ways. However, as described in chapter 4, a few of them were starting to drink at home as traditional social norms break down and the home, rather than the pub or street, becomes the centre of working-class social life (Saunders 1990). The reasons why most of the light drinking professionals decided against keeping a supply at home are less clear. Lack of interest and inclination, rather than lack of opportunity, seemed to be the main reason.

Regardless of the level of opportunity, not all women enjoyed drinking or found it relaxing. For the light drinkers, such as Marie and Liz, both professionals, or Judith, a non-professional, it was more or less irrelevant. These women did not enjoy drinking even if they had opportunities to do so and were unlikely ever to become heavy drinkers. For those who enjoyed it and found it relaxing, their chances of becoming an heavy drinker were high, especially if their circumstances provided many possibilities.

## Changed patterns of socialising

'We both drink less now. When you've got kids with you, you've got to be capable of taking care of them.' (Sandra, a heavy drinking non-professional)

*'We see less of single friends and more of ones with children.'* (Bernadette, a heavy drinking professional)

*'I don't really have friends. It's all family.'* (Jane, a heavy drinking non-professional)

*'I don't see enough of other mothers with small children. There aren't any groups locally and lots of my friends have moved away.'* (May, a light drinking professional)

Social networks usually provide a combination of emotional, moral and practical support as well as providing a source of information and advice. Such supports and contacts benefited their quality of life, as they reflected in chapter 4. Needless to say, opportunities for social contacts altered after the arrival of the child. Most reported marked changes in their social life, seeing less of their friends and more of their families. Many of them became involved in mother/child-centred social activities. Only Margaret, a heavy drinking professional, mentioned drinking as featuring in this context.

Several women, such as Diana, a heavy drinking non-professional, mentioned that they had been lonely in the first few months of being at home, before the child was old enough to join a toddler group. This is a well-known situation. In another study 18 per cent of young mothers were lonely (Graham and McKee 1980). By the time they were talking to me, when the children were getting on for two years old, there were four women in each group who still had no contact with women who like themselves had young children. But, only one or two of these were dissatisfied about this. No one group complained of being lonely more than any other. For several mothers, informal very localised social networks had grown out of contacts made at antenatal classes, playgroups or toddler groups.

Some were content with more individual contact, seeing a friend or relative once a week or so. For example, Lee, a heavy drinking professional, said:

*'I go to a friend's house once a week. I don't want to be part of a group. I don't suffer fools gladly and I'm not a buddy-buddy sort of person.'*

Overall, the non-professional women were slightly less in contact with other peers who had small children. They were less often involved in local social networks than the professional women. This is in keeping with Oakley and Rajan's (1991) study, which found that working-class women had fewer friends than middle-class women. As Allan (1996) describes it, working-class friendship patterns rely on chance encounters, rather than determined efforts to keep in touch. Despite the network of mother and baby groups which exist in most localities, the reality is that the likelihood of mothers at home making chance encounters have diminished as community facilities, such as local shops and transport facilities, have declined. In so far as the non-professional mothers had less access to their own transport their chances of social contacts were even more diminished. Further, going out for an evening with their partner, or simply going to see old friends, was a much less frequent occurrence for them than for the middle-class women.

A reduction of leisure time has frequently been commented on in the literature on the transition to motherhood (Piachaud 1984; Brannen and Moss 1988). This had an enormous influence on the lifestyles of these women. For many of them, negotiating the daily complex round required considerable skill and creativity (Hoskins 1989). Sandra, a heavy drinking non-professional, summed up the situation:

> 'Everything needs arranging now. We make lots of promises that we don't keep, particularly to single friends.'

Practical logistics, such as lack of time, the need to make arrangements in advance for a babysitter or the difficulties of transporting all the child's equipment with them, made it more difficult to go out, particularly if they did not have their own transport. Even though they tried to draw on family members for help, or to use reciprocal babysitting arrangements, paying for babysitters to maintain old contacts was often out of the question for the non-professional households.

Although almost all the women complained that they had very little leisure time, it was predominantly the heavy drinking professional group who maintained their previous interests, such as sports. For them adult-centred social life, involving going out for the evening, also dropped off after the birth, but certainly did not disappear altogether. Of all the four groups they were the ones who went out regularly in the evening. But simply being able to afford to go out was an insufficient explanation for the light drinking professionals had very similar patterns of going out to the heavy drinking non-professionals, but their leisure interests did not seem to revolve around drinking in the same way.

As suggested by the women themselves in chapter 4, an alternative explanation in terms of the greater enjoyment that heavy drinkers associated with such social activities seems a more plausible explanation. For within each social status group the heavy drinkers were more likely to go out more. Although the heavy drinking professionals were better off financially than their light drinking professional sisters, this seems an insufficient explanation on its own. Both middle-class groups would have been able to draw on their material resources, for example to pay for childcare, if they wished to go out. As it was, the light drinking professional group went out no more frequently than the heavy drinking non-professional women. Although they, too, were marginally better off than their lighter drinking peers this again seems to be only part of the explanation. Enjoyment seem to be the key.

All the activities the women enjoyed in an evening out, such as seeing friends, going for a meal, going to a club or disco, going to the cinema or to the theatre could have been accompanied by drinking. Certainly there were clear class preferences about what to do when they did get out. For example, going for a meal, or to the theatre or cinema – more expensive pursuits – were more popular amongst professional women, whereas simply going for a drink, to a club or disco, or possibly out for a meal, were preferred by the non-professionals. In terms of differences within social levels, all heavy drinking professional women listed going for a meal as one of their favourite activities, but only half the light drinking professional women did so. This lends some support to Savage et al.'s (1992) finding that a sub-group of middle-class people were particularly inclined to high and lavish consumption of food and drink as an integral part of their lifestyle.

Those activities which almost certainly involved drinking (going for a drink or a meal, or to a club or disco) were more favoured by both heavy drinking groups. This again suggested that drinking as a normal and necessary part of social activity was especially important to them. Furthermore, within each social status grouping, heavy drinkers had a more varied repertoire of activities, implying that for them social activities were more important than for the light drinkers. Additional evidence for this interpretation comes from the finding that of the 35 per cent who complained about not being able to get out socially enough, 23 per cent were heavy drinkers. It is of note that, as I commented in the previous chapter, 32 per cent of the women were initially disappointed with caring for their child, and 20 per cent were heavy drinkers. However, for these heavy drinkers, child care became easier and more satisfying as the child grew older and more sociable. As Emma, a heavy drinking professional, explained:

*'It's more fun. You're no longer the key character.'*

Anne, a heavy drinking non-professional, made a similar comment:

*'She'll play alone sometimes and communicate what she wants. She's a real person now.'*

On the other hand, some light drinkers found the opposite. As Frances, a light drinking non-professional, said:

*'When they're small they sleep and you can put them down to sleep.'*

Eileen, also a light drinking professional, expressed her frustration, saying:

*'I now understand mothers who feel like throwing them out of the window.'*

This again seemed to point to the heavier drinker's greater inclination for social interaction.

I now continue by seeing what role families and friends played in these women's social circles.

## Families, partners and drinking

I did not specifically ask the women about their childhood experiences of parental drinking, or their own first experiences with alcohol. This was because I was primarily interested in examining the lifecycle stage when they were building their own families. This is the principal time when community surveys suggest that for many women their drinking spontaneously decreases. However, some interesting asides emerged. Several women hinted that it had been important in shaping their own attitudes towards drinking. As noted in the introduction, drinking is a learned behaviour, and as chapter 4 outlined, it follows a career pathway. So, it makes sense that as they reviewed their adult drinking careers, these women remembered early encounters and experiences.

Many of the light drinkers, regardless of social grouping, spontaneously mentioned that their mothers had also been light drinkers, implying that it was quite natural that they should follow in their mothers' footsteps. Maybe this is a reflection of following an appropriate drinking model who was in no danger of offending the prevailing social expectation that women should not be seen to be drinking heavily. It was the heavy drinkers who were in the vanguard of social change, who dared to defy tradition and drink more heavily than previous generations. But this did not come through in their comments. None of the heavy drinkers mentioned that their mothers had been light drinkers. In fact, they did not mention them. For these women, the circumstances of their adult lives and their own preferences seemed to have been the main influence in establishing their drinking habits. Family tradition hardly figured for them, except for a few where the pattern of regular drinking every evening laid the basis for Eva's drinking. She certainly thought so, but the rest of the women made very few other such direct references.

Interestingly, nobody referred to their mother as a heavy drinker when they were children. In the rare instances when they did refer to their mothers drinking heavily this was much later on. For Mildred's mother it was around the time of her menopause. For Linda's mother it was a reaction to being badly treated by the men in her life. Both Linda and Mildred seemed to be trying to understand their mother's drinking as a rational response to circumstances. Perhaps the closeness of the bond encouraged them to step beyond the usual condemnations and stigma.

Where they were mentioned, childhood memories of heavy problem drinking referred to men. Fathers, unlike mothers, were either not mentioned or described as heavy drinkers. Eva had childhood experiences of problem drinking:

> *'My step-father is an alcoholic. It was bad news every night from when I was about 12 years old onwards.'*

The links between heavy paternal drinking and their own were unclear and contradictory. For example, of the two women who specifically mentioned their father's drinking, Eva went on to be a heavy drinker and Judith to be a light drinker.

Religious affiliation is frequently closely intertwined with family background. All the women either listed a Christian denomination or said they had no religion. Of the 13 Roman Catholics, a denomination notably liberal towards drinking behaviour, nine were heavy drinkers. All four members of nonconformist Christian denominations who are traditionally disapproving of drinking were light drinkers. It was interesting to note that of the 13 Roman Catholics the five who were of Irish or Polish origin were heavy drinkers. These are cultures traditionally associated with a high consumption of alcohol (O'Connor 1978; Jolly and Orford 1983; Douglas 1987).

Fifty-eight per cent of the sample had close family living locally and saw them once a week, or more frequently. This was the case for 80 per cent of the non-professional women but only 37 per cent of the professional women. As in earlier studies, this frequent contact afforded a good deal of social and practical support, especially for the non-professional women (Brannen and Moss 1991). As Helen put it:

*'We see each other as often as possible, because we need each other.'*

Daily contact, revolving around regular childcare arrangements, was not uncommon for them. Drinking did not feature in this contact principally because it would have involved breaking sanctions about 'drinking indoors' and socialising as something that took place outside the home.

Many more of the professionals were living at a distance from their families, whereas most of the non-professional women had been born in London. This was more true for the heavy drinking professionals than the light drinking professionals. Most of those professional women who had family living at a distance maintained weekly telephone contact and saw each other about once a month. They were, after all, more able to afford the required travel, in terms of financial and time costs.

Overall contact patterns were very similar in each non-professional groups, but there were obvious differences between the two professional groups. The heavy drinking professionals frequently had family living locally, but their light drinking peers were more likely to have family outside London. Drinking at home with other family members was not frowned upon in these light drinking professional households, but remained less likely, partly because of less desire and partly because there was less frequent contact. Their heavy drinking counterparts were more able to keep up contact with family drinking companions and if necessary to substitute family companionship for friends if those friendship ties were loosened through changing circumstances.

Although, the professional mothers were less likely to rely on kin for regular help, when it came to a crisis there were no differences between them and the non-professional women. Curiously, both groups of heavy drinkers felt they would be able to count on a wider range of people to help in an emergency – monso than their light drinking counterparts. Presumably, this was yet a further reflection that, as previously noted, they seemed to be more socially outgoing.

In all, 28 per cent of women felt they would have liked more contact with their families. These included six women from each professional group. In reality, more of the heavy drinkers were likely to see their families at least once a week than their light drinkers, whose families were more likely to live at a distance. Similarly even though the heavy drinking non-professional drinkers saw their families as frequently as their light drinking counterparts they were less content with this. Five heavy drinking non-professionals would have liked more contact, but all the light drinkers were quite satisfied. Once again, this seems to be an indication that the heavy drinkers were more outgoing and needed more social contact than the light drinkers.

Alcohol has long been associated with sexual activity, either as an aphrodisiac, as part of the social prelude or as an aid to reducing inhibitions (Ford 1989; Flannigan et al. 1990; Temple and Leigh 1990; Abbey and Harnish 1995). I was given a graphic example of this when talking to a woman who was not part of the research but who had had major alcohol-related problems in the past. She now works helping others who have problems. In the course of a radio interview about alcohol harms, she was asked how much she used to drink. As she said:

> 'When I told the interviewer he nearly fell off his perch. He then said, "And I guess you woke up with a different bloke each morning." He nearly fell off his perch again when I said "Actually I've only ever had two lovers".'

Whilst none of these women linked their current drinking behaviour with sexual activity the reader will remember that some of them described closer links at earlier stages of their lives. However, certainly in professional households, as we saw in chapter 4, there was an assumption that drinking with partners was a shared and routine activity. Not only did they often have similar occupations, which yielded common groups of friends, but those occupations could also involve both partners in entertaining business contacts.

Earlier studies had demonstrated similar drinking levels and styles between partners as being especially characteristic of higher consumers (Waterson and Murray Lyon 1990a). It was noticeable amongst these women that a convergence of pattern was most pronounced amongst the middle-class groups. They were less traditional in their orientation to gender roles, and in practice had more egalitarian attitudes towards housework and childcare. Given that shared social and leisure pursuits between partners are more typical of middle-class than working-class people (Allan 1996) the emphasis on shared family drinking norms in these households becomes understandable. Whilst shared family drinking norms may be important, drinking with friends is also important and this is the next topic.

## Friends and drinking

For the non-professional mothers, friends had been very much work-based or opportunistic, as Allan (1996) would describe them. As so many of them gave up work after the birth, these friendships dropped off as well. This echoes findings in another survey of mothers with young children (Brannen and Moss 1991). It was the heavy drinking non-professional women who most felt this keenly. As Anne lamented:

> *'I've lost touch with a lot of my friends. They either live far away or they're busy working.'*

For these women, for whom 'going out' was essential to having a 'good time', the result was a serious reduction in the amount of contact with the friends who had been their drinking companions. Although the professional drinkers also complained that they saw less of their friends than previously, the reduction for them was less marked. They were more likely to have kept on working, to be able to afford babysitters and transport themselves to see friends and maintain links.

In addition, it should be remembered that friendship patterns differ between social classes. Allan (1996) describes these in full. He distinguishes a traditional working-class pattern, consisting of an extensive social network of overlapping kinship and neighbouring links. In this pattern, social contacts are framed by specific activities and are thus very dependent on context, interaction often taking place haphazardly rather than by design. There are strong differences between the sorts of contacts that take place in the home and those that occur outside the home. Interaction at home is confined to the family. Non-family or friendship contacts are largely conducted outside the home. Marital partners have separate friends.

These traditional norms are now breaking down because of geographical mobility, increasing affluence and changes in the housing market. As more working-class people become owner-occupiers, so their social activities become more home-centred. In this study this is evidenced by the few heavy drinking non-professional women who described drinking and socialising at home. For example, Moira mentioned it as something of a novelty instituted after the baby's arrival. But the traditional norms still remained influential as the experiences of the majority of the non-professional women testify.

Remembering these norms helps to explain why the non-professional mothers were so severely restricted in their access to the friends who had once been their drinking companions. Giving up work deprived them of a social milieu. Their culture did not encourage continuing those friend-ships independently of context, for example by reciprocal home visiting. Put these social constrains alongside the practical constraints and the decline in contact with friends becomes obvious. It was also these women who were most likely to follow the traditional working-class taboo against 'drinking indoors'. For them drinking was part of socialising and that took place outside the home. Opportunities were now lacking.

Other studies have documented how some women use their pleasur-able drinking behaviour as a symbol of resistance or freedom, as they reclaim public spaces which have hitherto been male-dominated (Waterson and Stringer 1998). Organising their drinking activities for such reasons was out of the question for non-professional women once they had a child, and irrelevant to the middle-class women who could quite easily drink at home if they wanted to do so. The middle-class tradition of 'making friends' independently of context, where friends may be brought into the family circle, and the home serves as a con-text for such contacts was not automatic for the non-professional women (Allan 1996). In this scenario, home becomes a place where individuals can display their sense of identity, as exemplified by the dinner party. Dinner parties were mentioned by professional women only and largely by heavy drinking professional women, and those occupations or that of their partners may have demanded such entertaining. In this way, they were much more easily able to maintain previous friendships. Even their cultural norms sanctioned such links by encouraging the use of their homes as a suitable venue for meeting. Such norms are pervasive. Middle-class norms of friendship continued to influence the small group of heavy drinking non-professional women who grew up in such households, such as Eva and Joy. For both of them, as we saw in chapter 4, daily drinking at home was an established and quite legitimate routine for them, as it was for heavy drinking middle-class women.

At the time I was interviewing them, the majority of women (two-thirds), were dissatisfied with the amount of contact they had with their friends. This was most marked amongst precisely those groups who had more potential for maintaining their contacts, the two profes-sional groups. It will also be remembered that they were slightly older and had had more time to acquire friends before becoming pregnant. Despite having less contact the non-professional women were appar-ently less dissatisfied. Maybe for them it was inevitable that they should lose contact with their workmates once they were no longer working and the context gone. What was remarkable was that they did not appear to resent it. This may have something to do with cultural expectations of friendship.

When asked whether there was anybody, other than their partner, in whom they could confide, only two or three women in each of the four groups said they had nobody. Such a generally high level of confiding would be characteristic of most women (Allan 1996; O'Connor 1991). However, in keeping with the descriptions of social contact patterns given earlier in this chapter there were particular class differences. Among professional women, friends as well as family were valued confidantes. It was more usual for non-professional women to depend primarily on female relatives and especially their mothers. There were no reported differences between the drinking groups in terms of the availability of a confidante. Contrary to the Breeze (1985) study, heavy drinkers were no less likely to have a confidante – a fact she suggests may encourage turning to the bottle for solace. But it was the two professional groups that particularly looked to their friends as well as family as confidantes and any perceived diminution of contact might be resented. Once again, although the heavy drinking professionals saw more of their friends than the light drinking professionals they were equally likely to complain about this, indicating once again how much they valued these social contacts.

## Drinking alone

These different friendship customs or traditions of drinking indoors went some way to explaining why all but two of the heavy drinking professionals would drink alone, but only a very small number in the other three groups would do so. The light drinking professionals were not very interested; whereas for the heavy drinkers it was available and they liked it. It was part of their daily life and routine. For them having a drink served as a reward, a transition to adult time, a time-keeping mechanism and, contrary to many of the activities in their lives, something they did for themselves, that gave them, and them alone, pleasure. Perhaps not surprisingly, in view of prevailing double standards, nobody mentioned having a drink as an aid to creativity, even those whose work required creativity. However, a few, such as Liz, a light drinking professional, had mentioned previous male partners who had used it that way (see chapter 4).

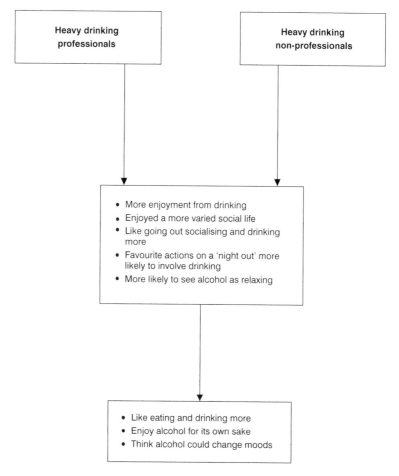

Figure 6.1   **Heavy drinkers' personal attitudes towards drinking**

Most commonly, lighter drinkers appeared to regard drinking alone as the first step to problem drinking. Many were fearful. May, for example, claimed she would never drink alone because she once had a friend whose severe drinking problems were made worse by secretive solitary drinking. She did not want to follow in her footsteps. On the other hand, the middle-class heavy drinkers seemed content to manage their own drinking and any attendant risks. Maybe they would pour themselves a drink when they felt their mood needed it, but they did not see this as a one-way road to drinking problems. Such emotional self manipulation was a matter of seeking temporary respite, not the start of a permanent addiction. Unsurprisingly, although 37 per cent of heavy drinkers said their favourite 'pick-me-up' when feeling tired was to pour themselves a drink, 30 per cent were heavy drinking professionals. They were the group who enjoyed a drink, had ready access to it at home and who were unlikely to be bothered about the cost. The heavy drinking non-professionals were more constrained in their use. Pouring a drink as a 'pick-me-up' was hardly a viable option for them. Even if tempted, there was no ready supply to hand and drinking indoors was more likely to be socially proscribed. Certainly, this does seem to suggest that drinking for enjoyment needs to be established before women start using it to help them cope with difficulties and a ready supply encourages such usage. This argument will be examined in more detail in the next chapter.

## Conclusion

Whilst the sociology of friendship and intimacy may in general be a neglected area (Pahl 1998) it is a profitable one for exploring influences on drinking patterns. Heavy drinkers seemed more likely to come from a family and cultural background that did not discourage alcohol use and which attached particular importance to social activities that might involve drinking. As adults, once past the stage of youthful excesses they continued to derive a great deal of satisfaction and enjoyment from alcohol, having much more positive attitudes towards it than light drinkers. These points are summarised in Figure 6.1. They enjoyed drinking and valued their social lives, going out to socialise and drink. Compared with the lighter drinkers they were much more likely to see alcohol as relaxing.

Above all, they prized their social lives and resented any constraints on it. Regardless of the reality of their situations, compared with their socio-economic peers they were more likely to complain of insufficient contact with their families and that they could not get out enough. Alcohol was something they enjoyed, and they would make the most of any drinking opportunities as they presented themselves.

There were important distinctions between the class groups. The middle-class heavy drinkers enjoyed a variety of different sorts of alcoholic drinks, often experimenting for its own sake. They were more likely to keep a ready supply at hand than the light drinking professional women, who were not very interested. For the non-professional heavy drinkers, drinking was associated with going out and enjoying company, rather than simply for its own sake.

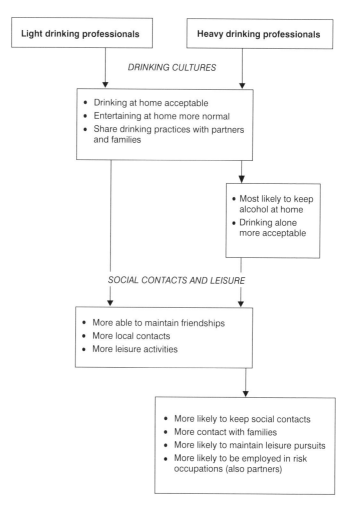

**Figure 6.2   Cultural and social opportunities for drinking for professional women**

In short, all professional women were in a much more favourable position to drink than the non-professional women (see Figure 6.2). For them drinking at home was not taboo and keeping drink in the home common. Entertaining at home was more normal and it was customary that drinking practices were shared with partners and families. They were more able to keep contact with drinking companions through employment. Work as a valued activity was more satisfying to these

middle-class women. For non-professionals working was more instru-
mental, an economic necessity rather than something to be intrinsically
valued, and therefore their work contacts were less integrated into their
social life. As many of them gave up work these links were severed.
Middle-class friendship norms enabled those women to maintain previous friendships by using their homes as a base for entertaining. They
were also more able to afford to pay babysitters if they did want to go
out, and to use their own transport when they did. Maintaining the old
pleasures of wining and dining and going to the theatre was possible.
But for many of the non-professional women their social circles were
very diminished once their child arrived.

This general distinction is sharpened if we look at the heavy drinking
professional group. They shared the basic middle-class drinking norms,
but for them it was even more acceptable that they kept a supply in the
home and quite usual that they would drnk alone. They were most
inclined to say they used alcohol routinely as a positive self-reward and
on occasions to modify their mood. This was not true of the light
drinking professional group.

Middle-class women were more able to lead varied social lives,
maintain old contacts, develop local ones and actively pursue leisure
interests. This was most true of the heavy drinking professionals, who
seemed remarkably sociable and outgoing. Not only did their personal
attitudes predispose them to enjoying an active drinking life, but the
drinking culture in their social circle, extended social contacts and, as
we saw in chapter 5, their employment links enhanced their opportunities. It is hardly surprising that heavier drinking in community
surveys should be associated with social advantage in women. But
what has been demonstrated here, even if not picked up by community surveys, is that this distinction is maintained after the birth of
their first child.

This chapter has begun some analysis of the notion of drinking associated with difficulties and stresses. As we saw in the previous chapter,
the non-professional groups as a whole were more disadvantaged then
the middle-class women. This made their lives materially harder and
impacted on the ways they could structure their social lives. Their social
circles became far less extensive than the middle class women (see
Figure 6.3). This created dissatisfactions, which were most keenly felt by
the heavy drinking non-professionals.

A third of all the women, all heavy drinkers, that is those well accustomed to drinking as part of their everyday life, used it to relax. Indeed,
all but one of the heavy drinkers spontaneously remarked on alcohol

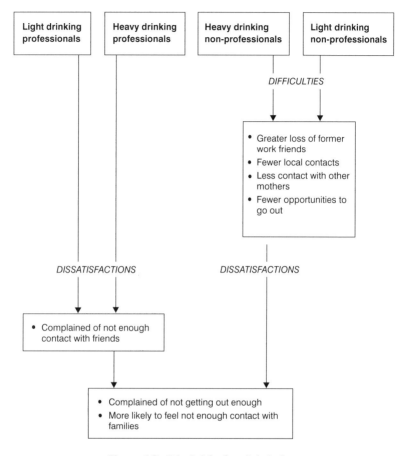

**Figure 6.3   Diminished social circles**

being a relaxant. However, nobody claimed to use alcohol to counteract nervous or worried feelings, despite Monica's comment that:

> *'Some women under stress drink a lot. It calms them down and they find it relaxing'.*

It seems reasonable to suppose though that women who find alcohol helps them to relax might be more prone to turn to it at times of difficulty. As Helen, a light drinking non-professional, reasoned:

> *'If you enjoy it, it could escalate from there.'*

In this sample, those women who had easiest access and enjoyed drinking, the heavy drinking professional group, were most inclined to say they used alcohol to modify their mood. The next chapter looks in more detail, at how using alcohol to cope with difficulties worked in all groups, both in terms of what the women were well aware of, and also at the effect of their situations more generally.

# 7
## Bottling it up

In the last two chapters we have looked at the implications of paid employment and social contacts. On the whole we have concentrated on drinking in response to social, material and cultural opportunity and the importance of personal enjoyment of drinking. We have only touched on the other main theme outlined in chapter 2, that of drinking to cope with difficulties, which is the focus of this chapter.

When were the women themselves aware of drinking to deal with unpleasant feelings, literally drowning their sorrows? This sort of drinking practice was in marked contrast to early adolescent flings, student freedoms or the early working days they described so colourfully. In this section we meet four of the women, who as the others did in chapter 4 tell their stories. This time they tell stories of instances when they knew they were drinking to blot out painful, unbearable feelings. The four, all heavy drinkers, recalled periods of very serious drinking as they tried to cope with serious difficulties.

In attempting to chart the stresses these women experienced over a period of about four years, I looked at three sources of stress. As in chapter 2 I have referred to long-term social and material stresses as disadvantages, distinguishing them from difficulties and dissatisfactions. I have defined difficulties as events that happened during that period, such as physical problems, little social contact or sudden unexpected changes. In the third category, dissatisfactions, I am more concerned with subjective reactions, for example expressed disappointment with the realities of childcare. Obviously these are not discrete categories or exact measurements. Felt dissatisfactions almost certainly affected how the women fared psychologically, but for the purposes of trying to explore and map these factors I have treated psychological problems as difficulties.

In reality there was considerable overlap and interaction between the categories. For example, if income is tight there is little spare cash to pay for a babysitter in order to visit friends. Indisputably, the effects of longstanding disadvantages, including financial worries and housing problems, were exacerbated by the arrival of a baby. In my study only Eliza, a heavy drinking non-professional, consciously linked money problems, or other disadvantges with drinking. She mentioned drinking – in this instance, her husband's – to unemployment and his consequent loss of confidence and self-esteem:

> *'He knocks it back. He's got nothing else to do so he goes to the pub at lunchtime to meet people. He's supposed to be looking for work. He gets through four pints at lunchtime and more in the evening. He takes refuge in the pub and comes back the worse for wear on Saturday and collapses. It's the cause of most of our problems. We row every day about the amount of money he spends.'*

Whilst evidence about the effect of male unemployment on drinking behaviour is not clear-cut, there is a trend for those few unemployed men who do drink, like Eliza's husband, to do so quite heavily (Lee et al. 1990).

As in chapter 4, this chapter includes personal drinking stories, but from difficult periods, when the women were aware they were drinking negatively. This, as Ettorre (1997 p. 12) has emphasised, comes with 'a sense . . . that something is not right in the lives of these women'. It may be to do with difficult and painful feelings, but the important point is that at some level these women are ashamed of what they feel and wish to hide away, but of course eventually the drinking too becomes a form of self-harm.

I continue by looking more specifically at the difficulties and dissatisfactions in these 60 women's lives in the couple of years or so before we were talking. As well as the time when these women were aware of using alcohol to counteract personal difficulties, I focus on the impact of totally unexpected changes, the inevitable physical changes that are part of becoming a mother and changed ways of viewing the world. How did these potential areas of difficulty link with drinking?

## Times of low self-esteem

Joy and Jill, both heavy drinking non-professionals, and Margaret, a heavy drinking professional, described how they had drunk very heavily when their previous marriages broke up. It is significant that these were the only three women out of the 60 who mentioned previous marriages. I had not asked them to talk specifically about previous relationships. I had presumed that I could follow up my reworking of the issues on sex-role performance, so detailed in previous research (see chapters 1 and 2), quite adequately simply by looking at how the women coped with the transition to motherhood. After all the literature, particularly community surveys of drinking behaviour, had pinpointed this time as the one instance when women spontaneously decreased their consumption. Other sources showed that women with dependent children tended to be light drinkers. But, contrary to this research, more detailed investigation looking at the differential impact of social advantage showed that not all women with dependent children become light drinkers. As chapter 4 demonstrated heavy drinkers, especially heavy drinking professionals, were able to continue drinking heavily throughout the life transition of becoming a mother. So, although marital break-up is often cited in the literature on female problem drinking (see chapter 2), this emergent emphasis on the break-up of previous marriages was yet another surprise.

Margaret's story was as follows:

> 'My marriage broke up when I was in my early thirties. When the difficulties started I needed to drink. At least two or three times a week I was drinking until I felt an effect. It was an anaesthetic. I couldn't face him coming home. I'd get through at least a bottle of gin a week. I'd go to the pub at lunchtime with colleagues. Every day we'd have a bottle of wine with dinner. At weekends I drank even more. I'd start late in the morning and just keep going. The more we socialised the better it was for me, because I could drink. I knew I was possibly affecting my health, but I didn't care I was so unhappy.'

For her, the need to blot out the pain was paramount. She did this by accentuating her existing patterns of socialising, tipping over the balance into potential problem drinking. All other considerations were irrelevant.

Joy's experiences may have had a similar genesis, but the way she dealt with it was different. She drank alone:

> 'I drank a lot of vodka when I moved here after my divorce. I didn't get married to get divorced. I felt a failure. For several years afterwards I felt very low. I'd sit and listen to the dog barking next door. I thought it sounds

*upset just like I feel – that cheered me up a bit. Otherwise I'd just drink to dull the edges and ease the pain a bit. That's why people drink. When you've had a drink you sit back and think life's not so bad.'*

Again she needed to block out her pain, but in contrast to Margaret her drinking was not achieved through socialising. As we have seen, she was one of the few non-professional women who had been accustomed to drinking alone at home, perhaps pouring herself a drink on arriving home from work. For her this pattern was an extension of an existing routine. But both she and Margaret drank to feel better, to be able to go on in the face of what they felt was unbearable. Both were verging on developing long-term harmful drinking. At the time they were going through these difficulties they needed the drink. There was no way they could have cut down without help.

Jill related that when she was 28 her marriage broke up:

*'He left me for somebody else. I wanted to get sozzled. I drank to block it out. It hurt so much. I tried to cut down but I couldn'.'*

In time, as her distress subsided, she did cut down and avoided continued escalation into a definite problem drinking. In this context, Susan, a light drinking non-professional's comment about the time when she felt pressurised to drink at work – which also included a throw-away aside that she was getting over a relationship at the time – becomes much more significant.

Another heavy drinking non-professional, Sandra, a part-time nursing auxiliary married to a film technician, described a rather different situation. Her drinking escalated during a period of post-natal depression:

*'You don't realise how much you are drinking. We used to socialise a lot. Before I was pregnant I'd always go for a drink when I met friends. When I'd go and see people we'd always have a bottle.'*

Unlike most of even the heavy drinking women she continued drinking very heavily throughout:

*'I drank heavily when I was first pregnant. We were away camping most weekends. The wine was just pouring away. I don't know how we stood up. People can lie to doctors. My GP would ask me, did I drink at all, and I'd say I was a social drinker. In fact I'd go away and soak it up. All the time I was feeling guilty, thinking that I ought to tell the truth. Eventually, I said*

*to the hospital doctor that I'd been absolutely legless, but all he'd say was we must wait and see. She [her baby] was all right thank goodness. The first month after she'd arrived was great, but after that I felt alone and isolated. My husband would go off to work in the morning and at the weekend he'd go off to cricket. I'd feel neglected. It suddenly seemed that I was trapped and he was free. I didn't want to tell anybody. I rang a helpline about post-natal depression, and was told I was one in ten women who suffer from it. I thought where the hell are they all? I expected to see them walking down the street looking depressed. At the clinic everybody looks so capable and fine. You want to say, I feel mad, but there's no privacy at the clinic. When I was nursing I didn't really understand why the women on the post-natal ward were so vulnerable and why they cried. I think you've got to go through it to understand. When I was depressed I found one glass of wine made me feel better, but then I couldn't stop. At times I drank a whole bottle and by the time my husband came home from work I was in a dreadful state. I just couldn't cope. That frightened me. I had no control. I even tried to make sure that I'd not got more than one bottle in the house, but it didn't work. It destroys your personality and takes away your reasoning. Suddenly I'd find that the bottle was emptying faster than I'd noticed. I'd be absolutely legless by 7.00 pm.'*

Even though she was not alone in experiencing post-natal depression, she was the only one of the 60 who explicitly admitted turning to alcohol to ease such pain. For these women drinking to ease psychological pain is intensely shameful, not something to admit to readily and certainly not to a stranger such as me. Talking about situations that were in the past such as the break-up of past relationships seemed to be safer ground. Sandra was speaking of very recent pain.

When Sandra's depression finally lifted some months later, her drinking decreased. Wilsnack (1994) too found in her study that women in their twenties and thirties were able to move in and out of problem drinking as their social context, roles and relationships changed. This certainly fits with the picture of almost universal high rates of drinking which most of these women described in their youth. It will be remembered that new partnerships most often triggered a change, either up or down. 'Settling down' was a major turning point for the light drinking non-professionals especially.

Sandra's situation is an interesting case in the light of the lack of interest in women's drinking in the post-natal period, which was described in chapter 1. Like Jill, Joy and Margaret she too emphasised her feelings of loss, but for her it was not a relationship, but her freedom and the feeling that she could not behave as an ideal mother should. She resented this and found it hard to cope with. Drinking helped, but when it went out of control she was frightened. Like most of the women in this study, for her that signified real problems. She was beginning to demonstrate what Ettorre (1997) has termed an unfeminine dependency on the bottle. That is, substituting dependency on a man for dependency on a bottle.

All these four women felt their losses. There were no other references to times of heavy drinking triggered by other sorts of loss from any other women. Three out of this four felt the loss of a relationship. Sandra felt the loss of her freedom. Circumstances had prevented all four from living out their internalised image of what society expected. Theirs was not the romantic partnership or perfect motherhood experience of the storybooks or magazines (Smart 1992). Sandra spells this out. She notes how capable and calm the other mothers appeared in contrast to her own feelings of turmoil. But she asks the question, where were the other 10 per cent who were supposed to be depressed, not what is wrong with me? Individual difficulties in self-esteem relating to or performing female roles frequently appear as explanatory themes in the women's alcohol problem literature. However, in contrast to that literature, these women did not see it as a personal failing but more as an understandable response to the situations they found themselves in. Such a response is in keeping with the way Mildred and Linda described their mothers' drinking problems. Once again in these two instances the loss related to a traditional female role model, either as partner or as mother. One woman had relationship difficulties; the other had problems with the menopause.

These stories reinforce the idea, mentioned in chapter 2, that the sort of life-events, or major changes in circumstances, associated with drinking were those that specifically undermined this sense of self-esteem and self-concept as a woman. For three of them, the sorts of difficulties they offered as explanations for their own periods of intensive drinking were obviously very specific loss situations, relating to the loss of a defined dependency on a man, which was related to a sense of personal esteem and confidence. They report precisely the debilitating effects of lack of self-confidence and esteem, which fits with previous reports (Thom 1986; Breeze 1985; Plant 1990; Ettorre 1992, 1997). We have revisited the older literature on women's drinking problems, described in detail in chapter 2, with its emphasis on faulty sex-role performance. Some of the women who have been talking here had held, and continued to hold, responsible jobs. But, despite their apparently non-traditional positions, the emphasis remained firmly focused on domestic issues. The next section looks at the impact of other life events to check this hypothesis.

Although some women consciously linked their drinking with the need to cope with feelings of anxiety or tension, or their worries, they were in a minority. For example, nobody mentioned using alcohol to help cope with unexpected events, as will be discussed next in this chapter. It is possible that they may not have been consciously aware of them. Consequently, I was interested to see whether the frequency or types of difficulties or disappointments varied between the groups.

## Dealing with the unexpected

*'My dad died soon after he [my son] was born. It was awful. I thought I'd never cope.'* (Monica, a light drinking non-professional)

*'My mother-in-law retired a bit early to help look after him, so that I could continue going to work. That was great.'* (Christine, a heavy drinking non-professional)

The women were asked whether any major events had occurred either for themselves, or a member of their family or a close friend in the previous few years. Such occurrences included moving home, trouble with the law, sudden disabilities or illnesses, job changes, redundancies, retirements, marriages, separations, divorces or anything major to celebrate. They were precisely the sort of happenings, good or bad which might provoke an 'I need a drink' response. As noted in chapter 2, the cumulative effect of such events is important.

While five respondents claimed that there had been no such events, in all, the women recalled 142 such major events between them. Those women who reported changes were asked to describe them and then to say how they felt at the time. This is because the impact or potential psychological distress caused by an event is strongly influenced by context. The same event may provoke one response in one individual and another in another individual, depending upon the circumstances. Thus, the women's subjective evaluation, in other words how they felt about it, of any particular occurrence was deemed to be more significant then the objective event itself.

When analysing their reactions, it was clear that there were four categories: welcome, concerning, fairly distressing or very distressing and disturbing. Such a single measure obviously is crude and limited, but is useful in indicating broad differences between the groups. In fact, these four evaluative categories referred to quite different sorts of occurrences. Those that were welcome generally related to other people and included them getting married, moving house, being promoted at work, and having babies. This was one of the largest categories (see Table 7.1). Circumstances that were concerning but not really distressing included a brother-in-law's engagement being broken off, relatives with financial problems, relatives with minor illnesses, or moving house with few problems. Very few events fell into this classification. Ros, a heavy drinking professional, reflects on one of those events:

> '*My mother was diagnosed as suffering from high blood pressure. I was concerned, but I certainly didn't lose any sleep over it.*'

Incidents described as fairly distressing occurred most frequently. These included expected deaths, family illnesses and redundancies. For example, Josephine, a light drinking non-professional, described how her father had died when she was pregnant:

> '*He'd been ill with cancer for a long time. We'd been going up there every weekend. I was upset, but it really was a relief.*'

Very distressing occurrences were of a quite different order and included life-threatening illness or death and violent attacks. Linda, a heavy drinking professional, told how she had been mugged whilst pregnant:

> '*It was terrible. I was scared to go out alone for ages. I thought I'd never get over it.*'

In all, 30 individuals, evenly distributed between the four groups, had had at least one very distressing episode or more than one seriously distressing event. Sometimes, these occurred simultaneously. For example, Caroline, a heavy drinking non-professional, told how her child had gone into hospital with bronchitis when he was about a year old:

> '*I was so worried. I don't know how I kept my sanity, because while he was in there my father had cancer of the throat diagnosed and my father-in-law had a heart attack.*'

The non-professional women experienced more sudden changes altogether than the professional women (see Table 7.1). This was largely

Table 7.1   The incidence of life-events

| Type of event | Heavy drinking professionals | Light drinking professionals | Heavy drinking non-professionals | Light drinking non-professionals | Total |
|---|---|---|---|---|---|
| Very distressing | 6 | 6 | 6 | 6 | 24 |
| Fairly distressing | 13 | 18 | 15 | 9 | 55 |
| Concerning | 2 | 3 | 3 | 3 | 11 |
| Welcome | 11 | 8 | 16 | 17 | 52 |
| Totals | 32 | 35 | 40 | 35 | 142 |

accounted for by the greater number of welcome events in the in the non-professional groups. Overall, the professional groups experienced more upsetting occurrences than the non-professionals.

Three totals are significant because, as we saw in chapter 2, it has been argued that psychological impact occurs regardless of the nature of the event. Thus the impact was greatest in the non-professional groups. In view of their other disadvantages it could be expected that they would be less well placed to cope with the changes and adjustments such events bring. The heavy drinking non-professional group seemed especially vulnerable, experiencing more events in total than any other group. Within the middle-class groups the reverse was true. It was the light drinkers who had experienced more life-events.

In sum, heavy drinkers were only marginally more exposed to all events than the light drinkers, and they were equally likely to experience upsetting events. But this obscures important class differences. Within the middle-class groups it was the light drinkers who had been especially exposed to upsetting events. This suggests that incidence as such was not immediately connected with heavy drinking, or certainly not for middle-class women. On the other hand, the heavy drinking non-professional group were particularly exposed in comparison to the light drinking non-professional women to all events, and in particular to unwelcome ones. One could easily imagine that they would be particularly vulnerable to using alcohol to counteract psychological distress or discomfort.

Gorman and Peters (1990), when discussing life-events and alcohol problems, suggest that it might be helpful to look at the type of event, dividing them into 'loss' and 'danger' events. However, there were no differences between the groups in terms of the numbers of events that could be described as either an 'entrance', 'exit/loss' or 'danger' event. As we have seen, the sorts of loss situations that the women consciously linked with times of intense drinking referred to partnerships or mother-hood. These were not sudden events of the sort I am discussing here. The few recent events which affected the well-being of the partner, the child or the marital relationship were looked at. But again, there were no noticeable differences between the groups.

Despite being prompted, nobody mentioned using alcohol to cope with the psychological impact of such events, except as celebrating some welcome occurrences. In terms of unwelcome events they were more likely to say they just had to cope with it by themselves or relied on others, especially partners, for support. Almost all of them named their partners as the main source of support in a crisis. Although 13 claimed that at times the relationship had not been good during this period, again, there were no marked differences between the groups. Given that the women themselves had drawn attention to the import-ance of domestic difficulties, especially relationship breakdown, in accounting for a high consumption of alcohol this was unexpected. A likely explanation is that none of these difficulties was very serious. Certainly, none of the 60 had separated from their partners since becoming pregnant. Indeed five had got married and three others had started to live with their partner.

There were no differences between the groups in terms of being sure of help in a crisis, the quality of relationship with their partner, or in having a confidante other than their partner to turn to. So, despite predictions from the literature as shown in chapter 2, and the women themselves in chapter 3, that sudden occurrences, especially those asso-ciated with loss and bereavement, might precipitate heavy drinking, this was not borne out by their personal experience.

Objectively, the non-professional mothers were a little less likely to be in contact with women with children of a similar age or to keep up previ-ous friendships, but were uncomplaining about this. Additional import-ant differences were that all the professional women had partners whereas seven of the non-professional women did not. Their quality of life was lower, and their social networks more limited. Such networks frequently provide a combination of emotional, moral and practical support as well as a source of information and advice. Not only do they improve the quality of life, but almost certainly enhance women's ability to cope with changes and unexpected adversities. This makes it more likely that, in the absence of other supports, both material and emotional, and in the face of greater exposure not only to more life-events in total but more unwel-come ones, than their lighter drinking peers, the heavy drinking non-professionals might be tempted to seek bottle-shaped comfort.

## Adjusting to motherhood

*'It's a vicious circle. If women follow the general indoctrination that they should look after everybody else and always be available, then they're more likely to be ill.'* (Maureen, a heavy drinking professional)

There were no differences between the socio-economic groups in terms of longstanding physical health problems. Reactions to the confirmation of pregnancy were similar in all groups. Material difficulties were a very real concern for some of the non-professionals. More non-professional women (90 per cent), had physically troublesome pregnancies than their professional counterparts (77 per cent). Objective difficulties in giving birth were evenly distributed between all four groups. This picture only gives marginal support to previous reports linking heavy drinking and reproductive difficulties (Wilsnack 1985).

Common illnesses among other household members were no more prevalent at any time in any group. But amongst the women themselves, heavy drinkers were more susceptible to minor illnesses in early motherhood. Several, like Andrea, a heavy drinking non-professional, complained of being continuously run down. Likewise Chris, a heavy drinking professional, said:

*'I've been dreadful these last few months. It seems that I'm at the doctor's every other week. He must think I'm a hypochondriac.'*

Tiredness and the stress of physically demanding caring roles find little response in public policy or services (Graham 1994). It might have been expected that it would be the non-professional women who were least able to purchase their own services, would experience greater stress, given their greater shortage of practical and emotional supports.

In keeping with their worse experiences, the non-professional women were more likely to say that they had found the reality of pregnancy worse than they had expected:

*'I thought I was going to be all radiant, blooming and glowing with good health during pregnancy, but I was just tired.'* (Caroline, a heavy drinking non-professional)

They were more likely to complain of unpredictable mood swings during their pregnancy. As Eliza, a heavy drinking non-professional, described:

'*It got me down. I was like a yo-yo. I had my crying days and my good days. Then the joys of childbirth were lost on me*'

The fact that it was the non-professional women who experienced more mood swings may have been linked with their more difficult pregnancies, as described earlier. Such feelings might have resulted from feeling disappointed with the experience and particularly with giving birth. Marion, a light drinking non-professional, remarked:

'*I'd expected the birth to be like a holiday dream. Instead, it was long and painful.*'

In all, 66 per cent of non-professional women but only 53 per cent of professional women found the birth experience worse than they had expected. This was probably because their expectations were higher, embodying traditional views about fulfilment from being a mother. There were no differences according to drinking level.

As outlined in chapter 2, much of the literature presumes that subjective feelings of psychological discomfort are linked with drinking behaviour. I was interested, first, in the ways the women themselves experienced the degree and duration of any discomforts, rather than in any psychiatric diagnosis. Second, I wanted to know whether they would draw any direct links with their drinking behaviour. The ways the women described how they felt in themselves in the first few weeks after returning home with a new baby were grouped into three categories following Oakley's (1980) classification of post-natal psychological discomfort. The first category was unease/anxiety. This referred to short-term feelings of anxiety or of being let down, which were often accompanied by mood swings or feeling weepy. Elaine, a light drinking non-professional, described her experience thus:

'*It was a real let-down, I was crying and all over the place, but it suddenly wore itself out.*'

The second category was depressed mood. Lesley, a light drinking non-professional, experienced it as follows:

'*I'd cry over the least little thing.*'

This sort of mood could last for several weeks, as it did for Phyllis, a heavy drinking professional:

> *'I went through a spate of gloom, at about two or three months, when I realised how tired I'd been.'*

But it was not so intense or long-lasting as depression, which frequently lasted for many months, as described by Eva, a heavy drinking non-professional:

> *'I was really depressed for six months. It's only now that I'm beginning to feel really on top again. As soon as I had him I started to cry. I used to wonder how I was going to get through the day. It was like fighting a blanket.'*

For Karen, a heavy drinking non-professional:

> *'It was a continuous down, it seemed that I couldn't cope.'*

All those who were classified as depressed had actually sought medical help, but some had delayed doing so until all else had failed. Lee, a heavy drinking professional, had been continuously depressed, but eventually went to her GP after 18 months. She described her experience thus:

> *'My husband was out for 12 hours a day. It's awful if you're alone all that time and feeling bad. I found it very difficult to turn to anybody.'*

She was prescribed a lengthy course of anti-depressants and at the time we were talking was still attending individual and marital therapy.

According to this classification, problems were widespread. Only 28 per cent of the 60 women had no problems; 38 per cent of them experienced unease and or anxiety; 25 per cent reported depressed mood; and 9 per cent depression. This distribution seems to be typical of other studies, which have found that between 10 per cent and 15 per cent of women suffer post-natal depression (Pitt 1991). Oakley (1980) found that 34 per cent of her sample had suffered from depressed mood or depression.

As far as the actual birth experience was concerned, the reader will recall that there were no objective differences between the groups, but that the non-professional mothers expressed more subjective discontent with the experience. So, it is very interesting that slightly more (37 per cent) of the non-professional as compared with professional women (30 per cent) reported depression or depressed mood. Oakley (1980) and other reviewers of the clinical literature (Richards 1990; Pitt

1991; Littlewood and McHugh 1997) have drawn attention to the links between adverse social conditions, adverse reactions to the experience of giving birth and looking after a baby and post-natal depression. That picture is confirmed here.

The most significant point is that all five women who were depressed were heavy drinkers, of whom two were middle-class. Apart from Sandra, a heavy drinking non-professional whose experience we have already looked at, none of them indicated any direct links with their drinking. Neither did they mention any sudden increase in drinking in the post-natal period. However, the possibility or potential of drinking to ease depression, as suggested in chapter 2, must be strong. Whilst the non-professional heavy drinkers might be under more pressure, drinking would be made easier for middle-class heavy drinkers by the ready availability and acceptability of drinking at home and drinking alone. These suppositions become more meaningful when we hear Geraldine and Sophie's stories in the next chapter.

The women completed a standardised psychological questionnaire. The 28-question version of the General Health Questionnaire (GHQ) is a well-validated and widely used instrument which does not require special training to administer and is suitable for general populations (Goldberg 1978). It has been used in similar populations of women (Brannen and Moss 1991). It is not concerned with diagnostic niceties, but focuses on the borders of clinical disturbance, by distinguishing those respondents whose level of distress is sufficient to warrant psychiatric assessment.

The higher the total score, the more likely an individual needs psychiatric assessment. Researchers have differed about the most appropriate score to use as a threshold within the total range of 0–28 for identifying psychiatric illness. A prevalence rate of 25 per cent is expected in a community sample and Goldberg (1985) advises that a threshold of five or six discriminates best in the general practice context. Kumar and Robson (1984) used a threshold of six in their study of antenatal and post-natal women. The same score was used here.

Twenty-seven per cent scored more than six, implying that they could be considered in need of psychiatric assessment. Such a percentage was in keeping with expected estimates (Goldberg 1985). When considered by social status, as might have been predicted, 30 per cent of non-professional women were distinguished, but only 23 per cent of middle-class women. This fitted with the general picture in chapter 2 that it was the non-professionals who experienced more continuous social disadvantage and difficulties, which are known to be linked with mental ill-health. As we have seen in previous chapters, they received less daily practical and social support, were less satisfied with their current roles and found childcare less rewarding than they had anticipated. They had also been more exposed to life-events. By contrast, there were only two things that the professional women complained of more frequently than the non-professionals: time pressures and missing their friends.

Using the same threshold score of six, it was noticeable that 37 per cent of heavy drinkers, but only 17 per cent of light drinkers, were identified, thus confirming the general trend. Breeze (1985), in her community survey of women's drinking, also found that high drinkers were more likely to display signs of psychological distress.

Within both socio-economic groupings, more heavy drinkers than light drinkers were distinguished. Between the professional groups the ratio was 6:1, and in the non-professionals it was 5:4. What is striking is that difference between the two middle-class scores was much greater than that between the two non-professional groups. So far, the story has shown that it was the non-professional women that were most disadvantaged, and the heavy drinking non-professional group who had most difficulty with the changes in their lives over the past few years. So it was unexpected that the heavy drinking professionals, those who were least disadvantaged, seemed as vulnerable as the heavy drinking non-professionals. It seemed that their psychological discomforts were independent of the cumulative effect of disadvantage, difficulties or dissatisfactions. For example, the middle-class groups were less discontented with the realities of pregnancy, childbirth and, as noted in the previous chapter, with childcare than the non-professionals. One explanation might be the psychological pressure of maintaining a busy dual-earner life-style, with its associated time pressures, coupled with a felt loss of social contact. These were the only two areas where the middle-class groups were more likely to complain.

As far as the heavy drinking non-professionals were concerned, their greater number of difficulties, disappointments, life-events in total, and more upsetting life-events, must have been more difficult to deal with in the face of less social advantage and in some cases real hardship. For example, whilst both groups of heavier drinkers were highly dissatisfied with the amount of contact they were able to have with their families, it was the heavy drinking non-professional women who felt it most keenly. For them, female relatives rather than friends were their confidantes. Not enough contact was a real limitation.

## It's all due to stress?

Putting this all together, drinking as a means to cope with difficulties was for these women far less common than drinking either because they simply liked doing it and took pleasure in it, or because social circumstances encouraged and enabled their drinking. Drinking to cope with difficult feelings was far more likely to be mentioned by the heavy drinkers. Whilst many of the women as a whole had mentioned drinking to cope with difficult feelings as a possible explanation for women in general developing drinking problems, past personal experience of really intense drinking, verging on the problematic, was only described by four women. These were all heavy drinkers, who recalled trying to cope with very painful personal difficulties, before they 'hit the bottle'. All four had already got easy access to alcohol, were moving in circles where heavy usage was sanctioned, enjoyed drinking and had become accustomed to associating it with relaxation before their difficulties arose. This meant that, contrary to some of the theoretical views and stereotypical assumptions, drinking to drown sorrows was of itself not a trigger to heavy drinking for these women. It was rather a trigger to move from heavy to problematic drinking. These women who turned to alcohol for relief only did so after they had become accustomed to using alcohol for other reasons. In their circumstances it was a readily available prop. Indeed, all those who had used alcohol to cope with difficulties were already heavy drinkers who took pleasure from drinking and were accustomed to using it for pleasure before they drank to 'drown their sorrows'. They were well aware that they were drifting into what they would have seen as problem drinking. Their behaviour changed. Although this may not have been in public, they provided a sufficient audience for themselves to be conscious of the changes and concerned that their difficulties should not escalate.

What is important is to tease out what distinguishes the sort of difficulties and contexts which might lead women to use alcohol as a main means of coping over a prolonged period, from those that are short-lived. Using alcohol for temporary relief, such as a lift at the end of hard day, or for 'Dutch courage' to counteract temporary nervousness, is one thing. Prolonged drinking that is out of control is another.

What were these difficulties? What sorrows needed drowning? The significance of domestic issues is clear when looking at the type of difficulties recounted by the four women who told their stories earlier in this chapter. Their memories were often tinged with more than hint of self-reproach and shame. Key themes were the loss of a marital partner or a perceived failure to demonstrate competent mothering ability. These losses left them feeling unable to perform what they saw as an expected female role: dependency on a man or appearing to be a proficient and able mother. Thus their sense of personal esteem was seriously undermined. A similar emphasis ran through the women's own ideas about the causes of heavy drinking in women (see chapter 3). In general, they described highly individualised situations, not mentioning the wider social implications such as gender inequalities, or interactions with social disadvantage. I have tried to disentangle these issues in this chapter.

Looking at these women's lives, some sorts of stress were experienced equally by all groups and appear unconnected with drinking behaviour. However, some were clearly experienced more by certain groups. In chapters 5 and 6 we saw how material and social disadvantages not only reduced the non-professionals opportunities to drink, but also their quality of life. We know from other research that material and social disadvantage makes women more vulnerable to physical and psychological difficulties, which in turn are often linked with low self-esteem and mental ill health. This makes it harder to cope with problems and dissatisfactions as they arise, which they inevitably do, especially at times of major transition such as the birth of a first child.

Not only were the non-professional women more disadvantaged, but they experienced more difficulties than the professional women. Figure 7.1 summarises the main point from this chapter, and also includes disadvantages, difficulties and dissatisfactions outlined in chapters 5, 6 and 7. For example, in chapter 6 I pointed out that maintaining social circles was an issue for them. Whilst they received a great deal of day-to-day support from their families, and were no less likely to have a confidante, their social networks were much more restricted than those of the middle-class women. In this context, the size of networks is probably not as important as the quality of the relationships and the support they offer. So, it is important that the non-professionals had less contact with other women who had children of a similar age. As a group they faced more sudden changes or life-events, and more physical problems in their pregnancies; more psychological problems in pregnancy, the post-natal period and in early motherhood, but had less back-up to deal with them.

We know from general population studies, as well as this study, that disadvantage and its attendant problems alone are not associated with increased drinking, which is more often associated with social advantage. Both heavy drinking groups, regardless of social status, experienced

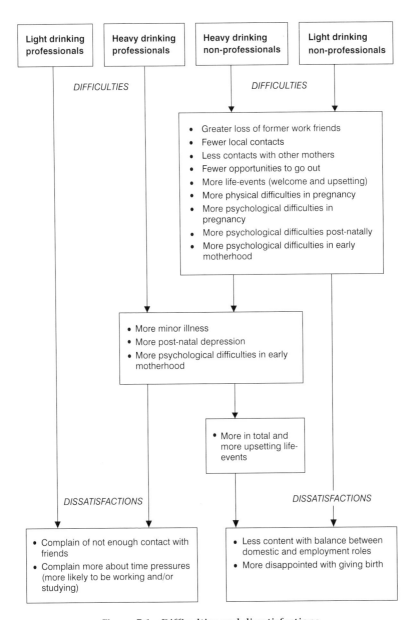

Figure 7.1  Difficulties and dissatisfactions

heightened personal difficulties in comparison to their light drinking counterparts. In comparison with their socio-economic peers, they were more likely to have suffered from more minor physical illnesses in the last few years, and more psychological difficulties in the post-natal period and at the time when they were talking to me. Whilst the women themselves did not make a conscious link, their drinking may often have been a constructive way of coping with feeling a bit down. After all, they were accustomed to seeing drinking as something to help them relax.

Difficulties were exacerbated for the heavy drinking non-professionals. They were most frequently exposed to unexpected changes, and especially upsetting changes. Looking at the overall picture of felt disappointments and dissatisfactions, detailed in chapters 5 and 6 (see Figure 7.1), we see that some were experienced by class groups only, some by all heavy drinkers as compared with their lighter drinking compatriots, but that heavy drinking non-professionals experienced the greatest number. If sheer numbers of difficulties and dissatisfactions, in a context of material disadvantage, create increased stress, as was suggested in chapter 2, then it was this group who were most likely to suffer. They were much less protected materially and socially then the heavy drinking professionals.

Drinking to cope at times was important for both groups of heavy drinkers, and both were at increased risk of psychological difficulties, but it is significant that the constellation of their potential stresses were quite different. There were some things in common; for example, both complained of more restricted social contacts than they would like, which I argued indicated their greater sociability. But it was the professionals who complained most and who did not have time to do everything that they wanted. Their expectations were higher. Notably, it was the non-professionals, especially the heavy drinking ones, who were more likely to find that the experience of actually becoming a mother was not as wonderful as they had imagined. This brings us back to our previous discussion of women assessing their performance as partners and mothers. The four stories in the earlier part of this chapter indicate that these women saw themselves as lacking. I will develop this theme further in the next chapter, where the differences between the two groups of heavy drinkers will be reviewed in the light of two stories told by women who developed severe drinking problems when their children were very young. I will also return to the other main theme of drinking in response to opportunities.

# 8
# Satisfaction or Solace: Two Case Studies

The earlier chapters have shown that the themes of opportunity and difficulty are deeply intertwined with women's drinking. My starting point was with the occupations of the women and their partners, both as a measure of relative social advantage and disadvantage and as a direct influence, providing opportunities for drinking. I then looked at the influence of the women's social contacts and the impact of difficulties and disappointments. This chapter examines how the two main themes fit together, one framing the other. Two case studies of women who developed drinking problems when their child was very young follow. The overview at the end assesses how pleasurable, constructive, controlled drinking can develop to become an uncontrollable, frightening problem.

## Pathways to drinking

Let us look in detail at the differing experiences of the four groups in detail. What overall model of the different pathways can be developed?

All the factors we have looked at, either those openly encouraging drinking or those generating stresses which might have stimulated them to use drink as a coping strategy, can be grouped under the following heads:

- personal attitudes towards drinking
- material situations – advantaged or disadvantaged
- drinking cultures
- social contacts and leisure
- difficulties
- dissatisfactions

In many instances the categories overlap, and what follows is an initial mapping of factors associated with positive drinking for pleasure, or drinking opportunities (see Figure 8.1) and factors potentially encouraging drinking as a coping device (see Figure 8.2). These include the themes developed in chapters 5, 6 and 7. In summary, obviously some of these factors are interlinked and, as already pointed out, their measurement was often crude. What the mapping in Figures 8.1 and 8.2 shows is considerable differences between heavy and light drinkers as influenced by socio-economic situation. Where a factor is indicated it means that it was more likely to feature in that group's experience. That does not mean that it did not feature at all for the other groups. What is important is the overall patterns these groupings make and the themes they suggest, rather than any exact quantitative or definitive analysis.

To start with, all the heavier drinkers were personally more positive about alcohol than the lighter drinkers, as shown in Figure 8.1. For them it was a source of pleasure. They took great delight in consuming it and talking about it. To summarise they:

- enjoyed drinking
- enjoyed a varied social life and social contacts
- liked going out socialising and drinking
- enjoyed all sorts of activities which involved drinking
- viewed alcohol as relaxing

It was the heavy drinking professionals who were most positive and who particularly enjoyed alcohol for its own sake, regardless of whether it was accompanied by food or other social activity. They were also most inclined to be aware of its mood-changing potential and use it to give them a boost.

Although all the heavy drinkers might have liked to drink, how far they were able to indulge was either constrained or encouraged by material circumstances. But, however favourable the social environment, if an individual did not like or enjoy alcohol very much, they were likely to remain light drinkers (see Figure 8.1)

The light non-professional drinkers had no positive drinking opportunities. On the contrary, the more advantaged group of heavy drinkers, the professionals, had especially positive attitudes towards drinking and, as we have seen, an especially favourable culture and many social opportunities for pleasurable drinking (see Figure 8.1). All the professionals had considerably more opportunity and access long before having a child and continued to do so afterwards. To begin with, they came from

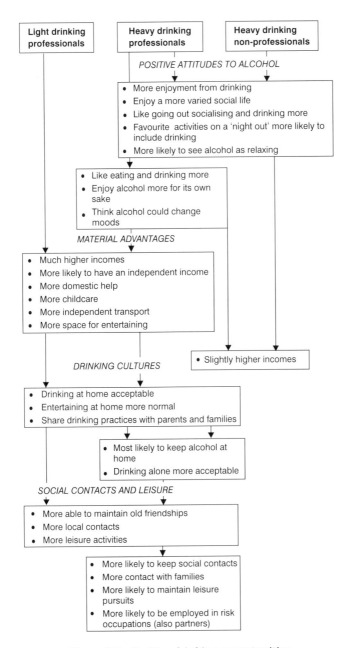

**Figure 8.1  Positive drinking opportunities**

wealthier households, they were much more likely to have a continued independent income and were easily able to purchase both leisure and pleasure. They had wider social circles. For them there were no vestiges of traditional taboos against 'drinking indoors'. Entertaining at home was commonplace. Drinking norms and cultures were similar to those of family members and partners. These basically encouraging factors were supplemented amongst the heavy drinking professionals. They and their partners were more likely to be employed in occupations where alcohol use was encouraged. Moreover, they were the most outgoing and sociable of all.

Life for the non-professional women was considerably tougher. Not only were they more likely to have housing problems, they were worse off, with some of them just about getting by. Many more of them gave up work after having a child, so their households were reliant on one income only, thus widening existing differentials from the professionals. For them there was no possibility of paying a babysitter several times a week so they could go out with their mates as they used to. They had no car that was specifically theirs, so just popping to the other side of town to see a friend for the afternoon was out of the question. They were fully occupied looking after their child and home, rather than paying some-body else to do it. No wonder the heavy drinking non-professionals found it hard to drink in the ways they used to, after the birth of their child. The national picture of the birth of a first child creating a water-shed in women's drinking behaviours was true for this group. They con-tinued to drink more than the light group and almost certainly exceeded national guidelines, but it was harder for them to maintain what they saw as part of their quality of life.

These differentials are highlighted when the position of the heavy drinking professional group is specifically contrasted with their experi-ence. Of all the groups, these women most frequently kept alcohol at home. Drinking alone was not taboo for them, whereas it was for the light drinking professionals. They were quite comfortable pouring themselves a drink, whenever they deemed it suitable. Moreover, they were sociable creatures, having lots of contact with their families. Opening a bottle was part of a family ritual, as it was with partners, many of whom were high consumers themselves, working in occupations that encouraged its use.

Certainly this picture goes a long way to explaining why heavy drinking is more common amongst advantaged groups of women. As with social advantage, disadvantage alone did not encourage heavy drinking. If anything, it discouraged it, for it will be remembered that heavy drinking was very much the exception among the non-professional women, which, as we saw in chapter 2, larger studies have also shown. It would be more appropriate to think of the effects of such disadvantages as making it harder for non-professional women to cope with difficulties. This could put those who liked drinking and had positive attitudes towards it at risk of drinking to cope or negative drinking.

They certainly had more than their fair share of difficulties (see Figure 8.2). Non-professional women in general were not only more disadvantaged, but were more likely to have more difficulties than their middle-class peers. Quite obviously, life had been most difficult for the heavy drinking non-professionals. They also reported more dissatisfactions and difficulties (see Figure 8.2).

Both groups of heavy drinkers had experienced more psychological and physical problems then their light drinking sisters. Amongst the middle-class women difficulties seemed to be more likely to start after their child's arrival, whereas for the non-professionals they were a more or less continuous background. Disappointments and dissatisfactions panned out in different fashions. To generalise, they fell into two categories: those relating to time available for social contact and those relating to experiences of motherhood. As a whole the professional managerial group emphasised time pressures and more limited social contact than they would have liked. Most notably, the heavy drinking professionals, despite their greater socialising, remained more likely to complain of limited contact with friends, and not surprisingly, given that of all the groups their lives were most hectic, of time pressures. For the non-professionals, dissatisfactions centred on their disappointment with their experience of the maternal role and the balance between domestic and employment roles. The whole experience did not live up to expectations and in practice was very far from how they would have liked it to be.

Although they were not necessarily of equal weight it is useful to have an indication of the cumulative experience of each group's experience relative to the other groups. This enables us to see which factors were more emphasised by which group and get a measure of the relative weightings between them. Looking at positive reasons for drinking first, each group was given a score of one for each factor indicated in Figure 8.1 that it experienced. For example, five initial positive attitudes towards drinking have been distinguished (Figure 8.1). Both groups of heavy drinkers displayed all five and thus scored five each, the light groups scoring nothing. But the heavy drinking professionals had an additional three positive attitudes towards using alcohol, making their

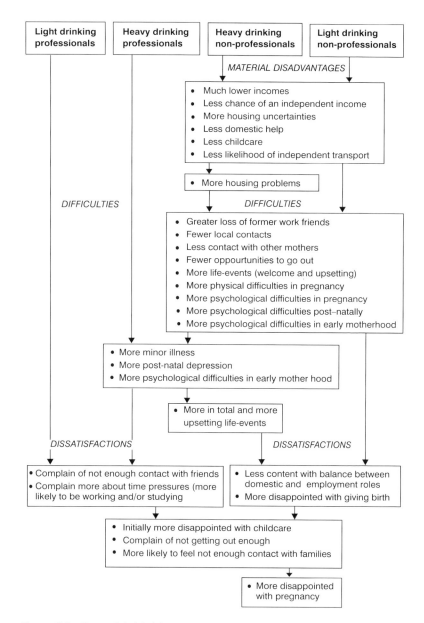

Figure 8.2   **Potential drinking pressures: material disadvantage, difficulties and dissatisfactions**

Table 8.1    Drinking opportunities

| Group of factors | Light drinking professionals | Heavy drinking professionals | Heavy drinking non-professionals |
|---|---|---|---|
| Positive attitudes | – | 8 | 5 |
| Material advantages | 6 | 7 | 1 |
| Drinking cultures | 3 | 5 | – |
| Social contacts and leisure | 3 | 7 | – |
| Totals | 12 | 27 | 6 |

total score eight for positive attitudes towards alcohol (see Table 8.1). The two professional groups each had six material advantages listed, and the heavy group a further one – slightly higher incomes – as compared with the lighter drinking professionals, making their total seven, as compared with six for the light drinking professionals. The heavy drinking non-professionals also had slightly higher incomes than their light drinking peers, so they scored one in this category of factors. As noted earlier, the light drinking non-professionals, unlike all the other three groups, did not experience any positive reasons for drinking, so that group is omitted from this table.

When all four relevant categories of factors linked with opportunity for drinking are looked at in this cumulative way it is obvious that both heavy groups were more encouraged to drink than their respective light groups. The heavy drinking professionals were the most favoured. However, the light drinking professionals, if they had been so inclined, would have found more drinking opportunities than the heavy drinking non-professionals, who would have valued it more. The net effect was a marked inequality of access between the two heavy drinking groups for whom regular drinking was part of their quality of life. Drinking as a response to opportunity was a very strong explanation for higher drinking levels amongst middle-class women.

Turning to the other theme of drinking to counteract stresses or negative drinking I have suggested that those women who liked alcohol and who were accustomed to using it to relax would be most likely to turn to it when under stress. When the accumulated totals of stress factors are looked at in the same way, they clearly demonstrate that circumstances for both non-professional groups were markedly more difficult than for the professional women (see Table 8.2).

In so far as the heavy drinking non-professionals were the most disadvantaged, and looking at these distributions which show that they had

Table 8.2   **Drinking pressures**

| Groups of factors | Light drinking professionals | Heavy drinking professionals | Heavy drinking non-professionals | Light drinking non-professionals |
|---|---|---|---|---|
| Material disadvantages | – | – | 7 | 6 |
| Difficulties | – | 3 | 11 | 7 |
| Dissatisfactions | 2 | 5 | 6 | 2 |
| Totals | 2 | 8 | 24 | 15 |

the most difficulties and dissatisfactions, it could be imagined that if any group would be likely to drink as a means of coping with difficulties it would be them. Although, the middle-class heavy drinkers had problems, it could be expected that the impact of some difficulties would be buffered by their social advantage.

None the less, the two heavy groups experienced different sorts of problems. It will be remembered that the four women highlighted in chapter 7 pinpointed certain difficulties pertaining to female role performance. These included separating from a partner and what they considered their less than ideal performance as a mother due to post-natal depression. In this context, physically difficult pregnancies, psychological troubles and dissatisfaction and disappointment with pregnancy, giving birth or motherhood could also be thought of as indications of a less than ideal maternal experience. All groups, apart from the light drinking professionals, experienced some of these difficulties, but it was the heavy drinking non-professionals who experienced more of them and felt them most keenly. They held the most traditional views about motherhood, but could not achieve them due to material constraints. This last point brings us back to chapter 2 where I argued that concepts of faulty female sex-role performance could be seen as a central theme in the past and current literature about women's drinking. The foregoing analysis suggests that there may be some truth in that focus, but that it needs redefining in a social context. Rather than such problems being due to individual irresponsibility, ignorance or psychological conflict they are quite clearly structurally and culturally shaped, and reflect other inequalities.

The heavy drinking professional women experienced fewer such role-performance difficulties. Their particular complaints seemed to centre on the highly organised, complex and pressured lives they led. It was these women who mentioned regular daily drinking and who were comfortable drinking alone. In this situation, it is easy to imagine that in certain stressful circumstances this habit could easily get out of control if they regularly used drink to maintain equilibrium, to restore a sense of balance and consequently their self-esteem.

Whilst not suggesting that all heavy drinkers will go on to become problem drinkers, this does begin to depict the sorts of circumstances in which different groups of women might drift into difficulties. The two women's stories, which now follow, illustrate how this can happen.

## Geraldine's story

Geraldine is in her mid-thirties. Her partner works in journalism. She developed a drinking problem a few years ago when her son was small. This is her story:

*'My parents drank. It was always a gin and tonic before and a glass of wine with, whether it was fish and chips or beef wellington. My dad and his mate started importing wine to sell, with a view to drinking the profits, not to make a million out of it. It was just that they got their wine cheap. So it's always been part of my way of life.'*

*I've always been very sociable. I went to college and was in all the drinking teams. It was fine, a bit over the top, but so what? It was the done thing. Everybody seemed to be doing it. There was a real swotty group, who weren't interested in drinking.*

*We used to drink socially, probably more, well definitely more, than the recommended amount, but not every day. Certainly we'd do it all of the weekend. We live in a little village. Village life revolves around going down the pub at lunchtimes at the weekends, quizzes in the pub – that sort of thing . . . that was life really. Up until I had my child I worked in finance. We used to commute into London every day.*

*I didn't drink at all, apart from about half a glass of wine every month, when I was pregnant. I found it quite a shock being at home with this baby. I'd thought it was going to be wonderful and fulfilling every minute of the day. It wasn't, because he screamed and I didn't know why. I hadn't really had much contact with young babies, so it was all a bit difficult. I didn't particularly enjoy the coffee mornings, mums and tots scene. I was bored. I didn't hit the bottle as soon as he was born. It was 18 months going on two years later, when I went for it. It was definitely boredom, going from a 13-hour day, commuting up to London, to being at home, when the highlight was doing the washing-up. I was his mother rather than me. Nobody noticed me. Everybody just assumes that's what you do because you're the mother. In my job it was me that gave the OK, said whether we'd got enough money to do this or that. I could say yes or no. We're talking hundreds and thousands of pounds. It's not like your own money. I was managing a small office. It was a responsible job. It was stimulating and rewarding. But it would have been impossible to continue those hours with a small child.*

*Anyway I made the decision that I was going to give up work because I wanted to. We'd really struggled to get pregnant. I had to go for fertility treatment. I wanted to be a mum at home. It was probably the biggest mistake I ever made for me, but it was what I thought I wanted. I thought it was going to be really fulfilling, a doddle and great fun. I found out it was hard work. You were tired all the time. I didn't always know the answer. When it wasn't all hunkydory, I felt even more guilty. We'd spent all this money on fertility treatment. But, there was this child, and it was crying. Even though you'd fed it and cleaned it up, it was still crying. I'd got the cottage in the village, but not the sunshine and roses. I expected him to be asleep in the corner while I was doing wonderful artistic things. It wasn't like that at all. I knit and make greetings cards. I dabble. Most of the things I wanted to do would have meant getting equipment out and that sort of thing. It wasn't the sort of thing you could drop and attend to this crying baby. So I thought I won't bother getting it out. I'd sit around waiting for him to cry again.*

*I think you get very strange impressions. You go round shops and see these mothers pushing their kids around. They look happy. You've got this bump and you don't think what happens to them behind closed doors, the sleepless nights, the screaming. You just see the lovely side. You ignore the ones lying on the floor banging their heels because their mother won't buy them a tellytubby.*

*It's for ever, even when he's thirty I'm still going to be his mother. Now he says, when I'm your age can I still live at home! I say, 'Oh you won't want to when you're my age."Oh I will,' he says. When I started my job in London I wondered what I'd let myself in for, but I knew I could give my notice in. But motherhood is for life. If it's not what you expected when this baby arrives, which I imagine 99.9 per cent of the time it isn't, it's hard luck. Nothing can prepare you for how you're going to feel: the responsibility and the burden. You can't say, right I'm giving in my notice, you've got to move out in a month. It's a tiny wriggling little thing, who's dependent on you. Even now he's at school it's always at the back of my mind – what if they need to contact me? Whether I do a job or not, it's got to be a job where I can say, sorry I've got to go. I've got to be contactable. Whoever's looking after him, in the end the buck always stops with me.*

*There's quite a lot of drinking in the village. In our road, there are several couples with young children. Friday nights always meant open house somewhere near. You didn't have to be invited. If you fancied going out, you just wandered over with your baby monitor. That's how life was – barbecues, garden parties, dropping in. It was me that started the street party. We're a different generation from my parents. Drinking's OK with us.*

*I started off by having a glass of wine when I'd got him to bed at night, thinking that's my day's work done. It progressed from there really. That was on my own. I started drinking more on my own, normally wine, as I would have done at the pub. Family and friends began to notice I was drinking more than I should, behaving a bit oddly and drinking at odd times of the day when it's not supposedly suitably acceptable. They went through all the stages of having drink taken out of the house and telling me I'd got a problem, when I wasn't ready to admit it to myself. Therefore I went on hard stuff, because it was easier. Anyway it's a bigger hit to drink vodka. Spirits are easier on the way back from the shop. Taking a corkscrew stuffed down your sock, to open the wine on your way back from the shop, isn't very comfortable.*

*It went on from there really. It wasn't an all day every day thing. I could keep off it for weeks at a time, and then have a major five-day vodka binge. I quite often saw my drinking as doing something adult, doing something for me. Everything revolved around where he [her child] needed to be and what he was doing. It was one thing I could do for me. If I'd been able to go out shopping or swimming or something, it would have helped. But I couldn't because I'd got the baby. It never crossed my mind to ask my parents to look after him or anything. No, it was I'll have a drink, that'll help. Whereas I could have been sensible and said, OK he's going to his grandparents every Wednesday, I'm going out. But I didn't and then it was too late. The drink had got me.*

*Being on my own was the trigger in the first place. I was bored. In hindsight, it might have been better if I'd gone back to work, but I couldn't have commuted to London. My husband works long hours. He still commutes and is often away. Obviously with him working the hours that he did, he never knew what he was going to come home to – the very sober acceptable wife, or I could be on the floor. He'd be out from very early in the morning until, well it could be 10.00. The earliest he'd be in was 8.30, so I'd have the baby from the time he got up until he went to bed. My husband hardly saw him at all during the week.*

*I got him into nursery just after his second birthday. I thought to myself, if I have a day to myself, it'll make all the difference. On that day I can start working, or figure out what I want to do, or get something going from home to make some money. But, I ended up taking him to nursery at 9.00 in the morning, getting a bottle of vodka on the way home and just being* out of it all day. Then, I'd stagger up to the nursery at 4.00 in the afternoon to pick him up. I'd look forward to the nursery day because I knew I could get really plastered that day. I could just lie and put videos on and do whatever I wanted on that day.

I was diagnosed with post-natal depression when my son was two. I was quite glad about that, because it gave me an excuse. I could say, I haven't got an alcohol problem. I'm depressed. At that stage I was hitting the bottle rather than seeking help in other directions. I got to the stage where somebody would always have to be around to make sure I was all right, or sober enough to go and pick him up from nursery. If I was found not to be sober, then he was trundled off to grandparents or friends or whoever.

The locals have been brilliant. There was somebody who lived over the road who was an all day, every day sort of chap, who kept topping it up. He wasn't a particularly pleasant bloke. I don't think I ever saw him sober, but I don't imagine he was nice even then. Everybody used to call him an alcoholic this and an alcoholic that. When I finally admitted that I'd got a problem and I was hitting vodka by the bottle, not just cider by the bottle, I thought what on earth is everybody going to think of me. But, the fact is that it has happened to me, and hopefully people used to and I hope still do, like me. Perhaps they look back at themselves and think well, if this has happened to her, well I ought to look at what I'm drinking. A lot of people in the gang have cut down on their drinking since I addressed the problem. I was quite open about it. I've been in detox and most of them knew. When I was apart from my child, [she'd lived alone for a time during her treatment], I'd every excuse to drink as much as I wanted. I expected to be treated like the two-headed monster and have curtains twitch at me and things like that. In fact, everybody's been fine. I'd built all that up myself, being prepared for being treated differently. Everybody's been absolutely wonderful and waited for me to bring the subject up.

I've since learnt that one or two of the neighbours thought I'd got post-natal depression. There's this one friend, who invited a friend to one of the local gatherings. This person had been through post-natal depression, and ended up being a counsellor or something for post-natal depression. She'd realised she'd got a drink problem and got out of it before she needed to seek help. She watched me. They asked her to watch me at one of these barbecues and apparently she went back to them and said, 'yeh...she's got postnatal depression.' But nobody until now has said anything to me. I was only told this last week. My child is now four! When I was hitting the bottle, apparently, I was a completely different person from the one they knew when I moved in. I think they were worried that I'd bite their *head off or something if they even suggested that I might need help. Nobody said anything. It's all water under the bridge now.*

*To this day I don't know whether I had post-natal depression or not. When I was first diagnosed I was put on anti-depressants, but I was still drinking. So I've no idea whether they were doing any good. For me it was something to blame it on and pretend that I hadn't got a drink problem.*

*Now I'm doing quite well. I'm not saying there won't be hiccups in the future. I'm sure there will. I'd love to think I could go down to the pub and have a couple of glasses of wine and that'd be OK, but I know if I had a sip, that'd be a bottle gone.'*

## Sophie's story

Sophie is in her mid-twenties. Like Geraldine her drinking problems came to a head when her daughter was very young. This is her story:

*I grew up in a home where my parents drank every single day and my mum especially. She was a secret drinker as well. You'd find her in front of the drinks cabinet with a bottle of gin in her mouth. They always got through a bottle of wine each, every evening and more at the weekends. You needed a brewery to supply all the drink. Kids were always given it. We were always round the table getting the empty glasses, throwing up in the toilets, having hangovers. I thought it was normal, as you do if you grow up in it.*

*My dad doesn't drink that much now. My mum still has, and always has had a bad drink problem. When we came home from school she'd either be flat out on the sofa, tearing at the house or dancing around. You'd never know how she was going to be. I still catch her now, with her head in the fridge and a bottle of martini in her mouth. I don't think she drinks gin any more, but that's what she always drank when we were kids. You'd hear the magnetic click go on the pull down thing on the drinks cabinet. She'd go into the dining room and you'd hear the click. You'd put your head round the door and she'd have a bottle of gin in her mouth.*

*I started drinking when I was 13 or 14, sneaking it out of the drinks cabinet on Friday night, or paying people, as they went into the off licence, to get a bottle of cider. I never saw it as a problem. By the time I got to 17 I started drinking a lot heavier, and various friends' parents had quiet words with me, but I didn't take any notice. I was still at school doing my A levels. After I'd finished school I moved into a house with seven other people. They were heavily into drugs and drinking. I smoked. [cannabis] I didn't do much acid or anything like that. It was mainly smoking and drinking. It was every day and every evening. I didn't see it as a problem.*

*Looking back, it obviously was a big problem. We'd go out most evenings. Then we'd drink at home.*

*I didn't see it as a problem until I was 21. After leaving school I'd worked for my dad. But by then I was working in an old people's home. The guy I'd lived with had just left. I started drinking at work, taking it out of the old people's cupboards or the drink cabinet, that sort of thing. I couldn't get through a shift without being drunk. I'd buy four cans of special brew on the walk home, which was about 45 minutes. I used to drink the same going there, only it was two cans. I didn't consider myself to have a drink problem. Looking back I had a very bad drink problem. I gave up work. I couldn't cope with it any more. That was the August.*

*I met my daughter's father in the following January He was a very big drinker. I fell pregnant in the May. I got a friend to go into town and buy a kit and a bottle of brandy. I drank half a bottle of brandy, tested myself. It was positive. I couldn't believe it and drank the other half of the brandy, but that was it. I stopped drinking the day I knew I was pregnant. The first two weeks were awful, but I had a very strong reason not to drink. I could not have a drink and I would not have a drink. I did not know with everything that I'd read on Fetal whatever it's called what would happen. They did not know whether even if you had one glass of wine what effect that would have on the baby. So to me, I wasn't going to drink, because they couldn't say what effect it was going to have.*

*I didn't have a drink again until about six weeks after she was born, by which time I was back living at my parents' house. I'd had problems with her father. My parents were pressurising me to drink saying, 'Oh, one glass of wine won't hurt.' I was still feeding her, so I only had a few glasses of wine at a time, before I stopped breast-feeding at 14 weeks. After that I went back to drinking every night, because it was expected of me.*

*I moved out from my parents, and went back to live with her father, when she was 20 weeks old. I had a lot of problems with her father. He always brought bottles of brandy and left them with me. That was when it went from bad to worse and in five months I was back drinking during the day again. It soon went back to how it was before. When she was 18 months old I took an overdose and they diagnosed post-natal depression. It was a very stressful time.*

*My parents are very racist and her father's black. We were in an on-off relationship. I'd not been having anything to do with my parents, but when I nearly lost the baby, when I was seven months pregnant. I called my parents to ask them to take me to the hospital. Then we were in contact again. Later on, when I moved back in with them, after she was born, my dad still wasn't talking to me and wouldn't hold her. It was very difficult living there. Trying to keep contact with her father was really difficult at that time.*

*When I left them and moved back into my home with him I thought it was all going to be wonderful. We would get back together, like a happy family. It was summer time. I was going to get the garden done. Everything was going to be perfect. It wasn't. But with the drink, everything seemed a little bit better. Things were very different from what I'd hoped.*

*When I went to antenatal swimming classes I saw that they had mums and toddlers ones. I thought I'll be coming back after six weeks. The babies were lying in their baby carriers on the side of the pool. When they've had their injections they can come in too. In fact, I got an infection where they cut me [She had an episiotomy during the delivery], so that put paid to that idea.*

*I remember the first night we got home. I thought, oh my God this is going to be the rest of my life. I can't cope with this. I'll have to give her back. It was like, wow what have I done? Now I wouldn't be without her. She was everything I'd imagined. I remember sitting there feeding her, just blanking out the whole world and that was perfect. Do you now what I mean? There was this little thing in my arms. I wanted a family. I didn't want to be on my own, stuck in the middle of a horrible council estate. I didn't want to have no money and to have to go to the post office with my giro. It just wasn't how I imagined things. I'd thought once the baby had come, I could get some sort of work, but when you've got a baby it's just not possible.*

*When I had the money, I'd go to great lengths and buy fresh fruit, a nice glass and buy a posh drink, cook a really nice meal and make a really nice long drink. It was always just for me, but it was like a treat. I'd enjoy sitting outside on the patio. She was asleep in bed. It was something grown up. It was such a change from ironing baby growers or clearing up sick.*

*When it wasn't all as I'd imagined I felt guilty. Everybody had told me to have an abortion, saying it's unfair to bring a child into the world in your situation. Her dad had left me, when I told him I was pregnant. We got back together later on. But everybody was saying it's not fair on the child . . . blah, blah, blah. I insisted that I didn't need anybody to help me. I could manage. But, there I was in the end messing up her life and people could say, I told you so.*

*I had imagined myself with this big career. I always intended to go back to university. I never did. Now I can't go back into care work, because it's shift hours. I need a job from 9.30 until 3.00, with however many weeks off during the year in the summer. It's impossible. I did think of going back and doing my teaching training. Even if I go back to college, I don't see how I can do it. I'm already in debt. I was going to go back to work when she was a year old, then when she was 18 months old, then when she was two. It was like it seemed endless. I was stuck. The house isn't horrible, but the area is. I'm living off income support. I wanted everything, but it seemed like I had nothing. I had nowhere to head for. I wanted to do so much, but I wasn't actually doing anything at all, apart from going down. I felt very incapable as a parent.*

*It was another year of heavy drinking, before I started to do something about it. It wasn't until I was drinking before I even got out of bed in the morning that I realised I'd got a problem. I did my first detox when she was two and a half and struggled with it. I've spent a lot of money on it and I've got a lot of debt now. I drank away my bank accounts and my credit cards.*

*Her father never lived with us, so I couldn't go out. I didn't go out until just before her second birthday. So all my drinking was done at home after I had her. The people I'd lived with when I was younger wanted to smoke dope when they had a drink. Most of the people I went out with or associated with before I was pregnant all smoked. Once she was born I then lost virtually all my friends, because my attitude was that they couldn't smoke in front of me, not when she was there as well. I was suddenly a responsible mother. They didn't like the change, so they went.*

*Mostly I don't feel so bad now. I can see the light at the end of the tunnel. But people have a very bad image of you, a single parent on the dole, with a mixed race kid, living on a council estate, with a drink problem on top. You may as well hang yourself as far as everybody else is concerned. I've had a lot of racist grief. I'm not in touch with her father now.'*

## Looking back

*'The baby was born premature due to alcohol as I now know (35 weeks) and I was tied to the house. Never having had a baby and no brothers or sisters, I was lonely. I was trying to act out a play, the perfect life as on television, with their gins and tonic and bottles of wine with a special meal. But then every night became a special night for me.'* (quoted in Long and Mullen 1994)

Despite common assumptions, that the birth of a first child is the main time when women are likely to cut down their drinking, experiences of turning to drink after the birth of a child are obviously not unusual. The above quote, Sandra's story in the last chapter and the two stories in this chapter graphically illustrate this. We have no real idea how commonly it happens or to whom. This book offers some pointers, not a complete picture.

Geraldine and Sophie were chosen to illustrate how the pathways, detailed earlier in this chapter, could potentially develop, as women moved from pleasurable, controlled drinking into major difficulties. These two women's material situations were quite different. Geraldine's situation relates to the heavy drinking professionals. She had held a professional job and was married to a professional. She did differ from many of them in that she gave up her job, but otherwise there are very many features in common. Sophie's story is more relevant to the non-professional heavy drinkers' experiences, especially the two who grew up in more middle-class households. She was now a single parent, living in difficult circumstances.

Turning first to opportunities for drinking, throughout her adult life, Geraldine had held most of the attitudes towards drinking identified in the heavy drinking professional group. Sophie's drinking was evidently a longstanding problem. Her experience as a young woman was reminiscent of the youthful extravagances of some of the heavy drinking non-professional women. However, still only in her mid-twenties, unlike many of those in the main study, she had not had time to settle into a more established pattern.

Both women grew up in households where alcohol was kept, freely available and part of the way of life. Drinking at home was part of usual family activities. Whilst Sophie's description of family drinking binges is not paralleled in the main sample, she comments that that has now changed, although her mother still has problems. She is less sympathetic to her mother than the women in the main sample who also had heavy drinking mothers, but where difficulties were more recent. Their situations are painted more sensitively, as their daughters explained their difficulties.

As both Geraldine and Sophie were sociable, enjoyed their drinking and although their social activities were markedly different, alcohol featured prominently, in shared activities with partners, friends and family. In other words, they shared the attitudes and drinking cultures associated with the middle-class heavier drinkers in the main sample (see Figure 8.1), even though their circumstances were very dissimilar. Geraldine had never left middle-class circles, whereas Sophie had taken her childhood ones with her as she moved on. In terms of leisure patterns and social contacts, Geraldine followed a variation of the middle-class pattern (see chapter 6). Her material advantages meant that she could afford an affluent lifestyle, much drinking, entertaining and leisure activities. She was outgoing, had many local links, and was well integrated into her circle. She and her husband, like many in the main study (see chapter 5), were both employed in occupations associated with drinking, and both worked in the private sector. Her positive opportunities were many and varied, and apart from changes in her working situation, largely unaffected by the arrival of her son. She could very easily carry on drinking as much as she had done before.

Like Geraldine, Sophie too had mixed in social circles where heavy drinking was the norm. She talks of her partner also being a heavy drinker. She goes back to live with her parents, who were also very heavy drinkers, expecting whoever was around to join them. But unlike Geraldine, she found that her drinking opportunities changed once her daughter had arrived and she had moved back to her own house. Although the baby's father, who did not live with them, would bring alcohol, finding the money for drink was difficult. She enjoyed a drink with a meal. It was a treat when she had the money. But doing it on a regular basis was difficult and going out was impossible. She had nobody who would look after her baby and could not afford to pay for childcare. She had less in common with old friends and acquaintances and they drifted away. She no longer had easy access to any of the positive and pleasurable aspects of her drinking, which she had seen as part of her quality of life. Certainly her relationship with drinking had mostly been problematic, but there were times when she had taken immense pleasure from it, as when she cooked a special meal and bought a certain drink she liked, even if she had to do it alone. For her it was a way of valuing herself and maintaining her self-esteem. As with Geraldine it was a positive reward and something they did for themselves rather than the baby. It was something adult, and different from childcare.

For both of them, drinking way over recommended limits was well established before they hit the problems that eventually brought them into treatment. For Geraldine this was the first time. Sophie has drifted in and out of problems since she was a teenager. Both managed to cut down radically when they were pregnant, but for both of them their problems started in earnest after the birth of their children. But unlike Sandra (see chapter 7), or the woman mentioned in Geraldine's story, they were unable to move out of their desperate drinking without skilled professional help.

Material disadvantages were a real issue for Sophie, whereas Geraldine was able to enjoy a materially comfortable lifestyle. In terms of similar difficulties to the ones the 60 women encountered, both Geraldine and

Sophie lost former social contacts. For Geraldine these were ones associated with work, for Sophie it was a more total change, as she shifted from one lifestyle to another. In contrast to Geraldine she had few local contacts and almost no opportunity to go out. Unlike the non-professional drinkers in the main study (see Figure 8.2), neither of them mentioned any sudden unexpected events or physical problems once they were pregnant, or difficulties around the birth. Their psychological problems and disappointments started well after their babies were born. Both found childcare difficult. Both were unhappy about not working and being at home, finding themselves totally enveloped in domesticity. Like the other middle-class women, Geraldine found that the status and identity she had gained through her work were important. Both were very lonely and felt isolated and trapped in motherhood. There was no escape. In their different ways neither could get on with more stimulating or creative activities – Geraldine with her craftwork and Sophie in finding the job and starting the career she had imagined.

There are strong parallels in their stories. Both found that their romantic expectations of motherhood were not realised. Geraldine was bored and tired. Sophie found childcare was not the main problem, but the circumstances surrounding her did not measure up to her dreams. No money, no job prospects, little social contact and living alone where she did not want to live – this was not how she felt it ought to be. Drinking heavily and getting into debt, simply set up a vicious circle, and her already precarious finances got worse. Both had very much wanted their children – Sophie refused to have an abortion and Geraldine had been undergoing fertility treatment. When reality failed to match the dream, they blamed themselves and felt guilty. They saw themselves as failed mothers. For Sophie this was compounded by relationship difficulties. She felt her esteem as a woman was at stake. Both felt they had only themselves to blame and then who could they talk to?

Both started drinking more at home. Whilst this is often cited as an indication of greater pathology among women drinkers, in their situations it is hard to see what else was available. But as Ettorre (1997) has commented, drinking at home, as in many 'risk' occupations (see chapter 5), is unsupervised. For women, without help, support or close social contact, comfort from a bottle can seem very attractive. However, drinking occasionally to lift a negative mood, as many of the heavier drinkers in the main study did, is very different from a situation where alcohol has become the main support, helpmate and source of relief from unacceptable and unbearable feelings, which cannot be talked about. Neither of them felt able to ask for help or mention their problems to anybody else. Drinking numbed their disappointments and killed the pain. In Geraldine's situation periodic binge drinking became something to look forward to for the rest of the week.

Whether depression came before drinking or came with it is unclear in both stories. What is clear is that as in so many studies of women's drinking problems (Conte et al. 1991), they went together. Both women evidently felt the stigma of having a drinking problem. Sophie felt stigmatised enough in her situation; having a drink problem made it much worse. Geraldine was glad of the diagnosis of depression. It was less discreditable than having a drink problem. Whether they were depressed before or not, certainly coping with the perceived stigma of alcohol problems must have compounded their difficulties. Again, low self-esteem and depression are often linked. These women felt they had failed as women. This has numerous echoes with other stories in this book. It is no accident that the first time Sophie recognised she had an issue with drink was when she was 21 and her partner had left her. Whilst social and material advantage may protect against depression it does not rule it out, nor does it protect against low self-esteem as a woman.

## Conclusion

This chapter has illustrated that for most women who enjoy alcohol, their drinking is a pleasurable part of their life. However, easy access as part of the quality of life is not equally available to all. Those who were more materially advantaged to begin with found other socially constructed opportunities to continue their easy access in very changed circumstances.

Problematic drinking must develop from somewhere. Those who already enjoyed drinking and who were accustomed to using it to cope with minor emotional upsets are most likely to drift into difficulties. For many women these will be temporary phases, but for some they will only be ended with skilled help.

The next chapter looks at the implications of these stories for preventing and recognising alcohol problems. Whilst I have been able to develop a very distinct picture of middle-class drinking, as far as non-professional heavy drinkers are concerned, the picture is less clear. To begin with, they were a more mixed group. In two instances, Christine and Sandra had middle-class jobs and carried on working throughout.

Eva and Joy, although classified as heavy drinking non-professionals, still followed their middle-class childhood drinking patterns, demonstrating how pervasive middle-class norms are. Of course, in society at large, fewer women in lower social classes drink heavily, so it is likely that those who do are likely to be a more heterogeneous group.

# 9
# Preventing Alcohol-related Harms

Whilst the principal concern of most of the heavy drinkers in this study was about accessing the pleasures of life, of which drinking was one, for some, drinking was more about blocking out their difficulties. They knew they were choosing a potentially unhealthy lifestyle, but it was a response to stressful realities. As we saw in chapter 8, it was positive in the short term because it enabled them to cope, but by choosing the lesser of two evils, they wondered what future troubles they were building up. For them increased pressure to cut down because 'it was bad for their health' could have turned what was a bad situation into something that was intolerable, making them feel even more guilty. The reality was that all the heavy drinkers, including those who were drinking for pleasurable reasons only, were putting themselves at some risk. They were all drinking more than officially recommended amounts. Their behaviour might not have been affected, but there is evidence to suggest that their bodies may have been. They were not necessarily dependent, but would, as we saw in chapter 1, count as new 'problem' drinkers. Health policy-makers may have been concerned, but were the women? As one woman said on a recent TV programme:

> *'I never think I'm damaging myself when I drink. That's inside me. That's a different matter.'* (BBC TV 'Drink for England', 1998)

This chapter considers the implications of the experiences of the four drinking groups and the two case studies for preventing harms. The dominant emphasis in health promotion policy has been on publicising information about risk levels of consumption. For our purposes, I am defining 'official' drinking information or advice as those behavioural injunctions, which come from health promotion publicity material or health care professionals. As a starting point, this chapter reviews how the dominant themes in the development of relevant of 'official' advice or information. It then reviews the women's awareness of such advice and how they rated it. I then discuss the implications of their views and stories for recognising potential risks and harm reduction. The implications of this material and the conclusions of the previous chapters are then developed into points for good practice in prevention and the recognition of potentially risky situations.

## Publicising alcohol risks for women

In terms of heavy drinking, women have not merited much special attention, Usually suggestions about appropriate levels of intake have been made along with suggested levels for men. As chapter 1 described, it is only pregnancy that has merited particular mention, other drink-related harms that women face have not been singled out in the same way.

Apart from difficulties in distinguishing and defining risks, and who should decide them, generating simple health advice is fraught with problems. Scientific knowledge, such as that generated by epidemiology, is couched in terms of probabilities. Translating that into clearly defined rulings is hard. In terms of drinking advice, three stances can be distinguished. One is a general maxim that beyond a very minimal level the more you drink the worse it is for you. The second is a strict observance of specific limits which delineate safe levels of drinking and those where there is a risk of potential physical harm and possible other alcohol-related harm. The third only comes into play in relation to pregnant women; that is, no level of intake has been shown to be safe (Poikolainen 1991). This position gives priority to the well-being of the foetus and encourages women to abstain altogether on the grounds that it is 'better to be safe than sorry'. A parallel with the use of thalidomide is often quoted. This drug was widely marketed and then removed from general supply in 1961, but medical reviews were still quoting it as harmless even in 1964 (Blume 1985). Such a position reinforces a classical female role position, the woman who suitably cares for all, even if that means denying herself. This stance presumes dangers until they are ruled out. Pertinently, abstinence as a health measure has only ever featured for pregnant women. It has never been officially recommended for women as a whole, or for men, even though the same logic could equally well apply to them.

Elements of all approaches have appeared in most countries. Given its emotive nature (see chapter 1), the issue of risk to pregnancy has frequently been overstated. For example, US publicity material in the

1980s and early 1990s frequently quoted Clarren, a worker at the Seattle Institute of Dysmorphology, as having stated that alcohol was the third most important cause of infant handicap. However, Clarren was referring to handicaps with known causes, which are only about 10 per cent of the total (Clarren and Smith 1978). Such problem inflation is easily fanned by press reports of cases of severe alcohol damage, and although scientists may dismiss isolated reports, they assume great importance in the minds of the public and consequently in the minds of policy-makers. We saw the important of the publication of *The Broken Cord* (McNeil and Litt 1992), a story of one child with FAS in chapter 1.

In the US no public warnings were issued until 1977. Women were then warned against consuming more than six drinks a day (Waterson and Murray-Lyon 1990). At the same time, moves to display compulsory public health warnings about the dangers of alcohol to the foetus were rejected. In 1980 a national workshop was held and the following year the American Surgeon General issued a warning to pregnant women against consuming alcohol, even in food. In spite of protests, this warning was widely publicised and increased research funding for nationally co-ordinated projects on the topic provided. In New York and many other parts of the country, bars, restaurants and liquor stores are required to display a sign stating that drinking can cause birth defects. Since 1989, every container of alcoholic beverage sold in the US has had to carry a label which gives a warning that women should not drink alcohol during pregnancy because of the risk of birth defects (Hilton and Kaskutas 1991).

Since the late 1980s the issue has become of increasing concern to the US legal system. Cases of physicians facing damage suits for failing to advise that alcohol could affect the foetus have been reported (*British Journal of Addiction* 1988). Since 1987 mothers who use alcohol and illicit drugs during pregnancy have become subject to increasing legal controls, compulsory treatment and may even face imprisonment. If their child shows positive signs of damage they may also face charges of child abuse (Chasnoff et al. 1990).

Interest developed later in the UK and in common with its approach to other alcohol problems at the time the government appeared to be reluctant to take a strong stand. In 1977 a question was asked in Parliament following a newspaper article about the potential effects of alcohol. The Secretary of State at the time replied that women who were at risk of affecting their offspring would be well advised to cut down for their own well-being, implying that harmful levels of drinking were fairly high. Nothing was said in a government publication on prevention and child health in 1980 (DHSS 1980). It was the press and a publication from the National Council of Women (1980) which drew serious attention to the topic. Pregnant women were first officially advised against frequent heavy drinking in a government publication entitled *Prevention and Health: Drinking Sensibly* (DHSS 1981). By 1982 the Royal College of Psychiatrists was warning against more than two drinks a day in pregnancy and this professional advice was subsequently endorsed by the government in 1983. The 'safe' amount was later reduced to no more than one or two drinks, once or twice a week (Royal College of Psychiatrists 1986, Royal College of Physicians 1987; Royal College of General Practitioners 1987).

The thrust of policy has been to encourage women to follow medically defined perceptions of what is a risk and what is not, with an overriding emphasis on pregnancy. Whilst there are clearly laid down recommendations about general drinking levels for women – what levels are of little physical risk, increased risk and harmful (see chapter 1), there are no warnings about other drink-related harms that women may be exposed to, for example male violence following drinking. The following sections investigate how far the 60 women were aware of these debates, how they evaluated such 'official' information and finally whether they would have defined the risks in the same way as official policy.

## Awareness of 'official' drinking advice

Were the women even aware of 'official' advice? What were their views on the three stances – cut out alcohol, because it is not proven safe, observe strict limits, or a more generalised approach – the more you drink the worse it is for you. Were they aware of the overriding emphasis in policy on drinking in pregnancy?

Most of these women viewed alcohol as a potential health hazard, had heard of 'sensible drinking' and 'units', but their knowledge about what these meant, exact mechanisms and levels of drinking associated with harm were, as with the rest of the population, rather vague (Department of Health 1997). Suggestions ranged widely from a bottle of spirits to one unit a day, with few differences between the groups. We have noted how important social contacts, and drinking cultures are in encouraging or discouraging drinking, so it seemed important to look at how the women's social circles viewed 'official' advice to watch levels of drinking. As in Breeze's (1985), survey where 86 per cent of her sample described excessive drinking as a health risk, women in all four groups were well aware of potential risks. As in another study, the professional managerial women had more accurate levels of knowledge (Mills-Hopper 1992). The heavy drinkers had a noticeably more detailed knowledge, but this may have been no more than a reflection that they were more likely to have had personal contact with somebody who had drinking problems.

All but two of the women considered that alcohol could be potentially harmful to the unborn child. Only seven specifically mentioned Fetal Alcohol Syndrome. Most remarked that alcohol could affect the baby's growth and several drew a parallel with the effects of smoking. A few, quite logically, thought that babies could be born alcoholic, as Mary, a light drinking professional, queried:

*'If a baby can be born a junkie, then why can't it come out alcoholic?'*

Contrary to 'official' advice, not all alcoholic beverages were ranked equally harmful. Some were good and others were not. Like Liz, a light drinking professional (quoted in chapter 3), three mothers spontaneously singled out spirits as particularly harmful. This ranking of dangerousness applied whether women were pregnant or not. In their minds, some sorts of alcohol, especially spirits, were always more hazardous than others. Phyllis, a heavy drinking professional, was even prepared to argue against what she saw as a globally bad press for all alcoholic drinks being seen in an equally bad light, commenting that:

*'There's a lot of good things about alcohol. Wine's a natural product. Spirits are another matter.'*

Members of both professional groups were more likely than the non-professional women to be aware that women were less physically tolerant to alcohol than men, and that there were recommended limits to consumption. Given that middle-class people are normally more specifically informed on health matters, (Blaxter 1990), this was to be expected. In time specialised medical knowledge gradually permeates general knowledge and becomes part of it (Cornwall 1984).

In terms of getting information, the middle-class heavy drinkers placed a lot of reliance on their own reading, whereas the non-professional heavy drinkers placed more reliance on friends. Reading about health matters is more a middle-class pursuit (Blaxter 1990). The influence of the mass media, particularly newspapers, was as important as any advice from a specifically health service source. Non-professional women were less likely than their professional counterparts to mention reading or hearing information on the radio and more concerned to follow advice gained from the television.

As in many other health promotion studies, knowledge did not necessarily influence behaviour (Tannahill 1995). Indeed, the heavy drinkers were not only more interested in talking about alcohol (see chapter 3), but noticeably more knowledgeable about its potential risks than the light drinkers. The heavy drinking professionals were particularly knowledgeable about the interaction of alcohol with other possibly deleterious factors, such as taking drugs, smoking, over-the-counter drugs, not eating properly, or not taking enough exercise.

Not surprisingly, there is little specific research on prevention activities with women, except those that refer to pregnancy. Most efforts have concentrated on giving information about the potential risks of drinking, either through the mass media or in the clinical context. But, again, when these types of intervention were evaluated, it was found that knowledge about potential risks was of itself insufficient to prevent high consumption. One American study even found that about a third of their study sample exceeded their own estimated 'safe' drinking level (Minor and Van Dort 1982). The overall effect of a multi-million dollar demonstration and publicity campaign about the effects of alcohol on the foetus, set up in Seattle was to shift the median level of drinking downwards. But it failed to reduce the proportion of women who were heavy drinkers in its target population (Streissguth et al. 1983). Continuing the theme of knowledge being no guarantee of behavioural change, we should remember that nurses and doctors, both professional groups who are well aware of the potential problems of alcohol, have a high incidence of alcohol problems (Clare 1990; Harz et al. 1990).

Previous studies have demonstrated that pregnant women are well aware that the more they drink the worse it might be for both them and their unborn child (Waterson and Murray Lyon 1990b). In terms of their own behaviour, even the women who drank most heavily had cut down, albeit they still drank more than the light drinking cohort. Similarly, Sophie and Geraldine, the two women who went on to develop severe alcohol problems, had cut down. As in other studies (Plant 1985; Sulaiman et al. 1988; Waterson and Murray Lyon 1989b) most of them had done so out of a generalised sense of responsibility, rather than any awareness that they should adhere to strict levels of intake:

> *'I read something about it somewhere. I didn't drink much anyway, but I stopped. It's better to be safe than sorry. I didn't want an alcoholic baby.'*
> (Judith, a light drinking professional)

This, coupled with the findings reported here, immediately renders much of the heated policy debate over how health education advice should be phrased as being largely redundant (Waterson and Murray-Lyon 1990b). In practice these women thought in general and relational terms, not in numbers. What also seems of great importance is the tone and way of imparting 'official' health advice.

## Evaluating 'official' drinking advice

*'Nothing's that straightforward.'* (Louise, a light drinking non-professional)

*'Nobody tells you why.'* (Josephine, a light drinking non-professional)

The real stumbling block is the way health promotion information is presented. Information that is simplistic, patronising and that glosses over complexities is likely to be rejected (Davison et al. 1992). This is likely to be all the more so if the suggested changes are unwelcome. About two-thirds of these women, drawn from all groups, complained that most of the advice they had ever received about drinking was insufficiently accurate or detailed. For example, Ruth, a light drinking non-professional, said:

*'They treat you as if you were without a brain.'*

Likewise, Bernadette, a heavy drinking professional, complained:

*'They deny your intelligence with their saying do this and don't do that, with no reasonable explanation.'*

Several women pointed out that advice from different sources was often contradictory. As Karen, a heavy drinking non-professional, wisely put it:

*'If they know, then why don't they all agree? If they don't know, they'd be better to keep quiet.'*

They were suspicious of absolutes:

*'The way the professionals talk about it, I don't go along with all that. Nothing's that black and white.'* (Monica, a light drinking non-professional)

In practice, adapting any health care advice to suit their circumstances proved the best option for these women. As Linda, a heavy drinking non-professional, put it:

*'I don't take any notice of any health care advice I don't like.'*

Maureen, a heavy drinking professional, objected to being coerced into behaving in a certain way:

*'I'm sensitive to propaganda and I wanted to sort it out for myself. It's such a moralistic thing to make people feel pressured.'*

As we have seen earlier in this chapter, these women thought of alcohol problems in terms of behavioural changes and risks arising from a dynamic interplay between the amount of alcohol an individual was drinking and their individual susceptibilities. Their models were more sophisticated than simple cause and effect. These women were more receptive to generalised notions of potential harms, preferring to think in terms of process, rather than specific levels of intake and types of harm. Notions of weekly totals and measuring their drinking in units seemed alien. How typical was one week? Whilst they may not have been very knowledgeable in any specifically factually accurate sense, they were interested in the general principles of how harm might occur. Simply being told this is what you must do, with no 'because' attached seemed to be irrelevant. Common-sense reasoning drawn from shared understandings in their social circles, and especially partner's advice and expectations, were most influential. Above all, they relied on their own creative lateral thinking. Their level of reasoning was less specific and, as already described, their assessment of what was necessary was not always congruent with 'official' health education advice.

However, there was one group who were the exception. Blaxter (1990), in a study of lifestyles, found that middle-class people were more likely than working-class people to accept health care advice founded on statistical probability. In this study, the middle-class lighter drinking group, who were heavily dominated by health workers, came down firmly on the side of 'official advice', advocating specific harm levels. Maybe this was because they cared little about drinking. Of all the groups they were most confident that individuals could largely safeguard their own health and the most authoritarian on this point. For them risk was a matter of going above certain medically proscribed levels. It was purely a matter of individual responsibility:

*'If people get liver cirrhosis they've only got themselves to blame.'* (Marie, a light drinking professional)

They advocated a simple message – do not drink more than $x$ units a day/week. Most of the rest of the women would have preferred to have been given appropriate accurate information, specifying the likelihood of possible risks, the mechanism of risk and other important consider- ations, and be left to make up their own minds.

Of all the groups, the heavy drinking professionals were the most insistent that it was up to the individual to decide their own drinking levels. Several of them argued that the case against drinking levels was not proven and strong advice was therefore unjustifiable. These well- informed objectors were quick to point out that smoking, food addi- tives and over-the-counter drugs could be just as damaging. In the face of these other threats why should they fore go their less threatening pleasure of drinking? Unfortunately, I was unable to determine whether this was some form of subtle justification for their own behaviour as described in chapter 4, or a more universal belief that health status was primarily the responsibility of the individual. Certainly another study carried out in GP surgeries has shown that higher consumers give higher estimates of 'safe' levels of intake than lower consumers do (Anderson and Wallace 1988).

Whichever point of view they adopted, the professional women were noticeably much more confident of their own opinions, and concerned about health promotion. They were quite confident to function as what Feathestone (1991) has called cultural intermediaries, disseminating norms about appropriate drinking behaviour. Likewise, Bunton and Burrows (1995) have noted that middle-class people are more comfort- able in the vanguard of lifestyle changes. For the two non-professional groups it was largely irrelevant, whereas they felt secure describing their experiences, they were much less secure in voicing their opinions in general. In terms of accepting official advice they were suspicious, but were less inclined to articulate their doubts, preferring to rely on their own generalised reasoning. Such scepticism led several women to suggest that health care advice should be geared to helping individual mothers make up their own minds. In other words, health care professionals should establish a partnership with women, by treating them on a more equal footing.

Giving credence to statistical evidence is unlikely, when one has personal experience to the contrary (Davison et al. 1991). After all it is perfectly reasonable to draw on personal experience, as Ruth, a light drinking non-professional, did about her smoking while she was pregnant:

> 'It's a load of poppy-cock, she [her child] was nine and a quarter pounds and I smoked 30 a day when I was carrying her.'

A further example of the way the women preferred to rely on their own experience and make up their own minds came from those few mothers who had been or were pregnant a second time. Several of the heavy drinkers who had cut down, however little, during their first pregnancy, felt in retrospect that it had been an unnecessary sacrifice. Their children had been born completely healthy. In view of this, they decided that it was not irresponsible if they continued to drink during the second pregnancy.

Taking a parallel from the smoking literature, and recalling Hart's (1986) discussion, which has recently been reframed by Graham (1995) as to why more middle-class than working-class people gave up smoking more quickly, they argue that for working-class people, much more than overcoming addiction is involved. What is at stake is cultural redefinition. For example, smoking may be a status symbol. So the real question becomes, do working-or middle-class people have more access to alternative status symbols? In this study, the professionals would have been able to use their material advantages to generate alternatives. Moreover, middle-class people have been more accustomed to change, more mobile, more individualistic and accustomed to greater personal autonomy. Following this line of thought, middle-class women, as here, could be expected to find health promotion, emphasising information given to individuals, encouraging individual autonomy might resonate with their way of thinking, whereas many of the non-professionals found it irrelevant. On the other hand, for the heavy drinking professionals, whose drinking was so integral to their daily round, a major reduction would have meant a cultural redefinition. Understandably, they resisted such an attack on their sense of personal identity and autonomy, attacking like with like by questioning the very basis of 'safe drinking levels'. The risk for them was the possibility of losing their pleasure.

## Recognising the 'risk'

There is no such thing as a risk-free world (Frankel et al. 1991), but there are differences of opinion on what constitutes a risk (Culpitt

1999). Defining what is 'safe enough' or a risk will always involve people in making choices. The way they do so will depend on the nature and context of their lives, their values as well as specific conditions affecting a particular judgement. Other studies have outlined how general stresses can prompt women into unhealthy responses, including heavy drinking (Graham 1993, 1994; Charles and Walters 1995). Whilst helping them to cope in the short term, long-term outcomes may be quite damaging. Such habits are hard to change if loneliness and lack of confidence contribute to establishing a vicious circle. The sort of problems the 65 women from South Wales who were interviewed in one study encountered were money problems, male unemployment and the demands of their double day, even if the man was unemployed:

> *'I know smoking, drinking, being overweight and not doing enough exercise are bad for me and I worry about the deleterious effects of doing these things on my health but I persist in doing them.'* (Interviewee – Charles and Walters 1995).

For this respondent, the short-term benefits outweighed possible long-term losses. For her the immediate risk was not being able to cope, not long-term physical problems. This was a rational response, even if it would not have accorded with 'official' health advice.

For the 60 women in this study, real alcohol risks or problems were what happened when drinking got out of control. In other words, nothing to do with medically defined information about levels, units or amounts. They were doubtful about the scientific accuracy of the derivation of these anyway, and well aware that they were challenging medical power.

> *'Giving more detailed information would involve saying it's a matter of opinion and challenging medical orthodoxy.'* (Ros, a heavy drinking professional)

They knew very well that what was so often portrayed as fact was more a matter of opinion or probability. They were asking for a less patronising approach, which gave them sufficient information to enable them to make up their own minds, in the context of their own lives. If they chose short-term gains, whilst laying themselves open to potential long-term harms, it was not because they were either ignorant or irresponsible, but because they chose to cope with any difficulties that way or to maximise their immediate quality of life as they saw it.

Their scepticism about the basis for public anxiety about women's drink-related harms may well be justified. The figures about increases have often been taken out of context, thus conflating impressions of the scale. For example, between 1979 and 1984 female deaths from chronic liver disease and cirrhosis of the liver increased by 9 per cent, and between 1977 and 1986 admission to psychiatric hospital for alcohol problems by 60 per cent (Alcohol Concern 1988). But as Foster (1995) points out, these increases are based on a very small incidence: in 1987 there were only just over 400 female deaths from alcohol-related liver disease. In addition, Foster (1995) argues that that there has been a lack of rigorous evaluation of the epidemiological studies on which many of the sensible drinking messages are based. She argues further that this lack of scrutiny is a subtle way of controlling women, emphasising an individualised approach concentrating on individual behavioural changes, which to women in poverty may be largely irrelevant and or, if costly, unattainable (Daykin 1998).

Returning to these women's experiences, for the heavy groups, drinking was associated with pleasure. Whilst they were well aware of dangers in a general sense, the times when they were aware of any personal risk were all times when they were depressed and lonely. Either a relationship had just finished or they were finding that looking after a small child could also be an isolating task. In each instance they described an increasing dependency. Notions of the numbers of units they could safely drink whether pregnant or not were not at the forefront of their minds. What they were interested in was some relief from their psychic pain. In those moments that was the real risk, not later alcohol dependency.

Like the 60 women in the main study, Geraldine and Sophie describe harmful drinking in terms of intoxication, altered behaviour and dependency. Geraldine started drinking at 'odd times of day, when it's supposedly not acceptable'. These changes were noticed by other people. It was at this point that she began to realise that she was drinking for negative reasons. Neither Geraldine nor Sophie appears to have been concerned with the personal physical risks she may have been taking.

These two, like the rest of those who told stories of times when they were drinking to cope, found it hard to tell when they might have drifted from physically risky levels to dependency. The frequency with which issues of loss, especially the loss of a relationship, fears of not performing perfectly as a partner or mother, events which appeared to threaten a sense of womanhood and attempts to conceal emotional pain came up is striking. Indeed Sophie says it was only when her partner left her, when she was 21 and after many years of problematic drinking, she first acknowledged it herself. There is plenty of anecdotal evidence that women commonly respond to bereavements, relationship difficulties and miscarriages by periods of solitary heavy drinking (Kent 1990). Long and Mullen's (1994) sample of women with alcohol problems, and all the women who speak here, talk of using alcohol to deal with emotional pain.

Recognising intoxication is obvious, but recognising the dividing line between regular drinking and dependency is hard. By the time Geraldine was prepared to admit that what had started out as an adult activity and a way of staying sane had begun to create problems of its own, she had become dependent. At some point the gains are outweighed by losses. The way of dealing with the immediate risk creates bigger, more long-term risks. In specific terms, clearly the public, these women included, are much less bothered about regular heavy drinking than drunkenness and dependency (Health Education Authority 1989). The implication is that prevention efforts need to focus on a continuum of harm, starting with physical dangers, long before dependency is established. It would also be helpful to alert the public to the warning signs, when an individual may be moving from one type of harm to another.

What was significant was that in all these stories the women felt they should be able to cope. That was what their romantic expectations of relationships and motherhood had promised. They thought the failing must be due to them and them alone. When feeling ashamed and guilty a bottle does not criticise. It offers instant comfort. They did not, or could not look to other people for support. They bottled up their feelings and temporarily drowned them. Of course, once established this pattern set up its own dynamic and very vicious circle. Even if they stopped drinking the feelings came back and became unbearable.

All the women were well aware of how stigmatised alcohol problems were. Geraldine speaks of an 'unpleasant neighbour who was an alcoholic' in much the same vein as the women cited in chapter 3 talked of people with alcohol problems. Mental health problems are also usually stigmatised, as Sandra's experience described in chapter 7 showed. Geraldine's neighbours, although suspecting she had post-natal depression, were reluctant to talk to her about it, until much later. But for Geraldine and to some extent Sophie, this diagnostic label was better than being categorised as a person with alcohol problems. It enabled Geraldine to maintain a semi-respectable public face, but the reluctance of neighbours to say anything about her drinking as well as her depression tells a different story. Whilst the real issues may have been to do with mental well-being, these women were equally unable to ask for help with their emotional turmoil. That was shameful too.

For most of the women in this study, such difficult times were resolved without any professional help. The alcohol literature frequently describes this as a spontaneous remission, implying that nothing changed in these women's lives. What did happen was that they somehow managed to regain a sense of their own self-worth and curb the destructive ways in which they were drinking. That was not the case for Geraldine and Sophie. They needed long-term skilled intervention before they could stop their negative drinking. But their internalised stigma and shame made it difficult for them to accept that was what they needed.

Friends and family frequently try to dissuade women from going for treatment (Baily 1990; Smith 1992). After all, it takes a certain amount of self-esteem before being able to ask for help. Women are well aware of stigma attached to such problems. Despite efforts by helping agencies to dispel their fears, many remain terrified of losing the care of their children (Thom and Green 1996). In such circumstances, avoiding asking for help for fear of censure can seem like the least painful solution (Thom 1986; Baily 1990; Copeland and Hall 1992).

Clearly health professionals failed to recognise potential alcohol problems in all the women here who were diagnosed as having postnatal depression. In Long and Mullen's (1994) sample of seven women who had had serious alcohol problems, all seven had been in contact with various health and welfare professionals in connection with other problems, such as the death of a child, but their use of alcohol had never been explored. Furthermore, other research has demonstrated that heavy drinkers are in frequent contact with their GPs (Wallace and Haines 1985). Anderson (1993) has estimated that some 20 per cent of all GP patients exceed sensible drinking levels. Anderson (1993) describes how GPs frequently lose opportunities to help with alcohol problems. But professionals are notably reluctant to ask about drinking. This was first noticed twenty years ago (Shaw et al. 1978) and the situation has not changed (Anderson 1993, Marshall 1996). Professionals are reluctant to look for things they feel they cannot deal with, so tend to wait until the crisis or something that cannot be ignored occurs (Anderson 1993).

Women's problems with alcohol are even less likely to be recognised then men's (Women's National Commission 1988; Smith 1992; Copeland and Hall 1992). Certainly, most women are likely to present for help with another issue and then it is difficult for professionals to raise the topic. Rosemary Kent (1990) suggests that social workers see alcohol problems as a male issue, whereas most of their clients are women and children. Other studies have also noticed this bias, in that professionals are more likely to notice male drinking problems (Smith 1992).

Whilst women may turn to negative drinking at any stage of their lives. This research shows that it is those that are already exceeding sensible limits that are most likely to use alcohol to manage difficulties. For many this will not become harmful. But anything a woman may perceive as a threat to her womanhood is a flash-point that health and welfare professionals should be aware of. Whilst checklists may be helpful in some instance to alert workers, unless they pay attention to the real lived experience of women their best efforts are likely to be frustrated. They need to be aware that if drinking is linked with difficult feelings, it almost always starts as a constructive way of controlling those feelings. It becomes a way of coping, a way of keeping going, when there do not seem to be any alternatives. That is to understand the rationale of women's behaviour, rather than drawing attention to their personal failings. It also does not minimise their problems, which now include drinking as well. Deciding upon any change, even if problems are intense, involves individuals in carrying out some sort of cost-benefit, losses and gains, analysis. Unless the benefits are seen to outweigh the costs, why change?

The result is that if professionals do not pick up alcohol problems early, brief interventions such as advice, counselling, physical assessment, short-term cognitive therapy, self-help materials, and follow-up (Bien et al. 1993) cannot be offered at an early stage. In the absence of any help or support, some problems will remit, but others will get worse and a crisis may well precipitate a woman into specialised alcohol treatment. This might have been forestalled if only a professional had been opportunistic in asking about her drinking, or more helpfully, had focused on her needs, had asked about her mental well-being, and not about her children or her partner. However, simple, short-lived interventions in primary care, of the sort listed above, are less successful for women than men (Wallace et al. 1987). It seems that women need to reassess the role that alcohol plays in the whole of their lives. For them it is not a self-contained issue. Problem usage develops from deep-seated, emotional unease. This seems to be different for men.

Simply asking sensitively about consumption levels may be sufficient to alert professional to situations where physical health may be being compromised. But, as we have seen, most women define drinking risks or problems in terms of intoxication or dependency. Drinking above sensible limits does not carry the same fear of stigmatisation. Indeed, the middle-class heavy drinkers in this study were likely to dispute the basis for any suggestion that they should cut down. They were intent on defining their own risks and alcohol was not one of them. The heavy drinking non-professionals, whilst almost certainly less confident about disputing with professionals, did not seem unduly bothered about any future physical risks they might be exposing themselves to. For them the risk was of not being able to have a good time, especially once children had arrived. Professionals need to be able to accept that individuals have the right to draw their own conclusions. As these women have indicated, unless health and welfare professionals are willing to engage in discussion with women about what the real risks are, they run the risk of being dismissed. Unless professionals take account of the lived experience of women they will be less effective in promoting health and quality of life for all.

As we have seen, the heavier drinkers saw their drinking as a pleasure. One of the outcomes of the increased levels of sensible drinking that came out of changed government guidance in the UK in 1995 was the recognition of non-harmful drinking. At that time medical research was indicating that light drinking could be beneficial for health. The Conservative government of the day may have been more anxious to promote good relationships with the alcohol trade than promote any notions of access to non-harmful drinking as a quality of life issue, but it did give publicity to the benefits that alcohol could bring. Certainly many of the women in this book knew that at first hand. Health messages could acknowledge that, as well as giving some indication of the epidemiological knowledge associating certain levels of intake with health risks. Most importantly, rather than creating a spectre of problems it would be most helpful to reduce stigma by stressing the ordinariness of alcohol problems, that many people move in and out of problem status and that it could happen to anybody. Pleasurable drinking might be one side of the coin, but negative drinking can easily become the other. An indication of some of the early signs of possibly becoming dependent, such as bottling up problems, feeling down and lonely, and not confiding in anybody would be helpful. Such experiences are common enough and could equally well lead to depression. Public encouragement to seek help at an early stage might be very beneficial. There is a message here for health promotion policy – to increase public awareness of the extent and nature of emotional and mental health issues as well as alcohol problems. There is also an urgent need to reduce the stigma attached to such difficulties.

## Conclusion

To summarise the main points in this chapter:

- Whilst 'official' alcohol advice emphasises level of intake, most of the women thought more generally in less directly mechanistic ways, for example, the more you drink the worse it is for you.
- The women, although generally reducing their intake, were less likely than 'official' sources to emphasise drinking in pregnancy.
- Light drinking professionals, many of whom were health professionals, were most likely to endorse the 'official' line.
- The groups were unaware of heavy drinking as a problem. They defined problems in terms of intoxication or dependency.
- Middle-class women were more knowledgeable and confident of their opinions than the non-professionals.
- Awareness of 'official' risk definition was not necessarily congruent with behaviour.
- The women wanted accurate health information about risks, mechanisms and influential factors, sufficient for them to make up their own minds.
- Information about the warning signs for drifting from heavy, potentially, physically damaging drinking, to dependency is needed.
- They requested that professional should treat them with respect, accepting that when women saw risks differently, this was almost always the result of a rational decision making process.
- Health and social care professional need to watch out for situations where women are concealing emotional pain, especially losses to do with their functioning as partners or mothers.
- There is a social need to reduce the stigma attached to women's mental health and alcohol problems.

Whilst there is much material here for preventative health policy to assimilate, it is the different definitions of risk that are most fundamental. For the women whose stories provide the material for this book, the real risks were usually not to their unborn children or their own health. For some, they were about not being able to access enough of the good things of life, including alcohol. For some, they were more about stresses, material, social or personal. Either way, simple exhortations about exact, appropriate drinking levels were wide of the mark, out of context, seen as moralising and, frequently, simply irrelevant. For the few who had been badly in need of help with drinking difficulties the probability of access to appropriately gender-sensitive help to deal with their negative drinking was paramount.

In a classic paper on health promotion, Tannahill (1985) argued that empowering those whose health may be at risk to participate in promoting their health is fundamental to health promotion. It is a short step to argue that this should extend to helping people decide on their own health risks in the context of their everyday lives. The way individuals and societies assess and confront the risks that face them can be a dynamic force in creating their own future (Franklin 1990). At an individual level it enhances self-esteem and is part of taking responsibility for one's own life. In this context that might be to drink at levels that might harm future physical health, or it might be to seek help with an alcohol problem because the risks of not doing so are greater than the risk of confronting painful feelings. Taking responsibility and deciding are a part of becoming an active citizen and this point will be developed in the concluding chapter.

# 10
# Promoting Fair Shares for All

The richness of the material these women presented through their stories has verified Room's (1975) assertion that studying the use of alcohol illuminates social structure and process, like some sort of social microscopic dye. By concentrating on changes in this one everyday behaviour, our understanding of how influences such as social class, cultural and social factors such as norms about appropriate drinking practices and employment situation, and individual preferences link together, to shape drinking careers through time. There were very distinct differences between the four groups of women – heavy drinking professionals, heavy drinking non-professionals, light drinking professionals and light drinking non-professionals. Contrary to previous surveys, which have suggested that when women begin building their own families their drinking decreases, these women's experience illustrates that for those who were previously heavy drinkers, this is not the case.

We have seen that for these women, heavy drinking was more commonly related to affluence rather than to disadvantage. Although social policy research is more accustomed to dealing with issues of disadvantage than advantage (Backett 1992), this picture corresponds to Burrows and Nettleton's (1995) findings in their analysis of UK national data. Furthermore, in this study, those heavy drinkers who are disadvantaged have less easy access to non-harmful drinking.

Second, some women drink to ease distress which is primarily related to gender role difficulties. These were not clearly related to social position, but affected women regardless of social advantage. However, it seems reasonable to suppose that social advantage does mitigate some personal psychological pressures. Thus, the traditional emphasis on drinking related to individual gender role difficulties, which we explored in chapter 2, needs reframing within a context of socio-economic position.

Traditional health promotion, which includes health education, prevention and health protection (Tannahill 1985), has suggested that opportunities for drinking should be curtailed, but the real policy and practice question is how to improve health for all, reduce harm and ensure access to quality of life for all women. For example, equalising the material position of all women would not only increase their quality of life, including opportunities for drinking, but also improve their health status (Graham 1998). Notions of equal opportunities in the alcohol field have typically focused on access to services (Gladish and Couter 1994), but these women's stories suggest a reframing in terms of fair shares for all in terms of access to positive drinking and protection from from harmful drinking. In other words, they call for a redefinition of what the real risk is, and question who should decide on risks – experts or women?

As Bunton (1992) has observed, risk discourse, and its calculation in an increasingly detailed way, have become central to the 'new' public health. This emphasis on risk discourse in the medical and health literature has been particularly marked since the late 1980s (Skolbekken 1995). Experts are telling us how to live, what risks and dangers we should avoid and, through public health promotion, are trying to make the easy choice the healthy one (Petersen and Lupton 1996). Thus, avoidance of risk becomes a moral imperative. Those who defy such officially constructed risk warnings suffer the moral connotations (Douglas 1992; Lupton et al. 1993; Culpitt 1999). Hidden in all of this is an implicit assumption that people want to be healthy, or at the very least healthier. Therefore, the more a certain risk behaviour is within an individual's control the greater the moral culpability if they do not avoid it. Whilst apparently shifting from some simplistic 'victim blaming' of those who suffer ill-health (Crawford 1977), by emphasising the importance of promoting healthy environments, this in fact becomes a more sophisticated version of it. Those who reject or disagree with official advice for whatever reason are deemed to be irresponsible (Foster 1995). Not only is this a failure to view women's behaviour – drinking in this instance – in context, but it is also a failure to address the question of whether everybody agrees with 'official' advice and, second, even if they do, is it relevant or important? As Thom (1997) has argued, women are broadly supportive of policies controlling alcohol consumption to prevent harms. The issue is, what harms are to be prevented? There is little or no discussion of who should define risks. One of the fundamental implications of these women's stories is that risks are not uniformly defined and agreed upon.

Half of these women were drinking at levels which have been linked with physical damage, but quite how heavy drinking leads on to identified problem drinking remains unclear. What their experiences have suggested are some pointers. These are echoed in Geraldine's and Sophie's experiences. Ettorre's (1997) distinction between negative and positive drinking is helpful here. Broadly speaking she defines positive drinking as moderate and life-affirming. The heavy drinking professionals description of the role of alcohol as a reward, pleasure or a way of markng a shift from child-focused time to adult time, (see chapter 4), is an example of positive drinking. We could also include what I would term respite drinking. An example would be the 'I need a drink' response on hearing bad news, or when a woman returns home after a very exhausting day at work, or pours herself a drink because she feels a bit down. Many of the heavy drinkers in this study talked of using alcohol to alter their mood in just such a short term way. This is very different from regular, out of control and dependent use to drown unbearable feelings. This is when women begin to drift towards negative drinking.

For Ettorre (1997), negative drinking occurs when women feel internalised shame and negative feelings arising from and associated with drinking difficulties. Certainly Sophie, Geraldine (see chapter 8), and Joy, Jill, Sandra and Margaret (see chapter 7), all felt very negatively about themselves when they were drinking very heavily. This obviously raises the question of whether we should be talking of risk of negative drinking or lack of positive drinking.

This chapter first looks at the implications of this research for positive drinking, how it can be promoted and harmful drinking discouraged. I then look at how negative drinking can be dealt with helpfully and finally suggest issues for an appropriate policy framework.

## Developing positive not harmful drinking

Any notion of positive drinking is in itself a contested position, especially where female drinkng is concerned (Ettorre 1997). Turning to a more general example, this book refers to some epidemiological studies which have suggested that a little drinking, far from being physically harmful, can even be beneficial. However, as Peele (1993) observes, there is very little public mention of the positive aspects of alcohol production or consumption in North America. This is because of the strength of the Temperance lobby, which refuses to counterance the possibility that alcohol use has any positive possibilities at all for men or women. Any prevention policy, which seeks to maximise the pleasures of alcohol, while minimising the problems, necessarily involves not only consideration of the most appropriate way of solving problems, but also a choice between social values, becoming inescapably ideological and political. We know from research carried out in the US that public support is most forthcoming for measures which impose fewest restrictions on non-harmful drinking (Hilton and Kaskuta 1991), but definitions of non-harmful may not be universally agreed.

First and foremost, we should remember that all the heavy drinkers in this research enjoyed drinking. For them alcohol was life-enhancing and generally non-harmful. For the light drinkers, regardless of social position and ability to purchase it, alcohol remained inconsequential. When comparing the two groups of heavy drinkers, it was obvious that opportunity played the major part in encouraging positive drinking, for pleasure and enjoyment. It was the heavy drinking professionals rather than the heavy drinking non-professionals who were able to maintain their levels of intake through into motherhood. They were more able to afford it, could purchase domestic help and create leisure time, and moved in employment and social circles where use was commonplace.

It was this group who were most likely to drink in excess of 'official' levels, but whose drinking would not be described as negative or dependent. The dilemma for health promotion lies in the area of heavy drinking, which is sufficient to generate possibilities of physical damage, but which is unlikely to be accompanied by the sort of behavioural changes that these women would recognise as problematic.

One option would be for policy to emphasise the positives of moderate drinking. At present it only emphasises the negatives of heavy drinking. Media representations of drinking tend to be either negative relating to drink driving, or romanticised images in advertisements promoting sales. Positive role models in health promotion material dealing with the issues of everyday life using alcohol safely and enjoyably would chime with these women's experiences.

Graham (1998) has criticised the way the UK 1992 *Health of the Nation* document defined its goals or outcome targets. As she points out, they are all to do with ill health and derived from morbidity or mortality statistics. They are not measures of health or estimates of risk exposure, derived from the way individuals protect their health in the context of their lives. For example, poverty is not mentioned as a risk factor, even though other research indicates very clearly that socio-economic position is very closely linked with health status (Davison et al. 1991; Wilkinson 1996), or as we have seen in this book, with opportunities linked to quality of life. Whilst it is beyond the scope of this book to suggest detailed alternatives, in terms of drinking behaviour perhaps more positive health-oriented measures could be developed, for example, an indication of the percentage of the population who are drinking non-harmfully or the number of years that those who had had help with problems managed non-harmful drinking behaviour, whether this meant abstinence or controlled drinking.

These women needed sufficient credible information covering the risks associated with drinking, and how other factors, both individual and social, affect those risks, to enable them to make up their own minds about how they should behave (Thomas 1995). As mentioned earlier, epidemiologically based knowledge is problematic. It is based on damage accumulated over time and affected by confounding variables, talks in terms of risks rather than symptoms, and is often hard to reconcile with individual experience. Most of these women did not have a scientific approach to epidemiology. Scientific epidemiology has been described as a 'web of causation' (Kriegler 1994). The web is presented as accurate and definite, weightings being ascribed to each influential factor. The presumption is that measurements are accurate. But looking at alcohol consumption, whilst these women knew they were generally drinking in excess of 'officially' defined limits, this did not necessarily apply every week, but was true of many more weeks than it was not. They would have been hard put to give detailed accurate measures of their intake, in terms of units per day. Similarly, as we saw in chapter 2, measurements of social class are social constructions, giving a broad ranking of social position. So many of the exact measurements become less exact when reconsidered. In addition, facts do not speak for themselves. 'Official' facts are defined and interpreted by experts and bureaucracies. In contrast, what might be termed a lay epidemiology is based upon personal observation in public and personal arenas. An acknowledgement of that dissonance rarely features in health warnings.

Specific knowledge in the form of guidance on units, levels or amounts rarely featured in these women's stories, whilst general rules of thumb, such as 'the more you drink the more likely you are to have problems' did seem to register with them. 'Official' advice emphasises the future (Petersen and Lupton 1996), but these women tended to view their behaviour in the immediate context of their lived experience and emotional well-being, that is the short term. Again, if health promotion material could recognise that it would be helpful.

One focus for health promotion would be to clarify the physical dangers of heavy drinking. Such information could include labelling containers with amounts and percentages or having information charts at sales outlets (Hilton and Kaskutan 1991). After all, many of the women emphasised how easy it was to obtain alcohol at sales points. Information about the alcohol content of drinks that they supposed might do them good, such as stout or Guinness, in comparison to those they generally regarded as harmful, such as spirits, would be helpful.

Equally importantly, information about the warning signs of negative drinking would be very useful. For example, when women find themselves turning to a bottle for comfort some suggestions of alternative sources of support would help (Thomas 1995). Individual health or welfare professionals need not only to be able to impart accurate and non-stigmatising information, but also to watch out for situations where women's self-esteem, in terms of their partnerships or their mothering ability, is threatened. For women accustomed to drinking, with the opportunity to do so and who enjoy it, such situations could presage more serious problems. For those at risk of drinking as a coping mechanism, additional social support and advice on alternative ways of coping could also be helpful. It seems sensible that similar suggestions on coping be incorporated into general health education advice targeted at those who enjoy drinking but who lead potentially stressful lives, like the heavy drinking professionals.

In other spheres of health and welfare, patient or service users' dependence on professionals are being challenged, and even government guidance emphasises choice and independent decision-making (Smale and Tuson 1993; Beresford and Trevellion 1995; Morris 1997). Exercising choice is part of individual active citizenship (Petersen and Lupton 1996; Culpitt 1999). But the possibility of this being extended to defining one's own health risks has so far been ignored. In this study the heavy drinking professionals were already demanding that right. From other research we know that exercising choice promotes self-esteem. We also know that low self-esteem is a key reason for women's negative drinking. A health promotion policy which was aimed at encouraging women to review available evidence critically and make up their own minds as to how it related to their situations might in the long term prevent more negative drinking and, by encouraging choice, be empowering (Tones 1995).

All of the above measures depend on individuals responding to policies designed to promote non-harmful drinking. One problem is that some of the measures designed to reduce opportunities to drink, most frequently favoured by governments, such as raising the price, could, unless accompanied by wider redistributive policies, increase inequalities in the quality of life. A series of options looking at the relative

merits of price, income, taxation systems, advertising, licensing, spon-
sorship, information policy and public education have been analysed in
terms of their implications for UK consumption, production and
employment (Maynard and Tether 1990; Godfrey 1997). Applying
those to this study suggests that simply increasing the price would
be unlikely to affect the heavy drinking professionals behaviour at all.
But it would more likely reduce the access of the heavy drinking non-
professionals even further. Drawing an analogy from work on women
and smoking, where proposals to increase tax on cigarettes have been
described as a tax on poverty (Woodhouse 1998), such notions could be
described as a tax on inequality.

Instead, it seems that most profitable options would be for policy to
focus on softer approaches, especially publicity emphasising the pleasurable side of moderate drinking, the potential physical problems that
come with heavy drinking and signs of problems drinking. As mentioned in the previous chapter, the tone of such material could do
much to reduce the stigma associated with alcohol problems. What does
come through most obviously from these stories is a need to change
long-established double-standards, that is change the 'governing images'.
Heavy female drinking is just as serious as heavy male drinking, no
more and no less. Stigmatising heavy female drinkers is both inaccurate
and unhelpful. It could encourage secretive drinking, particularly where
cultural norms sanction drinking at home or alone, and delay help-
seeking. Efforts should also be made to publicise issues of women's
emotional distress, and professionals need to view these issues in the
context of women's everyday lives.

## Dealing with negative drinking

The last section concentrated primarily on the implications of this
study for health promotion. This one briefly assesses some of the implications of dealing with negative drinking such as Sophie and Geraldine
experienced.

We need to disaggregate the notion of alcohol problems and think in
gender-sensitive terms of a range of alcohol-related harms, which for
women are largely physical and psychological health and relationship
issues. Whilst they may get drunk in public or be violent, women are
much more likely to be the victims of harm arising from such generally
male patterns of behaviour. Negative drinking is uncontrolled and
generally involves psychologically or physically dependent craving,
accompanied by intense feelings of shame (Ettorre 1997). When women

start drinking negatively to blot out their pain and avoid confronting their issues, they create other problems for themselves. Their source of comfort becomes a danger itself. Women who drink negatively are a group in great need. For instance, their suicide rate is higher than that of men who abuse alcohol (Harris and Barraclough 1997). As Margaret, a heavy drinking professional said:

> *'Women who drink really heavily often can't cut down. They need moral support to do so.'*

Sargent (1992) has extended this sentiment, emphasising that women need compassion and help, not treatment. The last thing they need is censure. As we have seen, their self-esteem is likely to have been damaged enough already. It takes courage to accept that they have got difficulties with their drinking and to ask for help. They need woman-friendly attitudes and atmosphere (Ettorre 1997). Their drinking was an integral part of their lives before it took over, and they need holistic help

There is very little research on gender differences and the form of intervention. What there is, is equivocal and inconsistent (Barber 1995; Thom and Green 1996). There is no real evidence that women do better with one sort of intervention than another, but they are more likely to need time to address issues of self-esteem and the relationship difficult-ies, which as we have seen, so often accompany women's drinking problems. There is much anecdotal evidence that they welcome oppor-tunities for single-sex work, including groups (Copeland and Hall 1992; Copeland et al. 1993). If single-sex facilities are not possible, then research shows that female staff are vital as well as specific women-only groups or times (Thom and Green 1996). This is fundamental when addressing intimate issues relating to womanhood. This does not mean having totally separate facilities. What is probably more important is to encourage women to choose for themselves from a range of intervention modalities which will match their needs (Bailey 1990).

Choice, taking control and taking responsibility are steps towards building self-esteem (Copeland and Hall 1992). As Sophie and Geral-dine's stories illustrate, low self-esteem and depression often accompany drinking problems (Conte et al. 1991). Negative emotional states are the most frequently reported reason for relapse after treatment (Rubonis et al. 1994). Therefore it is fundamental for women who have difficulties with alcohol to learn other ways of coping and finding support as they move away from negative drinking (Barber 1995). New supportive rela-tionships need to be formed and maintained; pleasures other than drinking found. As levels of self-esteem are powerful predictors of success (Allsopp et al. 1990; Long and Mullen 1994), women need to develop a positive self-image, become more assertive and move from a victim stance to a more active approach (Thomas 1995). They need help in confronting their difficulties as Sophie and Geraldine did as they recounted their stories to me. What is needed is for somebody else to hear their stories and see the meaning in them.

As Baily (1990) remarks, low self-esteem, feeling powerless, under-developed assertiveness skills are all part of socialisation into a traditional female role and do not equip women to deal with difficulties. Moving from the confessional to consciousness-raising becomes an important antidote, as these women recognise that they are not unique. At a societal level de-privatising this sort of gender-related pain, like post-natal depression, would make it easier for women to accept their emotional pain and be assertive in seeking support and help. Encouraging women to seek pleasure for its own sake and to take charge of their own range of pleasures would enhance their sense of control and esteem, helping to prevent negative drinking in the first place. They would be less susceptible to advertisements offering the good life and how to be the perfect woman, provided you drink whatever alcohol is being promoted. At a more general level, while traditional images and expectations of motherhood remain influential, some women will continue to feel disappointment when their experiences do not measure up to those ideals and expectations. Regardless of whether it is within their control to alter that reality or not, developing additional sources of self-esteem cannot but be beneficial.

A number of interesting links between gender and dependency have emerged which could usefully be followed up. Why, despite major changes in women's lives – for example, increased participation in the labour market – do their sources of self-esteem remain so traditional? Why is alcohol used when self-esteem is undermined rather than when other difficulties present? Why drink rather than use other coping mechanisms? The links between gender, dependency and stress could also usefully be examined further than these stories permit. For example, although doctors have reduced their drinking and smoking, rates still remain high amongst the predominantly female nursing profession (Hartz et al. 1990).

## Policy frameworks: measures for measures

I have been arguing that women's drinking issues need to be viewed in a gender-sensitive way as issues in their own right. Policy measures need to be developed specifically for women, to encourage their positive drinking and prevent and treat negative drinking. In terms of policy arenas these women's experiences have touched on two major concerns: health policy and the relationship between women and the state. The policy issues that are raised in the rest of this section, whilst drawing largely on UK experience, have relevance for other countries.

Most women enjoy using alcohol and it can add to the quality of life. In the UK total usage of alcohol far outweighs that of other drugs. Alcohol not only penetrates our patterns of consumption, but also our production (Maynard and Tether 1990). In this country, about 750,000 people are employed in the manufacture and distribution of alcohol. Central government receives in excess of £46 million in revenue from the alcohol trade per annum (Foster 1995). By the early 1980s the five biggest brewers were ranked amongst the most profitable 126 UK companies. About a third of the small group of multinational corporations which now dominate the international alcohol trade are British (Baggott 1990). In governmental terms those are the benefits. The downside is that the number of alcohol-related deaths is ten times that of illicit drugs (Noble 1994). The costs to the state are in the region of £10 billion per annum (Alcohol Concern 1999). The government of any country has to balance health and social costs with tax revenue needs, employment needs, the needs of trade and industry and ways of distributing taxation (Maynard and Tether 1990). Thus task of any government is to analyse conflicting interests, gains and loses of each option and outcomes for whom.

To date the UK government has proved singularly reluctant to implement an alcohol strategy (Baggott 1990). So many competing government departments have an interest in alcohol that their conflicts have weakened the chance of an integrated policy. For example, the Department of Trade and Industry might be interested in increasing production, whereas the Home Office, responsible for crime control, and the Department of Health might be more interested in limiting consumption. An integrated policy would also involve tackling the alcohol industry's huge vested interests with strong lobbies in a situation where the alcohol misuse lobby itself lacks thrust and where cross-party and electoral support for alcohol control is weak (Baggott 1990).

In terms of UK policy, a government-sponsored report on 'sensible drinking' was published in 1981 (DHSS 1981). In this, the government made it clear that encouraging individual behaviour change was the main plank of their policy. At its crudest, this reaction has been likened to victim blaming (Crawford 1977). It also coincided with the suppression of the report of an interdepartmental committee on alcohol problems, which recommended controlling overall consumption through price mechanisms. (It was subsequently published abroad [Bruun 1982].)

Following the election of a Labour government in 1997, the 1998 consultative document *Our Healthier Nation* (Department of Health 1998) appears to recognise the need to balance health and social well-being with industrial and commercial needs. Issues to do with alcohol were not dealt with in detail, pending the publication of another consultative document. Following widespread consultation with interested parties, Alcohol Concern, a national pressure group, produced *Proposals for a National Alcohol Strategy for England* in 1999. This is a wide-ranging document, covering taxation and prices, licensing, community safety, drink-driving, controlling the promotion of alcohol, changing attitudes, support and treatment. What concerns us here is how this strategy, if adopted by the government, will influence women's opportunities for positive drinking and how it is suggesting negative drinking can be prevented and helped.

To start with, this document has quite unequivocally recognised the distinctions between non-harmful and harmful drinking:

> *No strategy for limiting misuse of alcohol will succeed if it ignores the popularity and positive benefits that moderate drinking provides; the extent to which it is embedded in social life; and the significance to the economy of alcohol production, sale and trade.*

The suggested overall approach is strategic, noting that following the White Paper 'The New NHS: Modern and Dependable' (1998), Health Authorities are now required to develop, in association with other relevant agencies, broad-based public health needs assessments, through localised Health Improvement Programmes. Alcohol issues need to be included. It also emphasises links with the National Drugs Strategy (Anti-Drugs Co-ordinator 1998). As far as specific alcohol services are concerned, it advocates that local authorities and health authorities be required to adopt minimum standards of service provision and that specific funding be allocated, within a clearly defined planning and evaluating framework. It is recommended that services should be developed within an overall, integrated and wide-ranging network of services and measures, including outreach and rehabilitation facilities. The current legislative framework under the 1990 NHS and Community Care Act is permissive rather than proscriptive. Whilst the philosophical approach to care is one of normalisation, promoting user choice and empowerment, the realities of pressures on finance, which is not specifically allocated, and the lack of information about alcohol-related harms in local areas has meant that by the late 1990s services were very patchy (Harrison et al. 1996b). A government inspection reporting in 1995 noted a similar picture (Department of Health 1995).

Specific services for women are mentioned in the strategy and current difficulties of access noted. However, although the strategy singles out women as a group requiring special attention, what this means in practice is not spelled out. First of all services need to be available and well publicised, linked to existing women's organisations and services. Although the British Royal College of Psychiatrists called for specific services for women in 1986, and a national conference also drew attention to this need (DAWN 1988; Waterson and Ettorre 1989; Coupe 1992), services still remain patchy (DAWN 1994; Brisby et al. 1997). There is no statutory requirement on health or local authorities to provide alcohol services (Baker 1992), let alone services specifically for women.

Second, facilities need to be attractive and accessible. Voluntary organisations and especially community-based ones are more likely to be local, relevant to local needs and separate from statutory agencies. Women with children, despite agency efforts to change their public image, are still wary of agencies that have the statutory powers to institute enquiries or proceedings against them, with regard to their children (Thom and Green 1996). Opening times need to be appropriate for women with children. Crèche facilities and home visits help (Smith 1992). In 1994 25 per cent of agencies in the UK had no crèche and 50 per cent did not offer any home visits.

Where projects also offer help for children, then the needs of both child and mother must be given attention. Such projects are of immense importance, but because of meeting dual needs, funding may be difficult to obtain (Thompson 1997). This may also mean that the professionals working with the children are not necessarily the same as the ones working with the mothers. A collective approach is called for where any parent has alcohol problems (Dunne and Ellery 1997). Services need to be integrated with other health and welfare facilities. Localised services mean links are more possible with primary health care workers. Women need community-based support after intervention (Thomas 1995).

Similarly, whilst the need to train professionals, who frequently lack confidence and experience low success rates, is recognised in the report (as is the lack of support for front-line workers) there is no mention of how this applies to women's needs.

It is disappointing that there is little emphasis on any notion of inequality, social justice or recognition that exposure to alcohol cannot be reduced without reducing access, which, in a context of structured socio-economic status, will increase inequalities in access to positive drinking. As many researchers have pointed out, alcohol advice – or, as the strategy terms it informed choices about drinking – is of little benefit, if women have not got the required resources to find alternative sources of support (Petersen and Lupton 1998). There is no acknowledgement that women's wider social and economic position needs addressing. How does their access to transport or their income levels, for example, affect their relationship with alcohol? What about their employment possibilities? Lack of self-esteem is a constant theme linked with negative drinking. Social policies designed to give women resources and enhance their power cannot but benefit their esteem. In other words, a gender dimension is needed for all policies (Ungerson and Kember 1997, Doyal 1998), including any alcohol strategy.

Whilst it mentions research and recommends the establishment of a specific research unit, designed to monitor and evaluate the implementation of the strategy, which is to be welcomed, this narrow focus may be too restrictive. What these women's stories suggest is the importance of small-scale studies in depth, which illuminate the ways in which women construct their lives within their own social contexts and view the relevance of alcohol for them. Their perceptions may not only throw light on the implementation of the strategy itself, but also question some of its basic assumptions, for example about the nature of informed choice.

Whilst recognising the importance of consulting users, and indeed involving some user groups, but no women's group, in drawing up its recommendations, the report lacks detail on how this could be achieved as an integral and on-going part of an alcohol strategy. For example, although one of the objectives is to enhance the capacity of groups to make informed choices about their drinking habits, there is no mention of consulting users about how they perceive alcohol related harms or risks, which as we have seen vary from 'official' definitions.

What of the future? Supposing the government adopts these recommendations, how likely is it to be in implementing them? In the early 1980s an integrated approach failed. The Ministerial Group on Alcohol Misuse reached inertia with stalemate between the Departments of Trade and Industry and Agriculture, who had different and conflicting agendas to the Department of Health. The importance of the need for total government and ministerial backing cannot be overemphasised.

The situation and potential for conflicting interests is much greater than with drugs as the ten-year strategy plan for integrated action against drugs indicates (Anti-drugs Co-ordinator 1998). For example, it was not possible to include core alcohol industry organisations in developing the Alcohol Concern Strategy. But one of the strengths of the Alcohol Strategy is that it does include a plan for implementation. It is not simply a list of points requiring action.

But there are always parts that the state cannot reach very easily. Legislation will not eradicate private personal difficulties, but it can promote the position of women, helping them to develop their personal esteem and sense of self-worth in the public sphere. A woman who now works in providing services for people with alcohol problems, but who herself has had severe alcohol difficulties in the past, has made some relevant distinctions, which are useful here. She differentiated what she called drinking to feel better in the face of loneliness and boredom, from drinking to feel human or normal, where a sense of self-esteem and shame is so deeply ingrained that the woman is probably hardly conscious of whether she is lonely or bored. At times the former may precede the latter and it is here that policy frameworks can help by improving the status of women generally. If negative drinking is of the type where a woman is drinking to feel human or normal, then appropriate women-friendly sources of help, such as Geraldine and Sophie managed to access, can be assured through appropriate policy frameworks.

## Conclusion

This book has been an initial attempt to draw an outline map of some of the main pathways women follow in terms of their drinking careers, especially as they are shaped by social advantage. We have revisited mother's ruin and found it to be less ruinous and more pleasurable than might be expected. But we also found that for some women it retains its destructive power as strongly as ever.

As I indicated in the introduction, the book takes a broad-brush approach. This means that I have concentrated on developing the wider framework and contextualising women's drinking. Space has not permitted me to develop in detail the picture of women with alcohol-related physical problems or those who are aware they are drinking negatively, beyond Sophie and Geraldine's stories. Similarly, going forward in time, I have not been able to ascertain how subsequent children affect drinking patterns. Do higher consumers still have very different practices from lower consumers? Whilst nothing to do with 'mother's ruin', it would be interesting to examine how other life-cycle transitions, such as retirement, affect the gendering of drinking.

What is clear from these women's experiences, is that, as Ussher (1991), in concluding her book exploring the impact of misogyny on women's mental health, says, we need to 'listen to women'. These stories also tell us to listen to the whole of a woman's story, not the mother's story, not the partner's story, not even the child's story, but the woman's story.

# References

Abbey, A. and Harnish, R.J. (1995) 'Perception of sexual intent: the role of gender, alcohol consumption and rape supportive attitudes', *Sex Roles*, 32, 297–313.

Abbott, P. and Sapsford, R. (1987) *Women and Social Class*, Tavistock, London.

Abbott, P. and Wallace, C. (1996) *An Introduction to Sociology: Feminist Perspectives*, Routledge, London.

Abel, E.L. (1981) 'A critical evaluation of the obstetric use of alcohol in preterm labor', *Drug and Alcohol Dependence*, 7, 367–78.

Abel, E.L. (1984) *Fetal Alcohol Syndrome and Fetal Alcohol Effects*, Plenum Press, New York and London.

Abel, E.L. (1986) 'Publication trends for alcohol, tobacco, and narcotics in MED-LARS', *Annals New York Academy of Science*, 477, 103–4.

Acheson, D. (1998) *Independent Inquiry into Inequalities in Health*, Department of Health/The Stationery Office, London.

Ahmad, W.I.U. (1993) *Race and Health in Contemporary Britain*, Open University Press, Buckinghamshire.

Alcohol Concern (1988) *Women's Guide to Alcohol*, Alcohol Concern, London.

Alcohol Concern (1990) *Warning: Alcohol Can Damage Your Health*, Alcohol Concern, London.

Alcohol Concern (1996) *Women and Alcohol: Briefing*, Alcohol Concern, London.

Alcohol Concern (1999) *Proposals for a National Alcohol Strategy for England*, Alcohol Concern, London.

Alcohol Health and Research World (1994) 'Alcohol-related birth defects: special edition', *Alcohol Health and Research World*, 18, 1.

Allan, C.A. (1989) 'Characteristics and help-seeking patterns of attenders at a community-based voluntary agency and an alcohol and drug treatment unit', *British Journal of Addiction*, 84, 73–80.

Allan, G. (1996) *Kinship and Friendship in Britain*, Oxford University Press, Oxford.

Allatt, P., Kiel, T., Bryman, A. and Bytheway, B. (1988) *Women and the Life Cycle: Transitions and Turning Points*, Macmillan, Basingstoke.

Allsop, S. et al. (1990) 'Relapse prevention and management: a controlled trial with problem drinkers', *Drug and Alcohol Review*, 9, 143–53.

Anderson, P. (1993) 'Management of alcohol problems: the role of the general practitioner', *Alcohol and Alcoholism*, 28, 263–72.

Anderson, P. and Wallace, P. (1988) 'Safe limits of drinking: patients' views', *British Medical Journal*, 296, 1787.

Annandale, E (1998) *The Sociology of Health and Medicine: A Critical Introduction*, Polity Press, Cambridge and Oxford.

Anti-drugs Co-ordinator (1998) *Tackling Drugs to Build a Better Britain: The Government's Ten Year Strategy for Tackling Drugs Misuse*, The Stationery Office, London.

Arber, S. (1990) 'Opening the "black box": inequalities in women's health', in Abbott, P. and Payne, G. (eds) *New Directions in the Sociology of Health*, The Falmer Press, London.

Arber, S. (1997) 'Comparing inequalities in women's and men's health: Britain in the 1990's', *Social Science and Medicine*, 44, 773–87.

Backett, K. (1992) 'The construction of health knowledge in middle class families', *Health Education Research: Theory and Practice*, 7, 4, 497–507.

Baggott, R. (1990) *Alcohol, Politics and Social Policy*, Avebury, Aldershot.

Baily, S. (1990) 'Women with alcohol problems: a psycho-social perspective', *Drug and Alcohol Review*, 9, 125–31.

Baily, S. (1991) *Planning Prevention Strategies for Alcohol and Other Drug Related Problems among Women, National Centre for Research into the Prevention of Drug Abuse*, Curtin University of Technology, Perth, Western Australia.

Baker, S. (1992) 'Alcohol services and women', in Department of Health and Royal College of General Practitioners (ed.) (1992) *Women and Alcohol*, HMSO, London.

Balarajan, R. and Raleigh, V.S. (1990) 'Variations in perinatal, neonatal, postnatal and infant mortality by mother's country of birth', in Briton, M. (ed.) *Mortality and Geography: a Review in the mid-1980's*, HMSO, London, quoted in Payne, S. (1992) *Women, Health and Poverty*, Harvester Wheatsheaf, Hemel Hempstead.

Barber, J.G. (1995) *Social Work with Addictions*, Macmillan, Basingstoke.

Barker, D.J.P. (1994) *Mothers. Babies and Disease in Later Life*, British Medical Journal Publishing Group, London.

Barnes, M. and Maple, N. (1992) *Women and Mental Health*, Venture Press, Birmingham.

Barr, A. (1995) *Drink: An Informal Social History*, Bantam Press, London.

Bartley, M., Carpenter, L., Dunnell, K., and Fitzpatrick, R. (1996) 'Measuring inequalities in health: an analysis of mortality patterns using two social classifications', *Sociology of Health and Illness*, 18, 455–75.

Bartley, M., Popay, J. and Plewis, J. (1992) 'Domestic conditions, paid employment and women's experiences of ill health', *Sociology of Health and Illness*, 14, 313–41.

Beattie, J.O., Day, R.E., Cockburn, F. and McGlure, G. (1983) 'Alcohol and the foetus in the west of Scotland', *British Medical Journal*, 298, 795–801.

Beck, U. (1992) *The Risk Society*, Sage, London.

Beckman, L.J. (1978) 'Sex-role conflict in alcoholic women: myth or reality', *Journal of Abnormal Psychology*, 87, 408–17.

Behnke, M. and Eyler, F.D. (1993) 'The consequences of prenatal substance use for the developing fetus, newborn and young child', *International Journal of the Addictions*, 28, 1341–91.

Beory, M.D. and Merry, J. (1986) 'The rise in alcoholism in women of fertile age', *British Journal of Addiction*, 81, 142.

Beresford, P. and Trevillion, S. (1995) *Developing Skills for Community Care: A Collaborative Approach*, Arena, Basingstoke.

Berridge, V. and Edwards, G. (1981) *Opium and the People: Opiate Use in Nineteenth Century England*, Allen Lane, London.

Bhatt, A. and Dickinson, R. (1992) 'An analysis of health education materials for minority communities by cultural and linguistic group', *Health Education Journal*, 51, 72–7.

Bien, T.H., Miller, W.R. and Tonigan, J.S. (1993) 'Brief interventions for alcohol problems', *Addiction*, 88, 315–36.

Bifulco, A. and Moran, P. (1998) *Wednesday's Child. Research into Women's Experience of Neglect and Abuse in Childhood, and Adult Depression*, Routledge, London.

Bingol, N., Schuster, C., Fuchs, M., Aosub, S., Turner, G., Stone, R.K. and Gromisch, D.S. (1987) 'The influence of socio-economic factors on the occurrence of Fetal Alcohol Syndrome', *Advances in Alcohol and Substance Abuse*, 6, 105–18.

Black, J. (1983) 'Drinking habits during pregnancy', *Nursing Times*, 31 August, 25–6.

Blackburn, C. (1991) *Poverty and Health: Working With Families*, Open University Press, Buckinghamshire.

Blane, D. (1985) 'An assessment of the Black Report's explanations of health inequalities', *Sociology of Health and Illness*, 7, 423–45.

Blaxter, M. (1990) *Health and Lifestyles*, Tavistock, London.

Blume, S. (1985) 'Is social drinking during pregnancy harmless? There is reason to think not', *Advances in Alcohol and Substance Abuse*, 5, 209–19.

Borchorst, A. (1990) 'Political motherhood and childcare policies', in Ungerson, C. (ed.) *Gender and Caring*, Harvester Wheatsheaf, Hemel Hempstead.

Bott, E. (1959) *Family and Social Networks*, Tavistock, London.

Boulton, M. (1983) *On Being a Mother: a Study of Women with Pre-school Children*, Tavistock, London.

Bourdieu, P. (1984) *Distinction: A Social Critique of the Judgement of Taste*, Routledge, London.

Bourne, G. (1975) *Pregnancy*, Pan Books, London.

Brannen, J. (1988) 'Research note: The study of sensitive subjects: notes on interviewing', *Sociological Review*, 36, 552–63.

Brannen, J. and Moss, P. (1988) *New Mothers at Work*, Unwin Hyman, London.

Brannen, J. and Moss, P. (1991) *Managing Mothers: Dual Earner Households after Maternity Leave*, Unwin Hyman, London.

Breeze, E. (1985) *Women and Drinking*, HMSO, London.

Bresnahan, K., Zuckerman, B. and Cabral, H. (1992) 'Psychosocial correlates of drug and heavy alcohol use among pregnant women at risk for drug use', *Obstetrics and Gynecology*, 80, 976–80.

Brett, P.J, Graham, K. and Smythe, C. (1995) 'An analysis of speciality journals on alcohol, drugs and addictive behaviours in research methods reporting', *Journal of Studies on Alcohol*, 56, 24–34.

Brewers and Licensed Retailers Association (BLRA) (1997) *Statistical Handbook: A Compilation of Drinks Industry Statistics*, Brewing Publications Limited, London.

Brisby, T., Baker, S. and Hedderwick, T. (1997) *Under the Influence: Coping With Parents Who Drink Too Much*, Alcohol Concern, London.

British and European Social Attitudes Survey (1998) *How Britain Differs*, Ashgate Publishing, Aldershot.

British Journal of Addiction (1988) 'News and notes', *British Journal of Addiction*, 83, 118.

Broverman, I.K., Broverman, D.M., Clarkson, F.E., Rosenkrantz, P.S. and Vogel, S.R. (1970) 'Sex-role stereotypes and clinical judgements of mental health', *Journal of Consulting and Clinical Psychology*, 34, 1–7.

Brown, G. and Harris, T. (1978) *Social Origins of Depression*, Tavistock, London.

Brown, G. and Harris, T. (1989) *Life Events and Illness: A Reference Book for the Caring Professions*, Routledge, London.

Brown, P. and Scase, R. (eds) (1991) *Poor Work: Disadvantage and the Division of Labour*, Open University Press, Buckinghamshire.

Bruun, K. (ed.) (1982) *Alcohol Control Policies in the United Kingdom*, Sociologiska Instituten, Stockholm.

Bunton, R. (1990) 'Changes in the control of alcohol misuse', *British Journal of Addiction*, 85, 605–15.

Bunton, R. (1992) 'More than a woolly jumper: health promotion as social regulation', *Critical Public Health*, 3, 4–11.

Bunton, R. and Burrows, R. (1995) 'Consumption and health in the "epidemiological" clinic of late modern medicine', in Bunton, R., Nettleton, S. and Burrows, R. (eds) *The Sociology of Health Promotion: Critical Analyses of Consumption, Lifestyle and Risk*, Routledge, London.

Burghes, L. (1994) *Lone Parenthood and Family Disruption: The Outcomes for Children*, Family Policy Studies Centre, London.

Burrows, R. and Nettleton, S. (1995) 'Going against the grain: an analysis of smoking and "heavy" drinking amongst the British middle classes', *Sociology of Health and Illness*, 17, 668–80.

Busfield, J. (1974) 'Ideologies and reproduction', in Richards, M. (ed.) *The Integration of a Child Into the Social World*, Cambridge University Press, Cambridge.

Cahill, M. (1994) *The New Social Policy*, Blackwell, Oxford and Cambridge.

Calnan, M. (1987) *Health and Illness: The Lay Perspective*, Tavistock, London.

Calnan, M. (1996) *Modern Medicine – Lay Perspectives and Experiences*, University College London Press, London.

Calnan, M. and Williams, S. (1991) 'Style of life and the salience of health: an exploratory study of health-related practices in households from differing socio-economic circumstances', *Sociology of Health and Illness*, 13, 506–29.

Carley, M. (1981) *Social Measurement and Social Indicators: Issues of Policy and Theory*, Allen and Unwin, London.

Carob, A. (1987) *Working with Depressed Women*, Gower, Aldershot.

Carr-Hill, R. (1987) 'The inequalities in health debate: A critical review of the issues', *Journal of Social Policy*, 16, 509–42.

Cartwright, A.C.B., Shaw, S. and Spratley, T.A. (1978) 'The relationships between per capita consumption, drinking patterns and alcohol related problems in a population sample 1965–1974. Part I: Increased consumption and changes in drinking patterns', *British Journal of Addiction*, 73, 237–46.

Cavallo, F., Russo, R., Zotti, C., Camerlengo, A. and Ruggenini, A.M. (1995) 'Moderate alcohol consumption and spontaneous abortion', *Alcohol and Alcoholism*, 30, 195–201.

Central Statistical Office (CSO) (1991) *Social Trends 21*, HMSO, London.

Chalfant, H.P. (1973) 'The alcoholic in magazines for women', *Sociological Focus*, 6, 19–26.

Chan, P. (1996) 'Pride of place', *Community Care*, 1–7 February.

Charles, N. and Walters, V. (1995) 'Women's health: women's voices', *Health and Social Care in the Community*, 2, 329–38.

Charlton, B.G. (1993) 'The health obsession', *The Salisbury Review*, March, 31–5.

Chasnoff, I.J., Landress, H.J. and Barrett, M.E. (1990) 'The prevalence of illicit-drug or alcohol use during pregnancy and discrepancies in mandatory reporting in Pinellas County, Florida', *New England Journal of Medicine*, 322, 1202–06.

Cherpital, C.J. (1994) 'Alcohol and casualties: a comparison of emergency room and coroner data', *Alcohol and Alcoholism*, 29, 211–18.

Clare, A.W. (1990) 'The alcohol problem in universities and the professions', *Alcohol and Alcoholism*, 25, 277–85.

Clarren, S.K. and Smith, D.W. (1978) 'The fetal alcohol syndrome', *New England Journal of Medicine*, 298, 1063–7.

Clemmons, P. (1985) 'Reflections of social thought in research on women and alcoholism', *Journal of Drug Issues*, 15, 73–80.

Conte, H.R., Plutchik, R., Picard, S., Glanter, M. and Jacob, J. (1991) 'Sex differences in personality traits and coping style of hospitalised alcoholics', *Journal of Studies on Alcohol*, 52, 26–32.

Cooke, D.J. and Allan, C.A. (1983) 'Self- reported alcohol consumption and dissimulation in a Scottish urban sample', *Journal of Studies on Alcohol*, 44, 617–29.

Cooke, D.J. and Allan, C.A. (1984) 'Stressful life events and alcohol abuse in women: A general population study', *British Journal of Addiction*, 79, 425–31.

Copeland, J. and Hall, W. (1992) 'A comparison of women seeking drug and alcohol treatment in a specialist women's and two traditional mixed sex treatment services', *British Journal of Addiction*, 87, 65–74.

Copeland, K., Hall, W., Didcott, P. and Biggs, V. (1993) 'A comparison of a specialist women's alcohol and other drug treatment service with two traditional mixed-set services; client characteristics and treatment outcomes', *Drug and Alcohol Dependence*, 32, 81–92.

Cornwall, J. (1984) *Hard-Earned Lives: Accounts of Health and Illness from East London*, Tavistock, London.

Corrigan, E.M. (1980) *Alcoholic Women in Treatment*, Oxford University Press, New York.

Coupe, J. (1992) 'Why women need their own services', in Glass, I. (ed.) *The International Handbook of Addictive Behaviour*, Tavistock/Routledge, London.

Cox, B.D. et al. (1987) *Health and Lifestyle Survey: Preliminary Report*, Health Promotion Trust, Cambridge.

Crawford, R. (1977) 'You are dangerous to your health: the ideology and politics of victim blaming', *International Journal of Health Services*, 7, 663–80.

Crompton, R. (1998 second edition) *Class and Stratification: An Introduction to Current Debates*, Polity Press, Cambridge.

Crompton, R. and Mann, M. (1994) *Gender and Stratification*, Polity Press, Cambridge.

Culpitt, I. (1999) *Social Policy and Risk*, Sage, London.

Curlee, J. (1969) 'Alcoholism and the empty nest', *Bulletin of the Menninger Clinic*, 33, 165–71.

Curlee, J. (1970) 'A comparison of male and female patients at an alcoholism treatment centre', *Journal of Psychology*, 74, 239–47.

Cutler, S.F, Wallace, P.G. and Haines, A.P. (1988) 'Assessing alcohol consumption in general practice patients – a comparison between questionnaire and interview', *Alcohol and Alcoholism*, 23, 441–50.

Dahlgren, L. (1978) 'Female alcoholics: Development and pattern of problem drinking', *Acta Psychiatrica Scandinavia*, 57, 325–35.

Davey-Smith, G., Bartley, M. and Blane, D. (1991) 'The Black Report on socio-economic inequalities in health 10 years on', *British Medical Journal*, 301, 373–7.

Davidson, S., Alden, L. and Davidson, P. (1981) 'Changes in alcohol consumption after childbirth', *Journal of Advanced Nursing*, 6, 195–8.

Davies, H. and Joshi, H. (1994) 'Sex, sharing and distribution of income', *Journal of Social Policy*, 23, 30–40.

Davison, C., Davey-Smith, G. and Frankel, S. (1991) 'Lay epidemiology and the prevention paradox: the implications of coronary candidacy for health education', *Sociology of Health and Illness*, 13, 1–9.

Davison, C., Frankel, S. and Davey-Smith, G. (1992) 'The limits of lifestyle: reassessing "fatalism" in the popular culture of illness prevention', *Social Science and Medicine*, 34, 675–85.

Davidson, K. and Ritson, E.B. (1993) 'The relationship between alcohol dependence and depression', *Alcohol and Alcoholism*, 28, 147–55.

DAWN (1994) *Survey of Facilities for Women Using Drugs (Including Alcohol) in London*, DAWN, London.

Day, N.L. and Richardson G.A. (1991) 'Prenatal alcohol exposure: a continuum of effects', *Seminars in Perinatology*, 15, 271–9.

Daykin, N. (1998) 'Gender and health promotion in two different settings', in Doyal, L. (ed.) *Women and Health Services*, Open University Press, Milton Keynes.

De Boer, M.C. et al. (1993) 'Alcohol and social anxiety in women and men: pharmacological and expectancy effects', *Addictive Behaviours*, 18, 2, 117–26.

Deehan, A., Templeton, L., Taylor, C., Drummond, D.C. and Strang, J. (1998) 'Are practice nurses an unexplored resource in the identification and management of alcohol misuse? Results from a study of practice nurses in England and Wales 1995', *Journal of Advanced Nursing*, 28, 588–94.

Delphy, C. (1981) 'Women in stratification studies', in Roberts, H. (ed.) *Doing Feminist Research*, Routledge and Kegan Paul, London.

Department of Health (1991) *Health and Personal Social Services Statistics for England, 1991 Edition*, HMSO, London.

Department of Health (1992) *The Health of the Nation: A Strategy for Health in England*, HMSO, London.

Department of Health (1995) *Sensible Drinking: A Report of an Inter-departmental Working Group*, HMSO, London.

Department of Health/OPCS (1996) *Health Survey for England 1995*, HMSO, London.

Department of Health (1997) *Drinking: Adult's Behaviour and Knowledge*, HMSO, London.

Department of Health (1998) *Our Healthier Nation: A Contract for Health: A Consultation Paper*, The Stationery Office, London.

Department of Health (1998) *The New NHS: Modern and Dependable*: White Paper, The Stationery Office, London.

Department of Health and Social Security (DHSS) (1980) *Prevention in the Child Health Services*, HMSO, London.

Department of Health and Social Security (DHSS) (1981) *Prevention and Health: Drinking Sensibly*, HMSO, London.

Department of Health and Royal College of General Practitioners (1992) *Women and Alcohol*, HMSO, London.

Denzin, N.K. (1991) *Hollywood by Shot: Alcoholism in the American Cinema*, Aldine De Gruyter, New York.

Dorris, M. (1989) *The Broken Cord*, Harper & Row, New York.

Douglas, J. (1992) 'Black women's health matters: putting black women on the research agenda', in Roberts, H. (ed.) *Women's Health Matters*, Routledge, London.

Douglas, M. (1985) *Risk Acceptability According to the Social Sciences*, Routledge and Kegan Paul, London.

Douglas, M. (1987) *Constructive Drinking*, Cambridge University Press, Cambridge.

Douglas, M. (1992) *Risk and Blame: Essays in Cultural Theory*, Routledge, London.

Doyal, L. and Elston, M.A. (1986) 'Women, health and medicine', in Beechey, V. and Whitelegg, E. (eds) *Women in Britain Today*, Open University Press, Buckinghamshire.

Doyal, L. (1991) 'Promoting women's health', in Bandura, B. and Kickbush, I. (eds) *Health Promotion Research*, World Health Organisation, Copenhagen.

Doyal, L. (1995) *What Makes Women Sick?* Macmillan, Basingstoke

Doyal, L. (ed.) *Women and Health Services*, Open University Press, Buckinghamshire.

Drever, F. and Whitehead, M. (eds) (1997) *Health Inequalities: Decennial Supplement*, HMSO, London.

Dunne, F. (1988) 'Are women more easily damaged by alcohol?', *British Journal of Addiction*, 83, 1135–6.

Dunne, M. and Ellery, M. (1997) 'Drink problems', *Community Care*, July, 17–123.

Dzaldowski, A., Heather, N. and Crawford, J. (1988) 'Perceptions of drinkers and abstainers in a sample of Scottish adults', *Alcohol and Alcoholism*, 23, 7–16.

Edgar, N.C. and Knight, R.G. (1994) 'Gender and alcohol-related expectancies for self and others, *Australian Journal of Psychology*, 46, 144–9.

Edwards, G. (1983) 'Alcohol and advice to the pregnant woman', *British Medical Journal*, 286, 247–8.

Edwards, G., Anderson, P., Babor, T., Casswell, S., Ferrence, R., Giesbricht, N., Godfrey, C., Holder, H., Lemmens, P., Makela, K., Midanik, L., Norstrom, T., Osterberg, E., Romelsjo, A., Room, R., Simpura, J. and Skog, O. (1994) *Alcohol Policy and the Public Good*, Oxford University Press, Oxford.

Erikson, R. and Goldthorpe, J.H. (1992) *The Constant Flux*, Clarendon, Oxford.

Ernhart, C.B., Morrow-Tlucak, M., Sokol, R.J. and Martier, S. (1988) 'Underreporting of alcohol use in pregnancy', *Alcoholism Clinical and Experimental Research*, 12, 506–11.

Ettorre, B. (1989) 'Women and substance use/abuse: Towards a feminist perspective', *Women's Studies International Forum*, 12, 593–602.

Ettorre, E. (1992) *Women and Substance Use*, Macmillan, London.

Ettorre, E. (1997) *Women and Alcohol*, Women's Press, London.

EUROMAC (1992) 'A European concerted action: maternal alcohol consumption and its relation to the outcome of pregnancy and child development at 18 months', *International Journal of Epidemiology*, 21, Supplement 1.

Faculty of Public Medicine and The Royal College of Physicians (1991) *Alcohol and the Public Health*, Macmillan, London.

Farid, B., Elsherbini, M., Ogden, M., Lucas, G. and Williams, R. (1989) 'Alcoholic housewives and role satisfaction', *Alcohol and Alcoholism*, 24, 331–7.

Featherstone, M. (1991) *Consumer Culture and Postmodernism*, Sage, London.

Ferri, E. (1993) *Life at 33*, National Children's Bureau, London.

Ferrins-Brown, M., Dalton, S., Hartney, E., Kerr, C., Maslin, J. and Orford, J. (1998) '"Have a sip of this": the impact of family on the drinking patterns of untreated heavy drinkers living in the West Midlands, U.K.'. Paper presented at International Conference on Drinking Patterns and their Consequences, Perth, Australia.

Fillmore, K.M. (1985) '"When angels fall": Women's drinking as cultural preoccupation and as reality', in Wilsnack, S.C. and Beckman, L.J. (eds) *Alcohol Problems in Women: Antecedents, Consequences, and Intervention*, Guilford Press, New York.

Fischoff, B., Lichtenstein, S., Slovic, P., Derby, S. and Kenney, R. (1981) *Acceptable Risk*, Cambridge University Press, Cambridge.

Flannigan, B., McLean, A., Hall, C. and Propp, V. (1990) 'Alcohol use as a situational influence on young women's pregnancy risk taking behaviours', *Adolescence*, 25, 205–14.

Fossey, E. and Plant, M. (1994) *Growing up with Alcohol*, Routledge, London.

Foster, P. (1995) *Women and the Health Care Industry. An Unhealthy Relationship*, Open University Press, Buckinghamshire.

Ford, N. (1989) 'Urban–rural variations in the level of hetereosexual activity of young people, ' *Area*, 21, 237–41.

Frankel, S., Davison, C. and Davey Smith, G. (1991) 'Lay epidemiology and the rationality of responses to health education', *British Journal of General Practice*, 41, 428–38.

Franklin, J. (1998) *The Politics of Risk Society*, Polity Press, Cambridge and Oxford.

Franks, P. (1992) 'Social relationships and health: the relative roles of family functioning and social support', *Social Science and Medicine*, 34, 779–88.

Gabe, J. (ed.) (1995) *Medicine, Health and Risk: Sociological Approaches*, Blackwell, Oxford.

Gavron, H. (1966) *The Captive Wife*, Penguin, Harmondsworth.

Ghodsian, M. and Power, C. (1987) 'Alcohol consumption between the ages of 16 and 23 in Britain: a longitudinal study', *British Journal of Addiction*, 86, 1269–81.

Giddens, A. (1991) *Modernity and Self-Identity: Self and Society in the Late Modern Age*, Polity Press, Cambridge and Oxford.

Giddens, A. (1992) *The Transformation of Intimacy*, Polity Press, Cambridge and Oxford.

Gladdish, S. and Carter, R. (1994) *Opening Time: Opening up Alcohol Services to All Sections of the Community*, Alcohol Concern, London.

Glendenning, C. and Millar, J. (eds) (1987) *Women and Poverty*, Harvester Wheatsheaf, Brighton.

Goddard, E. (1991) *Drinking in England and Wales in the Late 1980s*, HMSO, London.

Goddard, E. and Ikin, C. (1988) *Drinking in England and Wales 1987*, HMSO, London.

Godfrey, C. (1999) 'The influence of price, income and taxation on UK alcohol consumption and problems', in Raistrick, D. (ed.) *Tackling Alcohol Together*, Society for the Study of Addiction, Abingdon.

Godfrey, C. and Robinson, D. (1990) *Preventing Alcohol and Tobacco Problems*, Avebury, Basingstoke.

Goldberg, D. (1985) 'Identifying psychiatric illness among general medical patients', *British Medical Journal*, 291, 161–2.

Gomberg, E.S. (1979) 'Drinking patterns of women alcoholics', in Burtle, V. (ed.) *Women Who Drink*, Thomas Books, Springfield, Illinois.

Gomberg, E.S. (1993) 'Alcohol, women and the expression of aggression', *Journal of Studies on Alcohol*, Suppl. 11, 89–95.

Gomberg, E.S. (1994) 'Risk factors for drinking over a woman's life span', *Alcohol, Health and Research World*, 18, 220–7.

Gorman, D.M. and Peters, T.J. (1990) 'Types of life events and the onset of alcohol dependence', *British Journal of Addiction*, 85, 71–9.

Government Statistical Office (GSO) (1998) *Annual Abstract of Statistics*, Government Statistical Service, London.

Graetz, B. (1991) 'The class location of families', *Sociology*, 25, 101–18.

Graham, H. (1993) *Hardship and Health in Women's Lives*, Harvester Wheatsheaf, London.

Graham, H. (1994) 'Gender and class as dimensions of smoking behaviour in Britain: insights from a survey of mothers', *Social Science and Medicine* 38, 691–8.

Graham, H. (1995) 'Cigarette smoking: a light on gender and class inequality in Britain?' *Journal of Social Policy*, 24, 509–28.

Graham, H. (1998) 'Health at risk; poverty and national health strategies', in Doyal, L. (ed.) *Women and Health Services*, Open University Press, Buckinghamshire.

Graham, H. and McKee, L. (1980) *The First Months of Motherhood. Health Education Monograph Series*, Health Education Council, London.

Graham, H. and Oakley, A. (1981) 'Competing ideologies of reproduction: medical and maternal perspectives on pregnancy and childbirth. In Roberts, H. (ed.) *Women and Health Care*, Routledge and Kegan Paul, London.

Grant, M. (1981) 'Drinking and creativity: a review of the alcoholism literature', *British Journal of Alcohol and Alcoholism*, 16, 88–91.

Green, E., Hebron, S. and Woodward, D. (1990) *Women's Leisure. What Leisure?* Macmillan, London.

Gutzke, D. (1984) 'The cry of the children': the Edwardian medical campaign against maternal drinking, *British Journal of Addiction*, 79, 71–84.

Hafner, S. (1992) *Nice Girls Don't Drink: Stories of Recovery*, Bergin and Garvey, New York.

Hamilton, K. and Jenkins, L. (1989) 'Why women and travel?' in Grieco, M., Pickup, L. and Whipp, R. (eds) *Gender, Transport and Employment*, Avebury, Aldershot.

Hampton, R.L., Senator, V. and Gullota, T.P. (1998) *Substance Abuse, Family Violence and Child Welfare*, Sage, London.

Hands, M.A., Banwell, C.L. and Hamilton, M.A. (1995) 'Women and alcohol: current Australian research', *Drug and Alcohol Review*, 14, 17–25.

Hanna, E., Duour, M.C., Elliott, S., Stinson, F. and Harford, T.C. (1992) 'Dying to be equal: women and cardiovascular disease', *British Journal of Addiction*, 87, 1593–97.

Harkin, A.M., Anderson, P. and Lehto, J. (1995) *Alcohol in Europe – a Health Perspective*, World Health Organisation Regional Office for Europe, Copenhagen.

Harris, E.C. and Barraclough, B. (1997) 'Suicide as an outcome for mental disorders', *British Journal of Psychiatry*, 170, 205–28.

Harrison, L., Harrison, M. and Adebowale, V. (1996a) 'Drinking problems among black communities', in Harrison, L. (ed.) *Alcohol Problems in the Community*, Routledge, London.

Harrison, L., Guy, P. and Sivyer, W. (1996b) Community care policy and the future of alcohol services', in Harrison, L. (eds) *Alcohol Problems in the Community*, Routledge, London.

Harrison, L. and Gardiner, E. (1999) 'Do the rich really die young? Alcohol-related mortality and social class Great Britain, 1988–1994', *Addiction*, vol. 94, 12, pp. 1871–80.

Harwin, J. and Otto, S. (1979) 'Women, alcohol and the screen', in Cook, J. and Lewington, M. (eds) *Images of Alcoholism*, British Film Institute/Alcohol Education Centre, London.

Harz, C., Plant, M.A. and Watts, M. (1990) *Alcohol and Health: A Handbook for Nurses, Midwives, and Health Visitors*, Medical Council on Alcoholism, London.

Health Education Authority (1989) *Beliefs about Alcohol*, Health Education Authority, London.

Health Education Authority (1996) *Health of the Nation – Monitoring Survey*, Health Education Authority, London.

Heather, N. and Robertson, I. (1989) *Problem Drinking*, Oxford Medical Publications, Oxford.

Heller, J., Anderson, H.R., Bland, J.M., Brooke, O.G., Peacock, J.L. and Stewart, C.M. (1988) 'Alcohol in pregnancy: Patterns and association with the socio-economic, psychological and behavioural factors', *British Journal of Addiction*, 83, 541–51.

Helwig-Larson, K., Knudsen, L.B. and Peterson, B. (1998) 'Women in Denmark – why do they die so young? Risk factors for premature death', *Scandinavian Journal of Social Welfare*, 7, 4, 266–77.

Herd, D. (1988) 'Drinking by black and white women: Results from a national survey', *Social Problems*, 35, 493–505.

Herd, D. and Grube, J. (1993) 'Drinking contexts and drinking problems among black and white women', *Addiction*, 88, 1011–110.

Hilton, M.E. and Kaskutas, L. (1991) 'Public support for warning labels on alcoholic beverage containers', *British Journal of Addiction*, 86, 1323–33.

Holmila, M. (1991) 'Social control experienced by heavily drinking women', *Contemporary Drug Problems*, 2, 547–71.

Holmila, M. (1994) 'Excessive drinking and significant others', *Drug and Alcohol Review*, 13, 431–6.

Holmila, M., Mustonen, H. and Rannik, E. (1990) 'Alcohol use and its control in Finnish and Soviet marriages', *British Journal of Addiction*, 85, 509–20.

Home Office (1995) *Aspects of Drunkeness 1993*, HMSO, London.

Home Office (1996) *Offences Relating to Motor Vehicles, England and Wales 1995*, HMSO, London.

Hoskins, D. (1989) 'Organising the domestic portfolio: gender and skill', in Grieco, M., Pickup, L. and Whipp, R. (eds) *Gender, Transport and Employment*, Avebury, Aldershot.

Houston, A., Kork, S. and MacLeod, M. (1997) *Beyond the Limit: Children Who Live with Parental Alcohol Misuse*, Childline, London.

Howarth, C. and Street, C. (1998) *Monitoring Poverty and Social Exclusion*, New Policy Institute and Joseph Rowntree Foundation, London and York.

Hunt, G. and Satterlee, S. (1987) 'Darts, drink and the pub: the culture of female drinking', *Sociological Review*, 3, 575–601.

Hyssala, L., Rautava, P., Sillanpaa, M. and Tuominen, J. (1992) 'Changes in the smoking and drinking habits of future fathers from the onset of their wives' pregnancies', *Journal of Advanced Nursing*, 17, 849–54.

Ihlen, B.M., Amundsen, A. and Tronnes, L. (1993) 'Reduced alcohol use in pregnancy and changed attitudes in the population', *Addiction*, 88, 389–94.

Jamieson, L. (1998) *Intimacy*, Polity Press, Oxford and Cambridge.

Jarvie, G. and Maguire, J. (1994) *Sport and Leisure in Social Thought*, Routledge, London.

Jerome, D. (1984) 'Good company: the sociological implications of friendship', *Sociological Review*, 32, 696–718.

Johnson, M.B. (1982) 'Sex differences, women's roles and alcohol use: preliminary national data', *Journal of Social Issues*, 38, 93–116.

Jolly, S. and Orford, J. (1983) 'Religious observance, attitudes towards drinking and knowledge about drinking amongst university students', *Alcohol and Alcoholism*, 18, 217–78.

Jones, B.M. and Jones, M.K. (1976) 'Women and alcohol: intoxication metabolism and menstrual cycle', in Greenblatt, M. and Schukitt, M.A. (eds) *Alcoholism Problems in Women and Children*, New York: Grune and Stratton.

Jordan, B., Jones, S., Kay, H. and Redley, M. (1992) *Trapped in Poverty? Labour Market Decisions in Low Income Households*, Routledge, London.

Kalant, O.J. (1980) 'Sex differences in alcohol and drug problems – some highlights', in Kalant, O.J. (ed.) (1980) *Alcohol and Drug Problems in Women*. New York: Plenum Press.

Kaplan, L.A. (1992) *Motherhood and Representation: The Mother in Popular Culture and Melodrama*, Routledge, London.

Kelly, M.P. and Charlton, B. (1995) 'The modern and the postmodern in health promotion', in Bunton, R., Nettleton, S. and Burrows, R. (eds) *The Sociology of Health Promotion: Critical Analyses of Consumption, Lifestyle and Risk*, Routledge, London.

Kemshall, H., Parton, N., Walsh, M. and Waterson, J. (1997) 'Concepts of risk as core influences on organisational structure and functioning within the personal social services and probation', *Social Policy and Administration*, 31, 213–32.

Kent, R. (1990) 'Focusing on women', in Collins, S. (ed.) *Alcohol, Social Work and Helping*, Routledge, London.

Knupfer, G. (1991) 'Abstaining for foetal health: the fiction that even light drinking is dangerous', *British Journal of Addiction*, 86, 1063–74.

Kreitman, N. (1977) 'Three themes in the epidemiology of alcoholism', in Edwards, G. and Grant, M. (eds) *Alcoholism: New Knowledge and New Responses*, Croom Helm, London.

Kriegler, N. (1994) 'Epidemiology and the web of causation: has anyone seen the spider?', *Social Science and Medicine* 39, 887–903.

Kroft, C. and Leichner, P. (1987) 'Sex-role conflicts in alcoholic women', *International Journal of Addictions*, 22, 685–93.

Kumar, R. and Robson, K. (1984) 'A prospective study of emotional disorders in childbearing women', *British Journal of Psychiatry*, 144, 35–47.

Lee, C. (1998) *Women's Health: Psychological and Social Perspectives*, Sage, London.

Lee, R. (1993) *Doing Research on Sensitive Topics*, Sage, London.

Leland, J. (1982) 'Sex roles, family organisation and alcohol abuse', in Orford, J. and Harwin, J. (eds) *Alcohol and the Family*, Croom Helm, London.

Lewis, J. (1980) *The Politics of Motherhood: Child and Maternal Welfare in England 1900–1939*, Croom Helm, London.

Lewis, V. (1997) 'Drunk in charge', *Community Care*, 11–17 September.

Lindbeck, V.L. (1972) 'The woman alcoholic: A review of the literature', *International Journal of the Addictions*, 7, 567–80.

Lisansky, E. (1957) 'Alcoholism in women: social and psychological concomitants', *Quarterly Journal of Studies on Alcohol*, 18, 588–623.

Litman, G. (1978) 'Clinical aspects of sex role stereotyping', in Chetwyn, J. and Hartnett, O. (eds) *The Sex Role System*, Routledge and Kegan Paul, London.

Little, R.E., Anderson, K.W., Ervin, C.H., Worthington-Roberts, B. and Clarren, S.K. (1989) 'Maternal alcohol use during breast-feeding and infant mental and motor development at one year', *New England Journal of Medicine*, 321, 425–30.

Littlewood, J. and McHugh, N. (1997) *Maternal Distress and Postnatal Depression*, Macmillan, London.

Llewellyn-Jones, D. (1978) *Everywoman: A Gynaecological Guide for Life*, Faber and Faber, London.

Long, A. and Mullen, B. (1994) 'An exploration of women's perceptions of the major factors that contrbuted to their alcohol abuse', *Journal of Advanced Nursing*, 19, 623–39.

Lowe, G. (1993) *Adolescent Drinking and Family Life*, Harwood Academic Press, London.

Lord President's Office (1995) *Tackling Drugs Together – A Strategy for England 1995–1998*, HMSO, London.

Lubotsky Levin, B., Blanch, A.K. and Jennings, A. (1998) *Women's Mental Health Services: A Public Health Perspective*, Sage, London.

Ludwig, A.M. (1990) 'Alcohol input and creative output', *British Journal of Addiction*, 85, 953–65.

Lupton, D. (1993) 'Risk as moral danger: the social and political functions of risk discourse in public health', *International Journal of Health Sciences*, 23, 425–35.

MacArthur, C. (1991) *Health After Childbirth*, HMSO, London.

MacDonald, J.G. (1987) 'Predictors of treatment outcome for alcoholic women', *International Journal of Addiction*, 22, 235–48.

McDonald, M. (1994) *Gender, Drink and Drugs*, Berg, Oxford.

McDonald, S. (1994) 'Whisky, women and the Scottish drink problem', in McDonald, M. (ed.) *Gender, Drink and Drugs*, Berg, Oxford.

McDowell, L. (1989) 'Gender divisions', in Hamnett, C., McDowell, L. and Sarre, P. (eds) *Restructuring Britain: The Changing Social Structure*, Sage, London.

McGlone, F., Park, A. and Roberts, C. (1996) 'Relative values: kinship and friendship', in Jowell, R. et al. (eds) *British Social Attitudes: the 13th Report*, Dartmouth, Aldershot.

McNeil, M. and Litt, J. (1992) 'More medicalising of mothers: Foetal alcohol syndrome in the USA and related developments', in Scott, S., Williams, G., Platt, S. and Thomas, H. (eds) *Private Risks and Public Danger*, Avebury, Aldershot.

MacRae, S. (1986) *Cross-class Families*, Clarendon, Oxford.

Macintyre, S. (1981) *Expectations and Experiences of First Pregnancy*. Occasional Paper 5. Medical Research Council Medical Sociology Unit, Aberdeen.

Macintyre, S. (1986) 'The patterning of health by social position in contemporary Britain: directions for research', *Social Science and Medicine*, 23, 393–415.

MacMillan, M. (1998) *Women of the Raj*, Thames and Hudson, London.

MacRae, S. (1986) *Cross-class Families*, Clarendon, Oxford.

MacRan, S., Clarke, L., Slogett, A. and Bethune, A. (1994) 'Women's socio-economic status and self-assessed health: identifying some disadvantaged groups', *Sociology of Health and Illness*, 16, 182–208.

Manthorpe, J. and Walsh, M. with Alaszewski, A. and Harrison, L. (1997) 'Issues of risk practice and welfare in learning disability services', *Disability and Society*, 12, 69–82.

Marmot, M.G., Davey-Smith, G., Stansfield, S., Patel, C., North, F., Head, J., White, I., Brunner, E. and Feeney, A. (1991) 'Health inequalities among British civil servants: the Whitehall II study', *British Medical Journal*, 337, 1387–93.

Marmot, M.G. (1996) 'The social pattern of health and disease', in Blane, D., Brunner, E. and Wilkinson, R. (eds) *Health and Social Organisation*, Routledge, London.

Marmot, M. (1997) 'Inequality, deprivation and alcohol use', *Addiction*, 92 (Supplement 1), S13–20.

Marsh, C. (1986) 'Social class and occupation', in Burgess, R.G. (ed.) *Key Variables in Social Investigation*, Routledge and Kegan Paul, London.

Marsh, S. and McKay, S. (1994) *Poor Smokers*, Policy Studies Institute, London.

Marsh, J.C. and Miller, N.A. (1985) 'Female clients in substance abuse treatment', *International Journal of the Addictions*, 20, 995–1019.

Marshall, R. (1996) 'Social influences on treatment outcomes', in Harrison, L. (ed.) *Alcohol Problems in the Community*, Routledge, London.

Martin, J. (1986) 'Returning to work after childbearing: evidence from the women and employment survey', *Population Trends*, 43, 23–30.

Martin, J. and Roberts, C. (1984) *Women and Employment*, HMSO, London.

Maslin, J., Dalton, S., Ferrins-Brown, M., Hartney, E., Kerr, C. and Orford, J. (1998) 'The "ups and downs" of drinking: the drinking careers of untreated heavy drinkers living in the West Midlands, UK'. Paper presented at International Conference on Drinking Patterns and their Consequences, Perth, Australia.

Maynard, A. and Tether, P. (eds) (1990) *Preventing Alcohol and Tobacco Problems – Vol. 1: Consumption, Production and Policy Development*, Aldershot, Avebury.

Maynard, M. (1990) 'The re-shaping of sociology? Trends in the sociology of gender', *Sociology*, 24, 269–90.

Megberg, A., Halvorsen, B., Holter, B., Ek, A.J., Askeland, A., Gaaserud, W. and Steinsvag, B. (1986) 'Moderate alcohol consumption – a need for intervention programmes in pregnancy?', *Acta Obstetrica Scandinavia*, 65, 861–4.

Melzer, H., Gill, B. and Petticrew, M. (1995) *The Prevalance of Psychiatric Morbidity Among Adults Aged 16–64 Living in Private Households in Great Britain*, HMSO, London.

Merrell, S. and Murcott, A. (1992) *Sociology of Food, Eating, Diet and Culture*, Sage, London.

Midanik, L. (1989) 'The validity of self-reported alcohol use', *British Journal of Addiction*, 84, 1419–25.

Miles, A. (1991) *Women, Health and Medicine*, Open University Press, Buckinghamshire.

Mills-Hopper Associates (1992) *Women and Alcohol – a Research-Based Evaluation*, Mills-Hopper Associates for Alcohol Concern, London.

Minor, M.J. and Van Dort, B. (1982) 'Prevention research on the teratgenic effects of alcohol', *Preventative Medicine*, 11, 346–59.

Morgan, P. (1987) 'Women and alcohol: the disinhibition rhetoric in an analysis of domination', *Journal of Psychoactive Drugs*, 19, 129–33.

Morris, J. (1997) *Community Care: Working in Partnership with Service Users*, Venture Press, Birmingham.

Mullen, K. (1994) 'Control and responsibility: moral and religious issues in lay health accounts', *Sociological Review*, 42, 414–37.

Nadieu, L. and Harvey, K. (1995) 'Women's alcoholic intoxication: the origins of the double standard in Canada', *Addiction Research*, 2, 279–90.

National Council of Women (1980) *Alcohol and the Unborn Child*, National Council of Women, London.

Nettleton, S. and Bunton, R. (1995) 'Sociological critiques of health promotion', in Bunton, R., Nettleton, S. and Burrows, R. *The Sociology of Health Promotion: Critical Analyses of Consumption, Lifestyle and Risk*, Routledge, London.

Nicolson, P. (1998) *Post-Natal Depression: Psychology, Science and the Transition to Motherhood*, Routledge, London.

Noble, B. (1994) 'Deaths associated with the use of alcohol', *Populations Trends*, 76, 7–16.

Oakley, A. (1974) *The Sociology of Housework*, Martin Robertson, Oxford.

Oakley, A. (1980) *Women Confined*, Martin Robertson, Oxford.

Oakley, A. (1984) *The Captured Womb*, Blackwell, Oxford.

Oakley, A. (1989) 'Smoking in pregnancy: smokescreen or risk factor? Towards a materialistic analysis', *Sociology of Health and Illness*, 11, 311–35.

Oakley, A. (1992) *Social Support and Motherhood*, Blackwell, Oxford.

Oakley, A. (1993) *Essays on Women, Medicine and Health*, Edinburgh University Press, Edinburgh.

Oakley, A. and Graham, H. (1981) 'Competing ideologies of reproduction: Medical and maternity perspectives of pregnancy', in Roberts, H. (ed.) *Women, Health and Reproduction*, Routledge and Kegan Paul, London.

Oakley, A. and Rajan, L. (1991) 'Social class and social support: the same or different?', *Sociology*, 25, 31–60.

O'Connor, J. (1978) *The Young Drinkers*, Tavistock, London.

O'Connor, P. (1991) 'Women's confidants outside marriage: Shared or competing sources of intimacy', *Sociology*, 25, 241–54.

Office of Health Economics (OHE) (1981) *Alcohol: Reducing the Harm*, Office of Health Economics, London.

Office for National Statistics (ONS) (1998) *Living in Britain: Results from the 1996 General Household Survey*, HMSO, London.

Office of Population Censuses and Surveys (OPCS) (1980) *Classification of Occupations 1980*, HMSO, London.

Office of Population Censuses and Surveys (OPCS) (1992) *Mortality Statistics 1992*, HMSO, London.

Office of Population Censuses and Surveys (OPCS) (1993) *Health Survey for England 1993. A Report Carried Out by OPCS on Behalf of the Department of Health*, HMSO, London.

Olsen, J., Pereira, A.C. and Olsen, S.F (1991) 'Does tobacco smoking modify the effect of alcohol on fetal growth?', *American Journal of Public Health*, , 81, 69–73.

Orford, J. (1989) *Excessive Appetites: A Psychological View of Addictions*, John Wiley and Sons, Chichester.

Orford, J. (1990) 'Alcohol and the family: an international review of the literature with implications for research and practice', in Kolowski, L., Annis, H. and Cappell, H. (eds) *Research Advances in Alohol and Drug Problems Vol. 10*, Plenum, New York.

Orford, J. and Edwards, G. (1977) *Alcoholism: A Comparison of Treatment and Advice, with a Study of the Influence of Marriage*, Oxford University Press, London.

Pahl, J. (1989) *Money and Marriage*. Macmillan, Basingstoke.

Pahl, J. (1990) 'Spending and control in marriage', *Sociology*, 24, 119–38.

Pahl, R. (1996) 'Friendly society', in Kraemer, S. and Roberts, J. (eds) *The Politics of Attachment: Towards a Secure Society*, Free Association Books, London.

Pahl, R. (1998) 'Friendship: the social glue of contemporary society', in Franklin, J. (ed.) *The Politics of Risk Society*, Polity Press, Cambridge and Oxford.

Payne, S. (1991) *Women, Health and Poverty*, Harvester Wheatsheaf, Hemel Hempstead.

Payne, S. (1996) '"Hit and miss": the success and failure of psychiatric services', in Doyal, L. (ed.) *Women and Health Services*, Open University Press, Buckinghamshire.

Pearson, M. (1993) 'Health on borrowed time? Prioritizing and meeting needs in low-income households', *Health and Social Care in the Community*, 1, 45–54.

Peele, S. (1993) 'The conflict between public health goals and the temperance mentality', *American Journal of Public Health*, 83, 805–10.

Pendleton, L., Smith, C. and Roberts, J.L. (1991) 'Drinking on television: a content analysis of recent alcohol portrayal', *British Journal of Addiction*, 86, 769–74.

Petersen, A. and Lupton, D. (1996) *The New Public Health: Health and Self in the Age of Risk*, Sage, London.

Phillimore, P., Beattie, A. and Townsend, P. (1994) 'Widening inequalities of health in Northern England, 1981–1991', *British Medical Journal*, 308, 1125–8.

Piachaud, D. (1984) *Round about Fifty Hours a Week: The Time Costs of Children*, Child Poverty Action Group, London.

Pitt, B. (1991) 'Depression following childbirth', *Hospital Update*, February, 133–40.

Plant, M.A. (1979) *Drinking Careers: Drinking Habits, Problems, and Occupations*, Tavistock, London.

Plant, M.A. (1981) 'Risk factors in employment', in Hore, B.D. and Plant, M.P. (eds) *Alcohol Problems in Employment*, Croom Helm, London.

Plant, M.A. and Plant, M.L. (1992) *Risk-Takers: Alcohol, Drugs, Sex and Youth*, Routledge, London.

Plant, M.L. (1985) *Women, Drinking and Pregnancy*, Tavistock, London.

Plant, M.L. (1990) *Women and Alcohol: A Review of International Literature on the Use of Alcohol by Females*. World Health Organisation Publications, Geneva.

Plant, M.L. (1997) *Women and Alcohol: Contemporary and Historical Perspectives*, Free Association Books, London and New York.

Plant, M.L., Plant, M.A. and Foster, J. (1991) 'Alcohol, tobacco and illicit drug use amongst nurses: a Scottish study', *Drug and Alcohol Dependence*, 28, 195–202.

Poikolainen, K. (1991) 'Abstain from poisoning your child', *British Journal of Addiction*, 86, 1060–2.

Pollitt, K. (1990) 'Tyranny of the foetus', *New Statesman and Society*, 30 March, 28–30.

Pollock, K. (1988) 'On the nature of social stress: production of a modern mythology', *Social Science and Medicine*, 26, 381–92.

Poskitt, E.M.E. (1984) 'Foetal alcohol syndrome', *Alcohol and Alcoholism*, 19, 159–65.

Power, C. and Estaught, V. (1990) 'The role of family formation and dissolution in shaping drinking behaviour in early adulthood', *British Journal of Addiction*, 85, 521–30.

Prandy, K. (1990) 'The revised Cambridge scale of occupations', *Sociology*, 24, 629–55.

Prescott-Clarke, P. and Primatesta, P. (1997) *Health Survey for England 1995: A Survey Carried out for the Department of Health*, Department of Health, London.

Priest, J. (1990) *Drugs in Pregnancy and Childbirth*, Pandora, London.

Razay, G., Heaton, K.W., Bolton, C.H. and Hughes, A.O. (1992) 'Alcohol consumption and its risk to cardiovascular disease', *British Medical Journal*, 304, 80–3.

Reid, I. (1989 third edition) *Social Class Differences in Britain*, Fontana Press, Glasgow.

Richards, J.P. (1991) 'Postnatal depression: a review of recent literature', *British Journal of General Practice*, 40, 472–6.

Robbins, C.A. and Martin, S.S. (1993) 'Gender, styles of deviance, and drinking problems', *Journal of Health and Social Behaviour*, 34, 302–21.

Roberts, H. (ed.) (1990) *Women's Health Counts*, Routledge, London.

Robinson, B.E. and Rhoden, J.L. (1998 second edition) *Working with Children of Alcoholics: The Practitioner's Handbook*, Sage, California and London.

Robinson, D. (1976) *From Drinking to Alcoholism: A Sociological Commentary*, John Wiley, London.

Room, R. (1974) 'Governing images and the prevention of alcohol problems', *Preventative Medicine*, 3, 11–23.

Room, R. (1975) 'Normative perspectives on alcohol use and problems', *Journal of Drug Issues*, 5, 358–68.

Rosett, H.L. (1980) 'The effects of alcohol on the fetus and offspring', in O.J. Kalant (ed.) *Alcohol and Drug Problems in Women*, Plenum Press, New York and London.

Royal College of General Practitioners (1986) *Alcohol – A Balanced View*, Royal College of General Practitioners, London.

Royal College of Physicians (1987) *A Great and Growing Evil*, Tavistock, London.

Royal College of Physicians, Royal College of Psychiatrists, Royal College of General Practitioners, (1995) *Alcohol and the Heart in Perspective: Sensible Limits Reaffirmed*, Royal Colleges of Medicine, London.

Royal College of Psychiatrists (1986) *Alcohol Our Favourite Drug*, Tavistock, London.

Rubonis, A.V., Colby, S.M., Monti, P.M., Rohsenow, D.J., Gulliver, S.B. and Sirota, A.D. (1994) 'Alcohol cue reactivity and mood induction in male and female alcoholics', *Journal of Studies on Alcohol*, 55, 487–94.

Sales, J., Duffy, J.C., Plant, M.A. and Peck, D.F. (1989) 'Alcohol consumption, cigarette sales and mortality in the United Kingdom: an analysis of the period 1970–1985', *Drug and Alcohol Dependence*, 24, 155–60.

Sargent, M. (1992) *Women, Drugs and Policy in Sydney, London and Amsterdam*, Avebury Press, Aldershot.

Saunders, P. (1990) *A Nation of Home Owners*, Macmillan, Basingstoke.

Saunders, J.H., Davies, M. and Williams, R. (1981) 'Do women develop liver disease more easily than men?', *British Medical Journal*, 282, 1140–3.

Saunders, J.H., Wodak, A.D. and Williams, R. (1985) 'Past experience of advice and treatment for drinking problems of patients with alcoholic liver disease', *British Journal of Addiction*, 80, 51–6.

Savage, M., Barlow, J., Dickens, P. and Fielding, T. (1992) *Property, Bureaucracy, and Culture: Middle Class Formation in Contemporary Britain*, Routledge, London.

Schools Health Education Unit (1997) *Very Young People in 1993–95*, University of Exeter, Exeter.

Schukitt, M. (1972) 'The alcoholic woman: a literature review', *Psychiatry in Medicine*, 3, 37–43.

Scott, S. and Williams, G. (1991) 'Introduction', in Scott, S., Williams, G., Platt, S. and Thomas, H. (eds) *Private Risks and Public Dangers*, Avebury, Aldershot.

Shaw, S. (1980) 'The causes of increasing drinking problems amongst women', in Camberwell Council on Alcoholism (ed.) *Women and Alcohol*, Tavistock, London.

Shaw, S., Cartwright, A., Spratley, T. and Harwin, J. (1978) *Responding to Drinking Problems*, Croom Helm, London.

Shore, E.R. and Batt, S. (1991) 'Contextual factors related to the drinking behaviours of American business and professional women', *British Journal of Addiction*, 84, 619–30.

Shore, E.R. (1992) 'Drinking patterns and problems among women in paid employment', *Alcohol Health and Research World*, 16, 160–4.

Simpura, J. (1995) 'Trends in alcohol consumption and drinking patterns: lessons from world-wide development', in Holder, H. and Edwards, G. (eds) *Alcohol and Public Policy: Evidence and Issues*, Oxford University Press, Oxford.

Skolbekken, J.A. (1995) 'The risk epidemic in medical journals', *Social Science and Medicine*, 40, 291–305.

Slattery, M., Alderson, M.R. and Bryant, J.E. (1986) 'Occupational risks of alcoholism', *International Journal of Addictions*, 21, 929–36.

Smale, G. and Tuson, G. with Biehal, N. and Marsh, P. (1993) *Empowerment, Assessment, Care Management and the Skilled Worker*, National Institute of Social Work and The Stationery Office, London.

Smart, C. (1992) *Regulating Womanhood: Historical Essays on Marriage, Motherhood and Sexuality*, Routledge, London.

Smart, R.G. (1994) 'Dependence and the correlates of change: a review of the literature', in Edward, G. and Lader, M. (eds) *Addiction: Processes of Change*, Oxford University Press, Oxford.

Smith, L. (1992) 'Help-seeking in alcohol-dependent females', *Alcohol and Alcoholism*, 27, 1, 3–9.

Sorell, G.T., Silvia, L.Y. and Busch-Rossnagel, N.A. (1993) 'Sex-role orientation and self-esteem in alcoholic and non-alcoholic women', *Journal of Studies on Alcohol*, 54, 566–73.

Stake, R.E. (1995) *The Art of Case Study Research*, Sage, London.

Stephens, C.J. (1985) 'Perception of pregnancy and social support as predictors of alcohol consumption during pregnancy', *Alcoholism: Clinical and Experimental Research*, 9, 344–8.

Streisguth, A.P., Darby, B.L., Barr, H.M., Smith, J.R. and Martin, D.C. (1983) 'Comparison of drinking and smoking patterns during pregnancy over a six-year interval', *American Journal of Obstetrics and Gynaecology*, 145, 716–24.

Streissguth, A.P., Grant, T.M., Barr, H.M., Brown, Z.A., Martin, J.C., Mayock, D.E., Ramey, S.L. and Moore, L. (1991) 'Cocaine and the use of other drugs during pregnancy', *American Journal of Obstetrics and Gynecology*, 164, 1239–43.

Strong, P.M. (1980) 'Doctors and dirty work – the case of alcoholism', *Sociology of Health and Illness*, 2, 24–47.

Sulaiman, N., Florey, C. du V. and Taylor, D. (1988) 'Alcohol consumption in Dundee primagravidas and its effects on outcome of pregnancy', *British Medical Journal*, 296, 1500–3.

Tannahill, A. (1995) 'What is health promotion?', *Health Education Journal*, 44, 167–8.

Taylor, C., Brown, D., Duckitt, A., Edwards, G., Oppenheimer, E. and Sheehan, M. (1985) 'Patterns of outcome: drinking histories over ten years among a group of alcoholics', *British Journal of Addiction*, 80, 45–50.

Taylor, M.E. and Wang, M.Q. (1988) 'Educational implications of alcohol use patterns among employed women', *Health Education*, October/November, 78–82.

Temple, M.T. and Leigh, B. (1990) 'Alcohol and sexual behaviour in discrete events, I. Characteristis of sexual encounters involving and not involving alcohol', Paper presented at the Alcohol Epidemiology Symposium, Ketill Bruun Society, Budapest, Hungary.

Tether, P. and Robinson, R. (1986) *Preventing Alcohol Problems: A Guide for Local Action*, Tavistock, London.

Thom, B. (1986) 'Sex differences in help-seeking for alcohol problems – 1. The barriers to help-seeking', *British Journal of Addiction*, 81, 777–88.

Thom, B. (1994) 'Women and alcohol – the emergence of a risk group', in McDonald, M. (ed.) *Gender, Drink and Drugs*, Berg, Oxford.

Thom, B. (1997) *Women and Alcohol: Issues for Prevention*, Health Education Authority, London.

Thom, B. and Green, A. (1996) 'Services for women; the way forward', in Harrison, L. (ed.) *Alcohol Problems in the Community*, Routledge, London.

Thomas, S. (1995) 'Planning the prevention of alcohol and other drug related problems among women', *Drug and Alcohol Review*, 14, 7–15.

Thompson, A. (1997) 'Home and dry', *Community Care*, 13–19 February.

Tomlinson, A. (1990) *Consumption, Identity and Style*, Routledge, London.

Tones, K. (1995) 'Making a change for the better', *Healthlines*, November, 17–19.

Townsend, P. (1979) *Poverty in the UK*, Penguin, Harmondsworth.

Townsend, P., Davidson, N. and Whitehead, M. (1988) *Inequalities in Health: The Black Report and the Health Divide*, Penguin, Harmondsworth.

Ungerson, C. and Kember, M. (1997 second edition) *Women and Social Policy*, Macmillan, London.

Ussher, J. (1991) *Women's Madness: Misogyny or Mental Ilness?* Harvester Wheatsheaf, London.

Valliant, G. and Milofsky, E.S. (1982) 'Natural history of male alcoholism IV: Paths to recovery', *Archives of General Psychiatry*, 39, 127–33.

Vannicelli, M. and Nash, L. (1984) 'Effect of sex bias on women's studies on alcoholism', *Alcoholism Clinical and Experimental Research*, 8, 334–6.

Vega, W.A., Kolody, B., Hwang, J. and Noble, A. (1993) 'Prevalence and magnitude of perinatal substance exposures in California', *New England Journal of Medicine*, 329, 850–4.

Vellaman, R. (1993) *Alcohol and the Family*, Institute of Alcohol Studies, London.

Vellaman, R. with Copello, A. and Maslin, J. (1998) *Living with Drink: Women who Live with Problem Drinkers*, Longman, Harlow.

Vogt, I. (1995) 'Women and addiction: a frame of reference for theory and practice', in Council of Europe, *Women and Drugs*, Council of Europe Publishing, Strasbourg.

Vollicer, B.J., Cahil, M.H. and Smith, J.L. (1981) 'Sex differences in correlates of problem drinking among employed males and females', *Drug and Alcohol Dependence*, 8, 175–87.

Wallace, P., Brennan, P. and Haines, A. (1987) 'Are General Practitioners doing enough to promote healthy lifestyles? Findings of the Medical Research Council's

General Practice Research Framework Study on Lifestyle and Health', *British Medical Journal*, 297, 663–8.

Wallace, P. and Haines, A. (1985) 'Use of a questionnaire in General Practice to increase the recognition of patients with excessive alcohol consumption', *British Medical Journal*, 290, 1949–53.

Ward, M. and Goodman, C. (1995 second edition) *Alcohol Problems in Old Age*, Wynne Howard for Staccato Training and Books, Henley.

Warde, A. (1990) 'Notes on the relationship between production and consumption', in Burrows, R. and Marsh, C. (eds) *Consumption and Class: Divisions and Change*, Macmillan, London.

Waterson, J. (1992) *Women and Alcohol: The Social Context of Changing Patterns in Pregnancy and Early Motherhood*, unpublished PhD thesis, London School of Economics, University of London.

Waterson, J. (1996) 'Gender division and drinking problems', in Harrison, L. (ed.) *Alcohol Problems in the Community*, London, Routledge.

Waterson, J. (1999) Redefining community care and social work: needs or risks led? *Health and Social Care in the Community*, 7, 276–80.

Waterson, J. and Duffy, J.C. (1992) 'Alcohol damage to the foetus and reproductive system', in Duffy, J.C. (ed.) *Health Risks Associated with Alcohol Consumption*. Edinburgh: Edinburgh University Press.

Waterson, J. and Ettorre, B. (1989) 'Providing services for women with difficulties with alcohol or other drugs: the current UK situation as seen by women practitioners, researchers and policy makers in the field', *Drug and Alcohol Dependence*, 24, 119–25.

Waterson, E.J. and Murray-Lyon, I.M. (1989a) 'Drinking and smoking patterns amongst women attending an antenatal clinic I: before pregnancy', *Alcohol and Alcoholism*, 24, 153–62.

Waterson, E.J. and Murray-Lyon, I.M. (1989b) 'Drinking and smoking patterns amongst women attending an antenatal clinic II: during pregnancy', *Alcohol and Alcoholism*, 24, 163–73.

Waterson, E.J. and Murray-Lyon, I.M. (1989c) 'Comments on a paper by M.L. Plant and M.P. Plant', *Alcohol and Alcoholism*, 24, 355–7.

Waterson, E.J. and Murray-Lyon, I.M. (1989d) 'Alcohol, smoking and pregnancy: some observations on ethnic minorities in the United Kingdom', *British Journal of Addiction*, 84, 323–5.

Waterson, E.J. and Murray-Lyon, I.M. (1990a) 'Is pregnancy a time of changing drinking patterns for fathers as well as mothers?', *British Journal of Addiction*, 85, 389–96.

Waterson, E.J. and Murray-Lyon, I.M. (1990b) 'Preventing alcohol related birth damage: a review', *Social Science and Medicine*, 30, 349–64.

Waterson, J. and Stringer, M. (1998) 'Women and alcohol: policies for drinking', Paper presented at British Sociological Association, York.

Weiner, L., Rosett, H.L., Edelin, K.C., Alpert, J. and Zuckerman, B. (1983) 'Alcohol consumption by pregnant women', *Obstetrics and Gynaecology*, 61, 6–12.

Wilkinson, H. (1994) *No Turning Back*, Demos, London.

Wilkinson, R. (1996) *Unhealthy Societies: The Afflictions of Inequality*, Routledge, London.

Willmott, P. (1987) *Friendship Networks and Social Support*, Policy Studies Institute, London.

Wilsnack, S.C. (1973) 'Sex role identity in female alcoholism', *Journal of Abnormal Psychology*, 82, 253–61.

Wilsnack, R.W., Wilsnack, S.C. and Klassen, A.D. (1984) 'Women's drinking and drinking problems: patterns from a 1981 national survey', *American Journal of Public Health*, 74, 1231–8.

Wilsnack, R.W. and Wilsnack, S.C. (1992) 'Women, work and alcohol: failures of simple theories', *Alcoholism: Clinical and Experimental Research*, 16, 2, 172–9.

Wilsnack, S.C. (1985) 'Drinking, sexuality and sexual dysfunction in women', in Wilsnack, S.C. and Beckman, L.J. (eds) *Alcohol Problems in Women: Antecedents, Consequences and Intervention*, Guilford Press, New York.

Wilsnack, S.C. (1994) 'How women drink: epidemiology of women's drinking and problem drinking', *Alcohol Health and Research World*, 18, 173–81.

Wilson, P. (1980) *Drinking in England and Wales*, HMSO, London.

Winick, C. (1983) 'Drinking and disinhibition in popular culture', in *Alcohol and Disinhibition: Nature and Meaning of the Link*. Research Monograph 12. National Institute on Alcohol Abuse and Alcoholism, Washington.

Wolfson, D. and Murray, J. (eds) (1986) *Women and Dependency: Women's Personal Accounts of Drug and Alcohol Problems*, DAWN, London.

Women's National Commission (1988) *Stress and Addiction Among Women*, Cabinet Office, London.

Woodhouse, K. (1998) 'Cause for concern: women and smoking', in Doyal, L. (ed.) *Women and Health Services*, Open University Press, Buckinghamshire.

World Health Organisation (WHO) (1992) *Women and Substance Abuse 1992 Interim Report*, World Health Organisation, Geneva.

World Health Organisation (1993) *European Action Alcohol Plan*, WHO Regional Office for Europe, Copenhagen.

Zajicek, E. (1981) 'Psychiatric problems during pregnancy', in Wolkind, S. and Zajicek, E. (eds) *Pregnancy: A Psychological and Social Study*, Academic Press, London.

# Index